Mountain Biking

The Pacific Northwest

*Dennis Coello's America by
Mountain Bike Series*

*Oregon
Washington*

Laurie and Chris Leman

Foreword, Introduction, and Afterword
by Dennis Coello, Series Editor

Formerly *The Mountain Biker's Guide
to the Pacific Northwest*

**Menasha
Ridge Press**

FALCON™

Published by Menasha Ridge Press and Falcon Press

10 9 8 7 6 5 4 3 2

Leman, Laurie.
   Mountain biking the Pacific Northwest : Oregon, Washington /
Laurie and Chris Leman ; foreword, introduction, and afterword by
Dennis Coello.—1st ed.
      p. cm.—(Dennis Coello's America by mountain bike series)
   Previously published under the title: The mountain biker's guide
to the Pacific Northwest, c1994.
   ISBN 1-56044-430-4 (pbk.)
   1. All terrain cycling—Oregon—Guidebooks. 2. All terrain
cycling—Washington (State)—Guidebooks. 3. Oregon—Guidebooks.
4. Washington (State)—Guidebooks. 5. Northwest, Pacific—
Guidebooks. I. Leman, Chris. II. Leman, Laurie. Mountain
biker's guide to the Pacific Northwest. III. Title. IV. Series:
America by mountain bike series.
GV1045.5.07L46 1996
796.6'4'09795—dc20   95-52532
                                                              CIP

Photos by the authors unless otherwise credited
Maps by Tim Krasnansky
Cover photo by F-Stock Inc., John Laptad

Menasha Ridge Press
3169 Cahaba Heights Road
Birmingham, Alabama 35243

Falcon Press
P.O. Box 1718
Helena, Montana 59624

  Text pages printed on recycled paper

CAUTION

   Outdoor recreational activities are by their very nature potentially hazardous. All
participants in such activities must assume the responsibility for their own actions and
safety. The information contained in this guidebook cannot replace sound judgment
and good decision-making skills, which help reduce the risk exposure, nor does the
scope of this book allow for disclosure of all the potential hazards and risks involved in
such activities.

   Learn as much as possible about the outdoor recreational activities you participate
in, prepare for the unexpected, and be safe and cautious. The reward will be a safer and
more enjoyable experience

Table of Contents

List of Maps

THE PACIFIC NORTHWEST   *RIDE LOCATIONS*

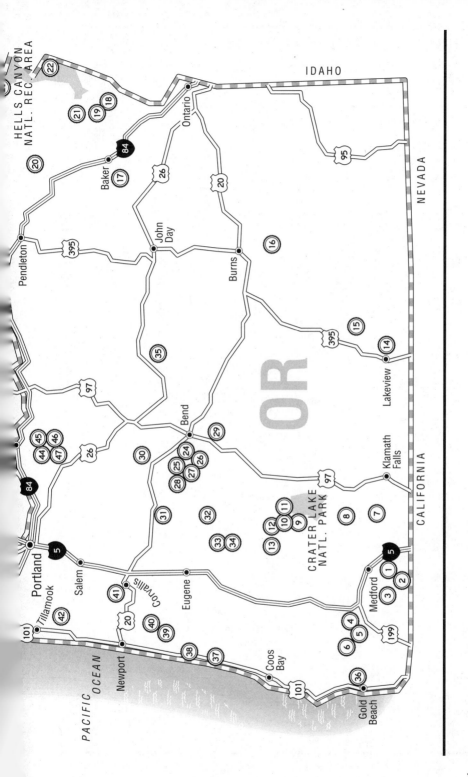

AMERICA BY MOUNTAIN BIKE   *MAP LEGEND*

Ride trailhead

Primary bike trail	Direction of travel	Optional bike trail and trailhead	Other trail	Hiking Only trail

Interstate highways (with exit no.)	U.S. routes	State routes	Dead Indian Highway — Other paved roads	Unpaved, gravel or dirt roads (may be 4WD only)

U.S. Forest Service roads	Seattle — Cities	Leavenworth ◉ Yakima — Towns or settlements	Dam — Lake — Intermittent stream / Perennial stream

0 ½ 1 MILES — Approximate scale in miles	True North	SISKIYOU NATIONAL FOREST — Public Lands*	State Border

✈ Airport

♥ Archeological or historical site

⛵ Boat ramp

▲ Campground (CG)

≡ Cattle guard

✝ Cemetery or gravesite

♠ Church

Cliff, escarpment or outcropping

Drinking water

Fire tower or lookout

Falls or rapids

Food

Gate

House or cabin

Lodging

Mountain or butte

Mountain pass

△ 3312 Mountain summit (elevation in feet)

✕ Mine or quarry

Observatory

Park office or ranger station

Picnic area

Power line or pipeline

Restrooms

Spring

Stable, corral or ranch

Swimming Area

Transmission towers

Tunnel or bridge

Remember, private property exists in and around our National Forests.

Foreword

Single-track excitement.

Welcome to *America by Mountain Bike*, a 20-book series designed to provide all-terrain bikers with the information they need to find and ride the very best trails everywhere in the mainland United States. Whether you're new to the sport and don't know where to pedal, or an experienced mountain biker who wants to learn the classic trails in another region, this series is for you. Drop a few bucks for the book, spend an hour with the detailed maps and route descriptions, and you're prepared for the finest in off-road cycling.

My role as editor of this series was simple: First, find a mountain biker who knows the area and loves to ride. Second, ask that person to spend a year researching the most popular and very best rides around. And third, have that rider describe each trail in terms of difficulty, scenery, condition, elevation change, and all other categories of information that are important to trail riders. "Pretend you've just completed a ride and met up with fellow mountain bikers at the trailhead," I told each author. "Imagine their questions, be clear in your answers."

As I said, the *editorial* process—that of sending out riders and reading the submitted chapters—is a snap. But the work involved in finding, riding, and writing about each trail is enormous. In some instances our authors' tasks are made easier by the information contributed by local bike shops or cycling clubs, or even by the writers of local "where-to" guides. Our sincere thanks goes to all who have helped.

All of the rides in this guide have been pedaled by our authors themselves, then compared with dozens of other routes to determine if they qualify as "classic"—that area's best in scenery and cycling fun. If you've ever had the experience of pioneering a route from outdated topographic maps, or entering a bike shop to request information from local riders who would much prefer to keep their favorite trails secret, or know how it is to double- and triple-check data to be positive your trail info is correct, then you have an idea of how each of our authors has labored to bring about these books. You and I, and all the mountain bikers of America, are the richer for their efforts.

You'll get more out of this book if you take a moment to read the Introduction explaining the "Trail Description Outline." The "Topographic Maps" section will help you understand how useful topos will be on a ride, and will also tell you where to get them. And though this is a "where-to," not a "how-to" guide, those of you who have not traveled the backcountry might find "Hitting the Trail" of particular value.

In addition to the material above, newcomers to mountain biking might want to spend a minute with the glossary, page 312, so that terms like *hardpack*, *single-track*, and *water bars* won't throw you when you come across them in the text.

Finally, the tips in the Introduction and Afterword on mountain biking etiquette and the land-use controversy might help us all enjoy the trails a little more.

All the best.

Dennis Coello
St. Louis

Preface

The Pacific Northwest is rich with public lands and opportunities for active recreation. The mountain biking in this region is exceptional. Gravel roads crisscross forests, climb mountains to stunning views, and reach across deserts. An inviting array of trails is found here. Single-tracks follow rivers, traverse rocky canyons, and wind through rainforests. Easy or demanding, long or short, road or single-track—the cycling opportunities in Washington and Oregon are limitless. Some places in the Pacific Northwest are home to networks of bike routes, making them attractive vacation destinations. Other areas offer trips through remote backcountry, longer trails over ridge tops, or easy pedals down forest roads. This part of the country offers routes suited to all skill levels and tastes.

We spent a year looking for outstanding mountain bike rides in Washington and Oregon. We visited ranger stations and bike shops, scoured guidebooks and brochures, and consulted maps. People we met recommended favorite outings. We rode the routes that seemed most promising—about 100 excursions in all. Eighty-two of those rides have been selected for this guidebook.

We have made every attempt to portray accurately the difficulty of each ride. Keep in mind that "difficulty" is a subjective matter. Some cyclists will find our descriptions understated, while others will find them overly cautious. We suggest that you start with an easier ride, especially if your fitness level is low or if your bike handling skills could use some work. This will give you a feeling for our rating scale and provide you with a setting in which to strengthen your riding abilities.

Mountain biking can be arduous. After logging many miles researching guidebooks, we half expected to tire of the sport. On the contrary, increased strength and bike handling ability make mountain biking more fun. Now we find ourselves looking for longer rides and technical terrain. Our explorations have become more fulfilling. Here's hoping that your adventures are gratifying too.

SAFETY, COURTESY, AND RESPONSIBILITY

Be completely self-sufficient. Be prepared to find your own way if you get lost. Use all available maps. Information is often inaccurate on maps; check their data and make comparisons. Take note of landmarks and keep track of where you are and where you have come from. Stop often and look behind you; it may be necessary to turn around and retrace your path. Tell someone where you plan to go, your route of travel, and your anticipated time of return. Tell them

Looking west from Mt. Hebo.

what to do if you do not return by the specified time. Ride with others who may be able to provide help in an emergency, especially in remote areas. Always call ahead to check on trail and road conditions, closures, or special circumstances that could affect your ride. Learn first aid and how to deal with hypothermia, dehydration, heat stroke, snake and tick bites, and other ailments and injuries that could befall backcountry users. Carry a good first-aid and repair kit. Keep your bicycle in good working order and know how to make roadside repairs (like how to fix a flat). Develop a checklist of what to take with you when you go riding. Wear a helmet, cycling gloves, and protective eyewear.

Ride within your limitations. Turn around if the weather becomes threatening or if you find the ride more difficult than you had expected. Keep your speed under control at all times. Play it safe on narrow roads and when approaching blind corners; someone may be coming from the other direction. Stay to the right and ride defensively and predictably. If the route involves highway or city riding, avoid rush-hour traffic. Wait until the off-season to visit areas popular with tourists. Steer clear of ongoing logging operations and backcountry rides during hunting season.

As relative newcomers, mountain bikers should make an extra effort to be courteous and ride safely. Announce your presence when approaching other trail users. Yield the trail when you meet others head-on. Be mindful of the special needs of equestrians. Horses have poor eyesight, are easily spooked, and can cause serious injury when startled. If you meet horses on the trail, dismount and move well off the trail to the downhill side. Take up a position where the horse will have a clear view of you. Ask the rider if the horse is spooked easily. If you come upon equestrians from behind, stop well in back of them. Do not attempt to pass until you have announced your presence and asked for permission. Pass on the downhill side if possible. Give these animals a wide berth, for they may kick out at you.

Be prepared for extreme riding conditions. Weather conditions can change rapidly—especially at higher elevations; carry raingear, warm gloves, and other protective clothing to change into. Dress in layers so you can adjust your clothing to meet any number of riding conditions. Ultraviolet radiation from the sun becomes more intense as you climb higher; wear protective sunglasses and apply sunscreen with an SPF of 15 or higher. Reapply sunscreen frequently. Lower air humidity and loss of water through increased respiration can cause rapid dehydration at higher elevations. Carry water from a safe source and bring more than you expect to need. Force yourself to drink even if you are not thirsty, especially on hot days. Once you become dehydrated, you will not be able to rehydrate and continue cycling. Carry high-energy foods and eat often; drink water with your snacks and meals.

Respect the environment you are riding through. Bicycles are not permitted in Wilderness Areas or on the Pacific Crest Trail. Some public lands restrict bicycle use to designated trails and roads only. Obey all signs indicating road or trail closings. Never trespass on private property or block access with your parked vehicle. Always stay on trails and roads; cross-country riding is inappropriate and often illegal. Never travel on worn trails where cycling will cause further damage. Carry your bike over degraded sections of the trail or turn around and return the way you came. Do not shortcut switchbacks or ride around waterbars placed in the trail; help control erosion instead of creating further degradation. It is never appropriate to skid your tires. If you cannot control your speed without skidding, dismount and walk your bike down the hill to gentler terrain. Skidding through switchbacks is extremely hard on trails. If switchbacks are too tight to roll through, walk your bike down them. Resource damage can result from riding on wet trails; call ahead to check on trail and road conditions. Wait until the spring thaw is over and trails are dry before riding. Pack out your own trash and, when possible, remove other people's litter as well. Leave gates as you find them—close them behind you if they were closed.

Call or visit the ranger station (or other land management office) that is responsible for the lands you will be traveling on. Ask to speak with a trail coordinator or a recreation specialist. Find out when the trail was last maintained and what condition it is in. It is also a good idea to inquire about ranger station office hours, for they vary widely from district to district. Forest Service maps are great sources of information. Obtain both the general map of the forest and the district map (district maps are sometimes referred to as "fire maps"). The general map will provide you with an overview of the region and helpful information about the area. The district map (topographic) is more detailed and is helpful as a directional aid. Feedback about trail conditions and your impressions of the ride are helpful to the rangers.

Become an informed participant and get involved in managing the lands you use for recreation. Many groups are active in trail building and maintenance efforts. Non-ATB off-road-vehicle users and equestrians have a record of involvement that speaks well of their concern for public lands. As newcomers, mountain bikers need to make an extra effort to get involved in volunteer activities and in the managing of our common lands. Get in touch with a local cycling club or bike shop that works to keep trails open to mountain bikes and promotes responsible riding. Attend meetings where management and recreation plans are discussed. Ask to be placed on a mailing list for volunteer work building or repairing trails.

Conflicts and closures are still with us, but mountain biking has grown out of its infancy to become an accepted form of recreation. We seem to be getting along better with other trail users. Land managers across Washington and Oregon welcome mountain bikers; they only ask that cyclists ride responsibly.

Laurie and Chris Leman

P.S.   In our trail descriptions you will come across the term *pummy* (rhymes with tummy). Volcanic activity in the Pacific Northwest produces soils with a high content of pumice. In some areas, trails become thick with pumice dust. These dusty (pummy) conditions usually occur during prolonged dry spells and on routes receiving heavy use. Negotiating a bike on a pummy trail is like riding through sand, but pumice is light, and it can often be pedaled.

Introduction

TRAIL DESCRIPTION OUTLINE

Information on each trail in this book begins with a general description that includes length, configuration, scenery, highlights, trail conditions, and difficulty. Additional description is contained in eleven individual categories. The following will help you understand all of the information provided.

Trail name: Trail names are as designated on United States Geological Survey (USGS) or Forest Service or other maps, and/or by local custom.
Length: The overall length of a trail is described in miles, unless stated otherwise.
Configuration: This is a description of the shape of each trail—whether the trail is a loop, out-and-back (that is, along the same route), figure eight, trapezoid, isosceles triangle, or if it connects with another trail described in the book.
Difficulty: This provides at a glance a description of the degree of physical exertion required to complete the ride, and the technical skill required to pedal it. Authors were asked to keep in mind the fact that all riders are not equal, and thus to gauge the trail in terms of how the middle-of-the-road rider—someone between the newcomer and Ned Overend—could handle the route. Comments about the trail's length, condition, and elevation change will also assist you in determining the difficulty of any trail relative to your own abilities.
Condition: Trails are described in terms of being paved, unpaved, sandy, hardpacked, washboarded, two- or four-wheel-drive, single-track or double-track. All terms that might be unfamiliar to the first-time mountain biker are defined in the Glossary.
Scenery: Here you will find a general description of the natural surroundings during the seasons most riders pedal the trail, and a suggestion of what is to be found at special times (like great fall foliage or cactus in bloom).
Highlights: Towns, major water crossings, historical sites, etc., are listed.
General location: This category describes where the trail is located in reference to a nearby town or other landmark.
Elevation change: Unless stated otherwise, the figure provided is the total gain and loss of elevation along the trail. In regions where the elevation variation is not extreme, the route is simply described as flat, rolling, or possessing short steep climbs or descents.
Season: This is the best time of year to pedal the route, taking into account trail condition (for example, when it will not be muddy), riding comfort (when the

1

weather is too hot, cold, or wet), and local hunting seasons.

Note: Because the exact opening and closing dates of deer, elk, moose, and antelope seasons often change from year to year, riders should check with the local Fish and Game department, or call a sporting goods store (or any place that sells hunting licenses) in a nearby town before heading out. Wear bright clothes in fall, and don't wear suede jackets while in the saddle. Hunter's-orange tape on the helmet is also a good idea.

Services: This category is of primary importance in guides for paved-road tourers, but is far less crucial to most mountian bike trail descriptions because there are usually no services whatsoever to be found. Authors have noted when water is available on desert or long mountain routes, and have listed the availability of food, lodging, campgrounds, and bike shops. If all these services are present, you will find only the words "All services available in . . ."

Hazards: Special hazards like steep cliffs, great amounts of deadfall, or barbed-wire fences very close to the trail are noted here.

Rescue index: Determining how far one is from help on any particular trail can be difficult due to the backcountry nature of most mountain bike rides. Authors therefore state the proximity of homes or Forest Service outposts, nearby roads where one might hitch a ride, or the likelihood of other bikers being encountered on the trail. Phone numbers of local sheriff departments or hospitals have not been provided because phones are almost never available. If you are able to reach a phone, the local operator will connect you with emergency services.

Land status: This category provides information regarding whether the trail crosses land operated by the Forest Service, Bureau of Land Management or a city, state, or national park, whether it crosses private land whose owner (at the time the author did the research) has allowed mountain bikers right of passage, and so on.

Note: Authors have been extremely careful to offer only those routes that are open to bikers and are legal to ride. However, because land ownership changes over time, and because the land-use controversy created by mountain bikes still has not completely subsided, it is the duty of each cyclist to look for and to heed signs warning against trail use. Don't expect this book to get you off the hook when you're facing some small-town judge for pedaling past a "Biking Prohibited" sign erected the day before. Look for these signs, read them, and heed the advice. And remember there's always another trail.

Maps: The maps in this book have been produced with great care, and, in conjunction with the trail-following suggestions, will help you stay on course. But as every experienced mountain biker knows, things can get tricky in the backcountry. It is therefore strongly suggested that you avail yourself of the detailed information found in the 7.5 minute series USGS (United States Geological Survey) topographic maps. In some cases, authors have found that specific Forest Service or other maps may be more useful than the USGS quads, and tell how to obtain them.

Finding the trail: Detailed information on how to reach the trailhead and where to park your car is provided here.

Sources of additional information: Here you will find the address and/or phone number of a bike shop, governmental agency, or other source from which trail information can be obtained.

Notes on the trail: This is where you are guided carefully through any portions of the trail that are particularly difficult to follow. The author also may add information about the route that does not fit easily in the other categories. This category will not be present for those rides where the route is easy to follow.

ABBREVIATIONS

The following road-designation abbreviations are used in the America by Mountain Bike series:

CR	County Road
FR	Farm Route
FS	Forest Service road
I-	Interstate
IR	Indian Route
US	United States highway

State highways are designated with the appropriate two-letter state abbreviation, followed by the road number. Example: UT 6 = Utah State Highway 6.

Postal Service two-letter state codes:

AL	Alabama		KY	Kentucky
AK	Alaska		LA	Louisiana
AZ	Arizona		ME	Maine
AR	Arkansa		MD	Maryland
CA	California		MA	Massachusetts
CO	Colorado		MI	Michigan
CT	Connecticut		MN	Minnesota
DE	Delaware		MS	Mississippi
DC	District of Columbia a		MO	Missouri
FL	Florida		MT	Montana
GA	Georgia		NE	Nebraska
HI	Hawaii		NV	Nevada
ID	Idaho		NH	New Hampshire
IL	Illinois		NJ	New Jersey
IN	Indiana		NM	New Mexico
IA	Iowa		NY	New York
KS	Kansas		NC	North Carolina

ND	North Dakota	TX	Texas
OH	Ohio	UT	Utah
OK	Oklahoma	VT	Vermont
OR	Oregon	VA	Virginia
PA	Pennsylvania	WA	Washington
RI	Rhode Island	WV	West Virginia
SC	South Carolina	WI	Wisconsin
SD	South Dakota	WY	Wyoming
TN	Tennessee		

TOPOGRAPHIC MAPS

The maps in this book, when used in conjunction with the route directions present in each chapter, will in most instances be sufficient to get you to the trail and keep you on it. However, you will find superior detail and valuable information in the 7.5 minute series United States Geological Survey (USGS) topographic maps. Recognizing how indispensable these are to bikers and hikers alike, many bike shops and sporting goods stores now carry topos of the local area.

But if you're brand new to mountain biking you might be wondering "What's a topographic map?" In short, these differ from standard "flat" maps in that they indicate not only linear distance, but elevation as well. One glance at a "topo" will show you the difference, for "contour lines" are spread across the map like dozens of intricate spider webs. Each contour line represents a particular elevation, and at the base of each topo a particular "contour interval" designation is given. Yes, it sounds confusing if you're new to the lingo, but it truly is a simple and wonderfully helpful system. Keep reading.

Let's assume that the 7.5 minute series topo before us says "Contour Interval 40 feet," that the short trail we'll be pedaling is two inches in length on the map, and that it crosses five contour lines from its beginning to end. What do we know? Well, because the linear scale of this series is 2,000 feet to the inch (roughly 2¾ inches representing 1 mile), we know our trail is approximately 4/5 of a mile long (2 inches × 2,000 feet). But we also know we'll be climbing or descending 200 vertical feet (5 contour lines × 40 feet each) over that distance. And the elevation designations written on occasional contour lines will tell us if we're heading up or down.

The authors of this series warn their readers of upcoming terrain, but only a detailed topo gives you the information you need to pinpoint your position exactly on a map, steer yourself toward optional trails and roads nearby, plus let you know at a glance if you'll be pedaling hard to take them. It's a lot of information for a very low cost. In fact, the only drawback with topos is their

Consulting a Forest Service map.

size—several feet square. I've tried rolling them into tubes, folding them carefully, even cutting them into blocks and photocopying the pieces. Any of these systems is a pain, but no matter how you pack the maps you'll be happy they're along. And you'll be even happier if you pack a compass as well.

In addition to local bike shops and sporting goods stores, you'll find topos at major universities and some public libraries, where you might try photocopying the ones you need to avoid the cost of buying them. But if you want your own and can't find them locally, write to:

USGS Map Sales
Box 25286
Denver, CO 80225

Ask for an index while you're at it, plus a price list and a copy of the booklet *Topographic Maps*. In minutes you'll be reading them like a pro.

A second excellent series of maps available to mountain bikers is that put out by the United States Forest Service. If your trail runs through an area designated as a national forest, look in the phone book (white pages) under the United States Government listings, find the Department of Agriculture heading, and then run you finger down that section until you find the Forest Service. Give them a call and they'll provide the address of the regional Forest Service office, from which you can obtain the appropriate map.

TRAIL ETIQUETTE

Pick up almost any mountain bike magazine these days and you'll find articles and letters to the editor about trail conflict. For example, you'll find hikers' tales of being blindsided by speeding mountain bikers, complaints from mountain bikers about being blamed for trail damage that was really caused by horse or cattle traffic, and cries from bikers about those "kamikaze" riders who through their antics threaten to close even more trails to all of us.

The authors of this series have been very careful to guide you to only those trails that are open to mountain biking (or at least were open at the time of their research), and without exception have warned of the damage done to our sport through injudicious riding. My personal views on this matter appear in the Afterword, but all of us can benefit from glancing over the following International Mountain Bicycling Association (IMBA) Rules of the Trail before saddling up.

1. *Ride on open trails only.* Respect trail and road closures (ask if not sure), avoid possible trespass on private land, obtain permits and authorization as may be required. Federal and State wilderness areas are closed to cycling.

2. *Leave no trace.* Be sensitive to the dirt beneath you. Even on open trails, you should not ride under conditions where you will leave evidence of your passing, such as on certain soils shortly after rain. Observe the different types of soils and trail construction; practice low-impact cycling. This also means staying on the trail and not creating any new ones. Be sure to pack out at least as much as you pack in.

3. *Control your bicycle!* Inattention for even a second can cause disaster. Excessive speed can maim and threaten people; there is no excuse for it!

4. *Always yield the trail.* Make known your approach well in advance. A friendly greeting (or a bell) is considerate and works well; startling

someone may cause loss of trail access. Show your respect when passing others by slowing to a walk or even stopping. Anticipate that other trail users may be around corners or in blind spots.

5. *Never spook animals.* All animals are startled by an unannounced approach, a sudden movement, or a loud noise. This can be dangerous for you, for others, and for the animals. Give animals extra room and time to adjust to you. In passing, use special care and follow the directions of horseback riders (ask if uncertain). Running cattle and disturbing wild animals is a serious offense. Leave gates as you found them, or as marked.

6. *Plan ahead.* Know your equipment, your ability, and the area in which you are riding—and prepare accordingly. Be self-sufficient at all times. Wear a helmet, keep your machine in good condition, and carry necessary supplies for changes in weather or other conditions. A well-executed trip is a satisfaction to you and not a burden or offense to others.

For more information, contact IMBA, P.O. Box 412043, Los Angeles, CA 90041, (818) 792-8830.

HITTING THE TRAIL

Once again, because this is a "where-to," not a "how-to" guide, the following will be brief. If you're a veteran trail rider these suggestions might serve to remind you of something you've forgotten to pack. If you're a newcomer, they might convince you to think twice before hitting the backcountry unprepared.

Water: I've heard the questions dozens of times. "How much is enough? One bottle? Two? Three?! But think of all that extra weight!" Well, one simple physiological fact should convince you to err on the side of excess when it comes to deciding how much water to pack: a human working hard in 90-degree temperature needs approximately ten quarts of fluids every day. Ten quarts. That's two and a half gallons—12 large water bottles, or 16 small ones. And, with water weighing in at approximately 8 pounds per gallon, a one-day supply comes to a whopping 20 pounds.

In other words, pack along two or three bottles even for short rides. And make sure you can purify the water found along the trail on longer routes. When writing of those routes where this could be of critical importance, each author has provided information on where water can be found near the trail— if it can be found at all. But drink it untreated and you run the risk of disease. (See *Giardia* in the Glossary.)

Cooling off in Paulina Creek.

One sure way to kill both the bacteria and viruses in water is to boil it. Right. That's just how you want to spend your time on a bike ride. Besides, who wants to carry a stove, or denude the countryside stoking bonfires to boil water?

Luckily, there is a better way. Many riders pack along the effective, inexpensive, and only slightly distasteful tetraglycine hydroperiodide tablets (sold under the names Potable Aqua, Globaline, and Coughlan's, among others). Some invest in portable, lightweight purifiers that filter out the crud. Yes, purifying water with tablets or filters is a bother. But catch a case of Giardia sometime and you'll understand why it's worth the trouble.

Tools: Ever since my first cross-country tour in 1965 I've been kidded about the number of tools I pack on the trail. And so I will exit entirely from this discussion by providing a list compiled by two mechanic (and mountain biker) friends of mine. After all, since they make their livings fixing bikes, and get their kicks by riding them, who could be a better source?

These two suggest the following as an absolute minimum:

    tire levers
    spare tube and patch kit
    air pump
    allen wrenches (3, 4, 5, and 6 mm)
    six-inch crescent (adjustable-end) wrench
    small flat-blade screwdriver
    chain rivet tool
    spoke wrench

But, while they're on the trail, their personal tool pouches contain these additional items:

channel locks (small)
air gauge
tire valve cap (the metal kind, with a valve-stem remover)
baling wire (ten or so inches, for temporary repairs)
duct tape (small roll for temporary repairs or tire boot)
boot material (small piece of old tire or a large tube patch)
spare chain link
rear derailleur pulley
spare nuts and bolts
paper towel and tube of waterless hand cleaner

First-Aid Kit: My personal kit contains the following, sealed inside double Ziploc bags:

sunscreen
aspirin
butterfly-closure bandages
Band-Aids
gauze compress pads (a half-dozen 4" x 4")
gauze (one roll)
ace bandages or Spenco joint wraps
Benadryl (an antihistamine, in case of allergic reactions)
water purification tablets
Moleskin / Spenco "Second Skin"
hydrogen peroxide, iodine, or Mercurochrome (some kind of antiseptic)
snakebite kit

Final Considerations: The authors of this series have done a good job in suggesting that specific items be packed for certain trails—raingear in particular seasons, a hat and gloves for mountain passes, or shades for desert jaunts. Heed their warnings, and think ahead. Good luck.

Dennis Coello
St. Louis

OREGON

Oregon encompasses a huge variety of spectacular landscapes. The coastal region offers hundreds of miles of beaches, rolling sand dunes, and sublime scenery. Coastal mountains and agricultural valleys quickly give way to the Cascades. The volcanoes that are part of this mountain range create a remarkable backdrop for central Oregon. Majestic snow-cones rise from verdant forests, filling the horizon with their great bulk. Sparkling snowfields and glaciers are created as moist ocean air is wrung dry by the mountains. Vast deserts have formed on the leeward sides of these giants. Heading northeast, sage and juniper give way to alpine terrain and the beginning of the Rockies. The extreme northeastern corner of the state is home to Hells Canyon, another world altogether. It is diversity like this that makes Oregon such an incredible playground for mountain bikers.

Southwest Oregon Area Rides

Mountain ranges and huge tracts of timber dominate southwest Oregon. This area is defined by the Siskiyou Mountains to the south, the Klamath Mountains and Coastal Range to the west, and the Cascades to the east. The northern limit of this region (for the purposes of this book) is the North Umpqua River.

The weather in the valleys of western Oregon is generally moderate. Extreme temperatures are rare. Rain is common in the winter and spring. Summers are often dry, with daytime temperatures seldom climbing higher than the 80s. Evenings are pleasantly cool. The higher elevations see snow in the winter and a wider range of temperatures year-round.

We begin this book with rides near the cities of Ashland and Medford. Today the area is a center of art, culture, and commerce. This broad, flat valley was once home to a tribe of Native Americans that fiercely defended its homeland. Early French-Canadian trappers called them *les Coquins*, "the Rogues." In the late 1880s, the valley was chosen as the route for the Oregon-California Railroad. A train depot was built at Medford, and the rails were pushed south over Siskiyou Pass. This route provided a link to a newly completed national network of railways and to a large degree shaped the future of southwestern Oregon.

Heading west, we explore rides near Grants Pass in the Siskiyou National Forest. The Galice and Illinois Valley ranger districts are becoming popular destinations for mountain bikers. The rangers in these regions are working hard to develop trails that meet the needs of this growing sport.

To the north are riding opportunities in the Rogue and Umpqua national forests. Crater Lake National Park is bounded by these forests and is an outstanding feature of the area. Mountain biking is almost nonexistent in this park, but the breathtaking beauty of the lake should not be missed. Not far from the park is Diamond Lake, which can provide some good cycling. Farther to the north is the North Umpqua River Trail. It follows the North Umpqua River for 80 miles and offers a variety of outstanding recreation experiences. The Tioga and Fox sections of the trail are explored in this guidebook; the remaining 65 miles are left to intrepid cyclist-adventurers.

RIDE 1 *WATERSHED LOOP*

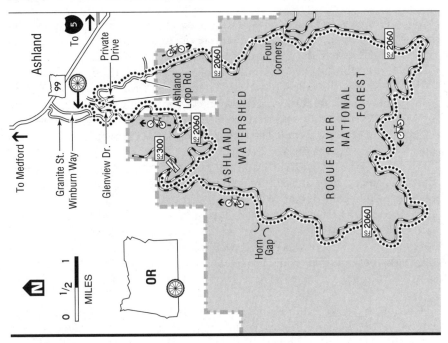

RIDE 1 WATERSHED LOOP

Ashland is a bustling tourist center known for its Shakespearean theater, splendid Victorian homes, and flower-filled landscapes. Two-wheel enthusiasts are drawn here by the area's outstanding mountain biking. A popular "local's ride" is the 27-mile Watershed Loop. The trip begins and ends in the center of Ashland in Lithia Park.

We rate this ride as difficult. The circuit's length and a steep five-mile climb make it strenuous. The 3,000-foot ascent is followed by 15 miles of level pedaling and easy hills. The loop ends with a six mile descent back into town. Most of the riding is on good gravel roads that see light traffic. (There are also 1.5 miles of pavement.)

General location: Ashland, Oregon is 15 miles north of the California border on Interstate 5.

Elevation change: The parking area in Lithia Park lies at 2,000′. The route

Forest Service Road #2060.

climbs to 4,400′ at an intersection of roads known as Four Corners. From Four Corners, you continue to ascend, but the climbing is hardly noticeable compared with the monster you just completed. You will encounter some rolling terrain before you reach a high point of 5,000′. These ups and downs add about 200′ of climbing to the trip. Total elevation gain: 3,200′.

Season: Snow may linger at higher elevations along the route in the spring. Most of the loop is within the Ashland Watershed. Entry into the watershed may be restricted during periods of high fire danger.

Services: Water is available at the trailhead in Lithia Park. All services can be obtained in Ashland.

Hazards: At Four Corners, Forest Service Road 2060 is gated and closed to most traffic. Ride defensively and assume that you may encounter some motor vehicles. The ride ends with a long descent that contains many curves. Control your speed and anticipate others approaching from around the next bend.

Rogue River National Forest.

Rescue index: Help can be found in Ashland.
Land status: The Rogue River National Forest and the City of Ashland.
Maps: The district map of the Ashland Ranger District is a good guide to this ride. USGS 7.5 minute quads: Ashland, Mt. Ashland, Siskiyou Peak, and Talent.
Finding the trail: From I-5 in Ashland, take Exit 14 and travel west on OR 66/Ashland Street. In 1.2 miles, turn right onto OR 99 North/Siskiyou Boulevard. In another mile the road's name changes to Lithia Way and it becomes a one-way street. Follow Lithia Way for .4 miles, cross a small bridge over Lithia Creek, and turn left onto North Main. This turn is signed "Southbound City Center." Once on North Main, get in the right lane, and turn right in .1 miles (follow the sign for Lithia Park). Bear right onto Winburn Way and follow it up through the park for .6 miles to the Upper Duck Pond and a parking lot on the left.

Sources of additional information:

Ashland Ranger District
645 Washington Street
Ashland, OR 97520
(503) 482-3333

Ashland Chamber of Commerce
P.O. Box 1360
Ashland, OR 97520
(503) 482-3486

Notes on the trail: From the parking lot, turn left onto Granite Street. The road changes to dirt after about .5 miles, and then you reach the intersection of Granite Street and Glenview Drive. Turn left onto Glenview Drive; follow it for .5 miles, then turn right onto Ashland Loop Road. Climb steeply to a T intersection and pavement. Turn left, then stay to the right and continue gently uphill on Ashland Loop Road. At the intersection with Morton Street, go right and uphill, remaining on Ashland Loop Road. Shortly, the pavement ends, the road enters the national forest, and its designation changes to FS 2060. At Four Corners, turn right and proceed on FS 2060 toward Horn Gap. Remain on FS 2060 to return to Lithia Park.

RIDE 2 *SISKIYOU CREST*

This is a demanding 30-mile out-and-back ride. It begins at Mt. Ashland Ski Area and follows gravel roads to the lookout on Dutchman Peak. The length of the trip and the amount of elevation gained make this a difficult outing. There is a lot of easy to moderately difficult climbing, and there are about two miles of steep uphills. The trip includes several long descents. The roads are in fair condition, with some washboarding and rocky sections. The return is almost as demanding as the first half of the tour.

Built in 1927, Dutchman Lookout is one of the few remaining cupola-style lookouts in the Pacific Northwest. The structure has two floors—a "fire-finder" room is stacked on top of the living quarters. The view from the lookout is panoramic. You may have the good fortune to meet Lillian Deala (the Lookout) and her faithful watchdog, Fluffy. Lillian pointed out the mountains for us; Fluffy let us play with her ball. On a clear day you can look north across nearly half of the state to Diamond Peak (near Waldo Lake). Closer peaks are Mt. Bailey, Mt. Thielsen (near Diamond Lake), and Mt. Scott (on the rim of Crater Lake). Mt. McLoughlin is prominent in the northeast. To the south, the ridge

RIDE 2 SISKIYOU CREST

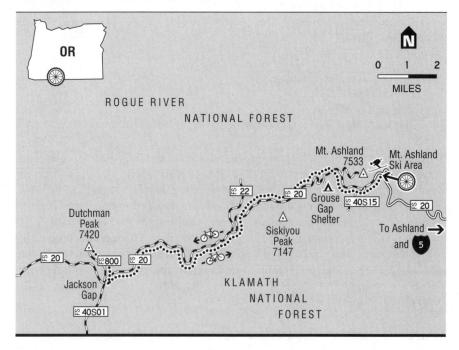

riding offers views of Cottonwood Valley, the Marble and Scott mountain ranges, Mt. Shasta, and Pilot Rock.

General location: Mt. Ashland Ski Area is approximately 18 miles southwest of Ashland, Oregon.

Elevation change: The ride begins at 6,600′ and tops out at 7,420′ on Dutchman Peak. Undulations along the route add an estimated 2,000′ of climbing to the trip. Total elevation gain: 2,820′.

Season: Generally, the roads are free of snow and open between July and mid-November. In the summer, the rocky meadows near Dutchman Peak contain many wildflowers. The route follows part of a popular 85-mile auto tour, and the roads can get busy on weekends and during hunting season.

Services: There is no water on this ride—bring all you will need with you. All services are available in Ashland.

Hazards: Loose rocks, gravel, ruts, and washboarding occur on the steeper sections of the route. The descent from Meridian Overlook to Siskiyou Gap is particularly rough. On bright days, this downhill stretch is made more treacherous by sun and shadow. Trees border the road and create patches of deep shade, which are followed by patches of blinding sunshine. Seeing the obstacles

Dutchman Lookout.

in the road becomes difficult under these conditions, so descend slowly. All of the riding is at high altitude; use sunscreen and drink plenty of water. Watch for traffic.

Rescue index: Help can be found in Ashland.

Land status: Rogue River National Forest.

Maps: The route travels through the Ashland and Applegate ranger districts. Used together, the district maps from these two agencies make a good guide to this ride. USGS 7.5 minute quads: Mt. Ashland, Siskiyou Peak, and Dutchman Peak.

Finding the trail: From Ashland, follow Interstate 5 south for 8.5 miles and take Exit 6 for Mt. Ashland. Follow the signs for Mt. Ashland. (You will be paralleling the highway for .6 miles.) Then turn right onto Colestin Road/Forest Service Road 20 and head toward Mt. Ashland Ski Area. Follow the road for 8.9 miles to the ski area parking lot on the right.

The view to the south from FS 20 is excellent, and there is a good pullout on the left just before milepost 5.

Sources of additional information:

Ashland Ranger District
645 Washington Street
Ashland, OR 97520
(503) 482-3333

Applegate Ranger District
Star Ranger Station
6941 Upper Applegate Road
Jacksonville, OR 97530
(503) 899-1812

Notes on the trail: Follow paved FS 20 southwest. The road surface changes to gravel in .3 miles (at a gate). At intersections, stay on FS 20 and follow the signs to Dutchman Peak. You will arrive at Jackson Gap and FS 800 after pedaling 13.7 miles. Turn right onto FS 800 and follow the sign to Dutchman Peak. You will reach the lookout in another 1.4 miles. Return the way you came. The Pacific Crest Trail parallels FS 20 for most of the route. It is closed to bicycles.

A brochure titled "The Siskiyou Loop" is available for $1 at the Ashland Ranger Station. It is filled with interesting information about the area.

RIDE 3   *APPLEGATE LAKE LOOP*

This 18-mile loop utilizes 12 miles of single-track, 3.5 miles of pavement, and 2.5 miles of gravel roads. The trail follows the fingered shoreline of Applegate Lake and climbs many short, moderately difficult hills. There are two steep climbs on the south side of the reservoir, both about one-quarter mile long. The trail is never too technical but is challenging enough to stay exciting. The majority of the trail surface is decomposed granite, and the trail is generally in good condition. Expect some rocks and windfalls. The roads are in good condition.

The most scenic portion of the ride occurs north of Watkins Campground. Wildflowers do well here, and there is a nice view of Elliott Creek Ridge across the lake. Harr Point is a good place for a lunch break. It is a sunny spot and surrounded by water.

General location: The ride starts at French Gulch Trailhead, approximately 25 miles southwest of Medford, Oregon.
Elevation change: The ride begins at 2,000′ and reaches a high point of 2,200′ at the top of Manzanita Creek Road. Many lesser ups and downs add an estimated 800′ of climbing to the trip. Total elevation gain: 1,000′.
Season: If the weather has been unseasonably dry, the spring is a nice time for a visit. The trails around the lake are often busy with hikers during the summer months. Typically, dry conditions contribute to good fall cycling, and a smattering of deciduous trees along the lakefront provide nice color that time of year.
Services: Water can be obtained on the north shore at Watkins Campground

RIDE 3 *APPLEGATE LAKE LOOP*

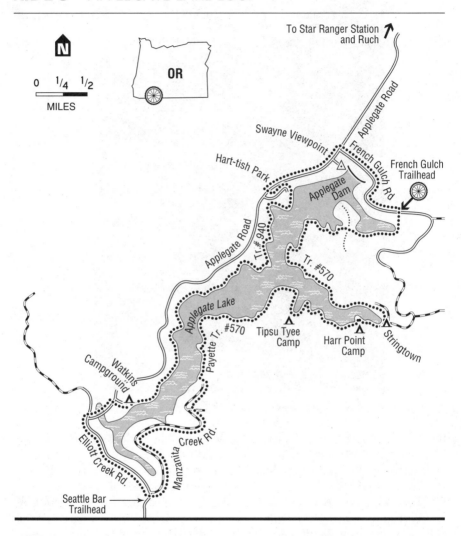

To Star Ranger Station and Ruch

N

0 1/4 1/2
MILES

OR

Applegate Road

Swayne Viewpoint

Hart-tish Park

French Gulch

French Gulch Trailhead

Applegate Dam

Applegate Road

Tr. #940

Tr. #570

Applegate Lake

Tr. #570

Tipsu Tyee Camp

Harr Point Camp

Stringtown

Payette Tr. #570

Watkins Campground

Manzanita Creek Rd.

Elliott Creek Rd.

Seattle Bar Trailhead

and Hart-tish Park. Limited groceries are available in Ruch. All services are available in Medford.

Hazards: In places, the single-track drops off steeply to the lake. Portions of the trail are rocky. Expect traffic on the roads.

Rescue index: Help may be found at the Star Ranger Station during regular business hours. There is also a pay phone at the ranger station.

Land status: Rogue River National Forest.

Maps: The district map for the Applegate Ranger District is a good guide to

Applegate Lake.

this route. USGS 7.5 minute quads: Squaw Lakes and Carberry Creek.

Finding the trail: From Interstate 5, take Exit #27 for Medford and Jacksonville. After exiting the highway, go west on Barnett Road (follow the signs toward Jacksonville). Get in the right-hand lane and turn right onto OR 99 North/Riverside Avenue. Follow OR 99 for 1 mile, then turn left onto OR 238/East Main Street. Bear right in .4 miles, remaining on OR 238. You will enter Jacksonville in 4 miles. About .7 miles into the town of Jacksonville, bear right, remaining on OR 238. This will take you through the "Old Town" section of Jacksonville. Note your mileage as you exit Jacksonville on OR 238. In 7.4 miles, turn left at the convenience store in the small town of Ruch onto unsigned Applegate Road. Follow signs for the Star Ranger Station and Applegate Dam. Follow Applegate Road for 14.5 miles to French Gulch Road on the left. Turn left onto French Gulch Road and follow it over Applegate Dam. Proceed on French Gulch Road for 1 mile and turn right into the parking area for French Gulch Trailhead.

Riding Da-Ku-Be-De-Te Trail

Sources of additional information:

Applegate Ranger District
Star Ranger Station
6941 Upper Applegate Road
Jacksonville, OR 97530
(503) 899-1812

U.S. Army Corps of Engineers
Portland District
P.O. Box 2946
Portland, OR 97208-2946

Notes on the trail: At the French Gulch Trailhead, follow the single-track Payette Trail #570. In approximately 1 mile (at the top of a steep little hill), stay left and descend as a trail goes right to a viewpoint and another trail goes hard left to signed Calsh Trail #971. Follow the signs to Stringtown. The trail becomes an overgrown double-track. At an intersection with a road (4.5 miles into the ride), go downhill and follow the road to a signed day-use area (Stringtown). Turn right and cross an earthen bridge that is bordered by a wooden fence. After a short uphill, turn right to go through a barbed wire fence at a "V" gate. Follow the trail past Harr Point and Tipsu Tyee Camp. Stay on the single-track as it follows the shoreline and passes innumerable inlets. The trail ends at an abandoned fire road and a sign for Payette Trail/French Gulch 9.2 miles. Go uphill through a narrow fence opening and ride up the steep road. Stay right at the Y intersection near the top of the hill, and immediately arrive at a main gravel road (unsigned Manzanita Creek Road). Continue straight (right) and descend on Manzanita Creek Road. Turn right when you reach paved Elliott Creek Road (Seattle Bar Trailhead is directly across from this intersection). Proceed on Elliott Creek Road for about 1 mile and turn right onto Applegate Road. Turn right into Watkins Campground after just .3 miles on Applegate Road. Signed Da-Ku-Be-De-Te Trail #940 heads northeast out of the campground and follows the shore of the reservoir. Trail #940 becomes a paved path after 3.3 miles (nearing Hart-tish Park). At the "No Bikes" sign, walk your bike to the left and uphill to a parking area. Stay left to exit the parking lot, and turn right onto Applegate Lake Road. Pass Swayne Viewpoint on the right, and then turn right onto French Gulch Road. Follow the road across the dam and return to French Gulch Trailhead.

RIDE 4   *BURNT TIMBER TRAIL*

Burnt Timber Trail forms a pleasant 1.7-mile single-track loop. It is well suited to beginning mountain bikers. There is a moderately steep one-quarter-mile climb near the end of the circuit where novices may have to push their bikes. The trail is well maintained and contains few technical difficulties.

The first portion of this interpretive trail passes through open woodlands and a meadow. Then it descends into a fern-filled old-growth forest. Live oak, madrone, and maples grow as understory trees below stately firs and cedars. After you cross lovely Burnt Timber Creek, your attention is focused on a challenging climb out of the drainage. The loop is short but fun enough to do twice—perhaps in the opposite direction.

General location: The trailhead is about 20 miles northwest of Grants Pass, Oregon.
Elevation change: The ride begins at 1,500', drops to a low point of 1,350', then ascends back to the trailhead. Ups and downs add approximately 50' of climbing to the loop. Total elevation gain: 200'.
Season: Early spring through fall.

RIDE 4 *BURNT TIMBER TRAIL*

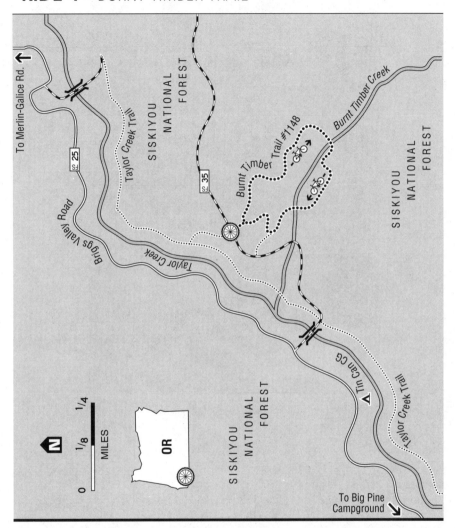

Services: There is no water on the ride. Water and a pay phone can be found at Indian Mary Campground. This campground is on the way to the trailhead on the Merlin-Galice Road. Food, lodging, groceries, and gas can be obtained in Merlin. All services are available in Grants Pass.

Hazards: The trail contains some tight turns and crosses some wooden bridges that can be slick when wet. Portions of the path are bordered by poison oak.

Rescue index: Help can be found in Merlin.

Land status: Siskiyou National Forest.

Burnt Timber Interpretive Trail.

Maps: Burnt Timber Trail was not shown on any maps at the time of our research. The Galice Ranger District was developing a mountain bike guide; contact the ranger station for updated information.

Finding the trail: Take Interstate 5 to Exit 61 (3 miles north of Grants Pass). Exit the highway and follow Merlin-Galice Road towards Merlin. Continue through Merlin on Merlin-Galice Road. From Merlin, it is 8.5 miles to Morrison's Lodge, on the right. After the lodge, Merlin-Galice Road crosses a concrete bridge over Taylor Creek and immediately comes to Briggs Valley Road/Forest Service Road 25. Turn left onto this paved one-lane road. Follow FS 25 for 4.9 miles to FS 35. Turn left onto FS 35 and travel .6 miles to the trailhead (on the right). Park in the pullout on the left.

Sources of additional information:

Galice Ranger District
1465 N.E. 7th Street
Grants Pass, OR 97526
(503) 476-3830

Notes on the trail: From the trailhead, descend on signed Burnt Timber Trail #1148. After passing an interpretive sign for "Poison Oak," you will immediately arrive at an interpretive sign describing "Forest Habitats." Stay left at the Y intersection at the "Forest Habitats" sign. Pass through a meadow and then enjoy a good stretch of downhill. A couple of small bridges span an intermittent creek, then you cross a couple of larger bridges over Burnt Timber Creek. After the second of these more substantial bridges, you arrive at an unsigned intersection of trails. To remain on Burnt Timber Trail, turn hard to the right and climb steeply. Bear left when you arrive back at the "Forest Habitats" sign. Pedal back to the trailhead.

RIDE 5 *CHROME RIDGE LOOP*

Chrome Ridge Loop is a demanding 20.5-mile ride. Pleasant views from the ridge and an exciting descent highlight the gravel road riding on this outing. The circuit ends on a fun note—four miles of single-track. The path follows a shady route through a forest of madrone, live oak, and conifers. This is a recently improved older trail. It contains rough areas and some stretches of loose tread, but it should improve with use.

The trip starts with a difficult five-mile gravel road climb to Chrome Ridge. This climb is followed by easier riding on rough and eroded Chrome Ridge Road. A fast descent back to the valley brings you to Minnow Creek Trail. The first 2.5 miles on the single-track are moderately difficult and technical. This section is quite soft, with hoof damage and loose rocks. The last 1.5 miles are an enjoyable descent, and the path is in good condition.

General location: Begins near Sam Brown Horse Camp, approximately 30 miles west of Grants Pass, Oregon.
Elevation change: The elevation at the trailhead is 2,080′. A high point of 4,240′ occurs on Chrome Ridge. Ups and downs on the ridge and trail add about 500′ of climbing to the loop. Total elevation gain: 2,660′.
Season: The higher elevations along the route are generally free of snow from June through October. Avoid hunting season. Stay off the trail when it is wet.
Services: Water can be obtained seasonally at Big Pine Campground (en route to the trailhead). Water pumps were being installed at Sam Brown Horse Camp

RIDE 5 CHROME RIDGE LOOP

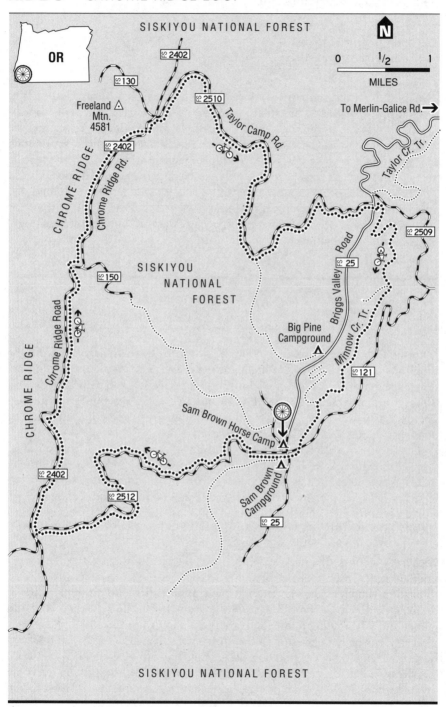

SISKIYOU NATIONAL FOREST

FS 2402

OR

N

0   1/2   1

MILES

FS 130

FS 2510

Freeland Mtn. 4581

Taylor Camp Rd.

To Merlin-Galice Rd. →

FS 2402

Taylor Cr. Tr.

CHROME RIDGE

Chrome Ridge Rd.

FS 2509

FS 150

SISKIYOU NATIONAL FOREST

FS 25

Briggs Valley Road

Chrome Ridge Road

Big Pine Campground

Minnow Cr. Tr.

CHROME RIDGE

FS 121

Sam Brown Horse Camp

FS 2402

FS 2512

Sam Brown Campground

FS 25

SISKIYOU NATIONAL FOREST

Riding Chrome Ridge.

and Sam Brown Campground at the time of our research. Food, lodging, groceries, and gas can be found in Merlin. All services are available in Grants Pass.

Hazards: The ride is long and exposed. Watch for traffic on the roads. Anticipate other trail users—the area is popular with equestrians. Control your speed on the descents and when approaching blind corners.

Rescue index: There is a pay phone at Indian Mary Campground on the Merlin-Galice Road (approximately 1.4 miles east of the intersection with Forest Service Road 25). Help can be found in Merlin.

Land status: Siskiyou National Forest.

Maps: Minnow Creek Trail was not shown on any maps at the time of our research. The Galice Ranger District was developing a mountain bike guide; contact the ranger station for updated information.

Finding the trail: Take Interstate 5 to Exit 61 (3 miles north of Grants Pass). Exit the highway and follow Merlin-Galice Road toward Merlin. Continue through Merlin on this road. From Merlin, it is 8.5 miles to Morrison's Lodge (on the right). After the lodge, Merlin-Galice Road crosses a concrete bridge over Taylor Creek and immediately comes to Briggs Valley Road/FS 25. Turn left onto this paved one-lane road. Follow FS 25 for 13 miles and turn right onto FS 2512 (1 mile beyond Big Pine Campground). Immediately (before the concrete bridge) turn right onto FS 011 and park.

Sources of additional information:

Galice Ranger District
1465 N.E. 7th Street
Grants Pass, OR 97526
(503) 476-3830

Notes on the trail: Turn right onto FS 2512 and begin the grind to Chrome Ridge. Turn right when you reach FS 2402/Chrome Ridge Road. Follow this main road for nearly 6 miles, to a major intersection where FS 130 goes left and FS 2510/Taylor Camp Road goes right. Turn right onto FS 2510 toward Briggs Valley Road. Proceed on the main road to FS 25 (Briggs Valley Road). Turn left onto FS 25; you will immediately arrive at the junction of FS 2509 (Onion Mountain Road) and Minnow Creek Trail. Turn right (south) onto Minnow Creek Trail. The single-track travels through the forest for 1.3 miles and then enters an open area on a hillside. Ride through the clearing and back into denser woods for .2 miles to an intersection of trails. Stay to the left, on the trail with a moderate descent, at the intersection where a secondary trail goes right and descends more steeply. You arrive at another intersection of trails in 1.7 miles. Bear left and continue to descend (the other trail goes right and climbs). Turn right when you reach unsigned FS 121. You will shortly arrive back at FS 25 and your vehicle, parked across the way.

The Galice Ranger District invites mountain bikers to explore this portion of the forest. The Briggs Valley area is fast becoming a prime destination for cyclists. New trails have been cut, signage has been upgraded, and new routes are being researched. The facilities at Sam Brown Campground and Sam Brown Horse Camp were being improved at the time of our visit. A brochure and map of mountain bike opportunities in the region is forthcoming.

RIDE 6   ILLINOIS RIVER ROAD

This 26.7-mile loop is strenuous, with many ups and downs. The trip begins with 14 miles on gravel Forest Service Road 4105. This stretch contains several long ascents and descents. The climbing on FS 4105 breaks down as follows: two miles of easy, four miles of moderately difficult, and two miles of steep

RIDE 6   *ILLINOIS RIVER ROAD*

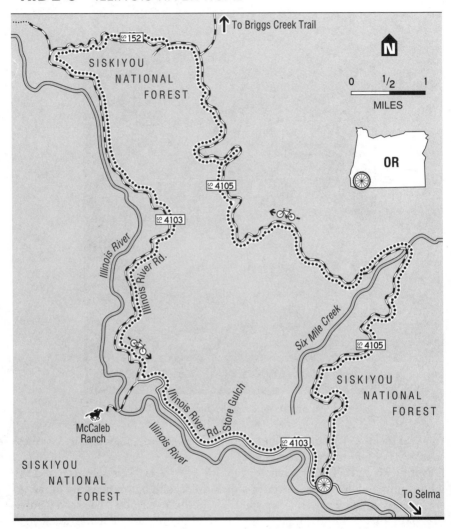

pedaling. This climb is followed by a rugged 1.2-mile descent to the Illinois River. Illinois River Road travels alongside the scenic waterway. The road is rough and the terrain is demanding. After 7.5 miles of unmerciful undulations, Illinois River Road changes to a paved surface. The last mile of the circuit is a grueling grind.

This loop makes a good training ride for powerful cyclists. The sight of your parked car may be a highlight of the trip. Reduced logging operations in the surrounding forest and the rough character of Illinois River Road help keep traffic light. The river is beautiful and is a favorite among kayakers and rafters.

Gazing down on the Wild and Scenic Illinois River.

General location: Begins 7 miles west of Selma, Oregon. Selma is 23 miles southwest of Grants Pass, Oregon.

Elevation change: The first part of the ride (on FS 4105) is characterized by long climbs and descents. The terrain over the second half is made up of many shorter ups and downs. The loop starts on FS 4105 at 1,500′. The road climbs to 2,480′ after 3.4 miles, then drops to 2,220′ by the 5-mile mark. The trip's high point of 2,800′ occurs in another 1.8 miles. This peak is followed by a 1.5-mile descent to 2,240′, then a 1-mile climb to 2,420′. Next, the route goes downhill for 3.2 miles to 1,520′. The intersection of FS 152 and FS 4105 is at 1,680′. FS 152 drops and connects up with Illinois River Road. Illinois River Road continues the descent to the ride's low point of 880′. From this low point, Illinois River Road rises and falls for the remainder of the circuit. The pedaling on this road contributes about 1,700′ of climbing to the ride. Lesser hills on FS 4105 add approximately 200′ of climbing to the trip. Total elevation gain: 3,800′.

Season: This excursion is suitable for year-round use.

Services: There is no water on this ride. Water, food, lodging, groceries, and gas can be obtained in Selma and Cave Junction.

Hazards: The greatest threat to a safe completion of this tour may be exhaustion. You may be fatigued by the time you reach Illinois River Road. The river road is exceedingly rough with rocks, and the hills seem never-ending. Control your speed on the descents and watch for loose gravel. FS 152 sees limited maintenance and can be strewn with windfalls.

Rescue index: Help can be found in Cave Junction.

Land status: Siskiyou National Forest lands and public right-of-way through private property.

Maps: The district map of the Illinois Valley Ranger District is suitable as a guide to this ride, but the map's depiction of the intersection of FS 4105 and FS 152 is incorrect. USGS 7.5 minute quads: Eight Dollar Mountain, Pearsoll Peak, Chrome Ridge, and York Butte.

Finding the trail: From Grants Pass, Oregon, follow US 199 southwest for 23 miles to Selma. From Crescent City, California, drive northeast on US 199 for 65 miles to Selma. In Selma, turn west onto Illinois River Road/FS 4103 and follow it for 6.8 miles to FS 4105, on the right. Continue on Illinois River Road for about 50 feet and turn left to park in a paved parking area.

Sources of additional information:

Illinois Valley Ranger District
26568 Redwood Highway
Cave Junction, OR 97523
(503) 592-2166

Notes on the trail: Head north up FS 4105. You encounter a short stretch of broken pavement after about 11 miles on this road. Then you find yourself cycling next to unsigned Soldier Creek and through some older stands of timber. You will pass a sign for Briggs Creek Trail #1132 (on the right) after a total of 13.1 miles on FS 4105. From this sign, it is about 1 mile to FS 152, on the right. FS 152 is signed, but the sign and the road are hard to see from FS 4105. The landmark to look for is a sign on the left of FS 4105: it identifies FS 4105 and reads, "Road 4103—14 miles, Selma—21 miles." Here, turn right onto FS 152 and follow it for 1.2 miles to Illinois River Road (signed for McCaleb Ranch, Store Gulch, Six Mile Creek, and Selma). Turn left onto Illinois River Road; the road to the right leads into private property. Stay on Illinois River Road for the remainder of the loop.

RIDE 7   *BROWN MOUNTAIN TRAIL*

This is a moderately difficult 13.5-mile loop (including 5.5 miles of single-track). The climbing on Brown Mountain Trail is mostly easy, but the riding is made more difficult by protruding obstacles like rocks and roots. The condition of the trail improves after the first mile. The route follows gravel roads for 4.7 miles, paved roads for 3.3 miles. The cycling on the roads is about half easy uphill pedaling, half level pedaling and downhill cruising. The ride ends with a moderately difficult (but short) ascent.

Brown Mountain Trail twists and turns its way through a lovely old-growth forest. Morel mushroom hunting in the late spring and huckleberry picking in the late summer can be productive. Orchids, trilliums, and other shade-loving wildflowers blanket the forest floor in the early summer. Near the end of the trail, you pass by 15,000-year-old lava flows at the base of Brown Mountain.

General location: Begins near Lake of the Woods, about 30 miles northeast of Ashland, Oregon and approximately 50 miles west of Klamath Falls, Oregon.
Elevation change: The trailhead lies at 4,850′. A high point of 5,730′ is attained on Forest Service Road 700. Undulations add about 200′ of climbing to the ride. Total elevation gain: 1,080′.
Season: Plan on cycling here from mid-May through October. Wildflower displays in the spring and summer provide seasonal interest.
Services: There is no water on this ride. Water can be obtained seasonally at Fish Lake Campground. Food, lodging, and pay phones can be found at Fish Lake Resort or Lake of the Woods Resort. All services are available in Ashland and Klamath Falls.
Hazards: Brown Mountain Trail is popular with hikers and equestrians. Watch for motorists while traveling on the forest roads.
Rescue index: Help is available seasonally at the Forest Service's Lake of the Woods Welcome Center during regular business hours.
Land status: Rogue River and Winema national forests.
Maps: The district map of the Ashland Ranger District of the Rogue River National Forest is a good guide to this ride. USGS 7.5 minute quads: Lake of the Woods South and Brown Mountain.
Finding the trail: From Interstate 5 at Ashland, take Exit 14 and go east on Main St./OR 66 east. Turn left (toward the airport) onto Dead Indian Road after .7 miles on OR 66. Drive 21 miles and turn left onto FS 37 (Big Elk Road). Follow FS 37 for 6 miles and turn right onto FS 3705. Stay on FS 3705 for 3.3 miles; there you will see the Brown Mountain Trail #1005 on the left. There is a parking area across from the trailhead.

From Klamath Falls, drive northwest on OR 140/Lake of the Woods

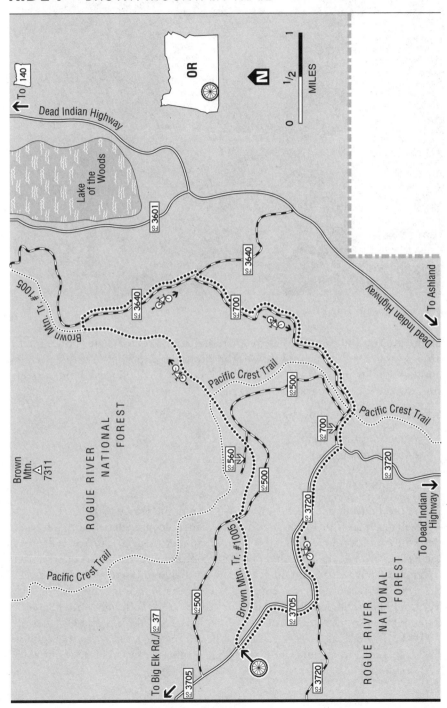

OR

N

MILES
0 1/2 1

To 140
Dead Indian Highway

Lake of the Woods

FS 3601

FS 3640

FS 3640

Brown Mtn. Tr. #1005

FS 700

FS 3640

To Ashland

Dead Indian Highway

Pacific Crest Trail

FS 500

FS 700

Pacific Crest Trail

FS 560

FS 500

FS 3720

FS 700

Brown Mtn.
7311

ROGUE RIVER NATIONAL FOREST

FS 3720

To Dead Indian Highway

Pacific Crest Trail

FS 500

Brown Mtn. Tr. #1005

FS 3705

To Big Elk Rd. FS 37

FS 3705

FS 3720

ROGUE RIVER NATIONAL FOREST

Brown Mountain Trail #1005.

Highway. You will pass the Winema National Forest Visitor Center (on the left) after 33 miles. Continue on OR 140 for 7 miles and turn left onto FS 37. Go another 2 miles and turn left onto FS 3705. Follow FS 3705 for 3.3 miles to the trail (on the left) and parking (on the right).

Sources of additional information:

Ashland Ranger District
645 Washington Street
Ashland, OR 97520
(503) 482-3333

Notes on the trail: Head east on Brown Mountain Trail #1005. In 1.7 miles you will reach FS 500. Turn right onto the road, then immediately turn left back onto the trail. Continue on Trail #1005 where it crosses FS 560. You will cross the Pacific Crest Trail in another .5 miles. Continue straight at this intersection to remain on Brown Mountain Trail; follow the sign for Lake of the Woods. At the next intersection (in over 2 miles), Lake of the Woods is signed to the left. Turn right here and pedal a short distance to FS 3640. Turn right onto FS 3640. After 1.5 miles, turn right onto FS 700. Follow FS 700 for 3.2 miles (past FS 500) to a T intersection. Turn right onto paved FS 3720, following the sign for FS 37. In 2 miles turn right onto FS 3705, continuing toward FS 37. Follow FS 3705 to your vehicle.

RIDE 8   *RUSTLER PEAK LOOKOUT*

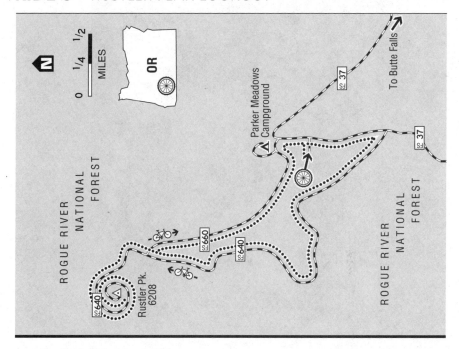

RIDE 8   *RUSTLER PEAK LOOKOUT*

This is a tough 9.3-mile loop with a one-way spur up to the top of Rustler Peak. The climbing starts out easy and becomes increasingly difficult as you near the summit. The ride follows gravel roads in mostly good condition. The final steep push to the top (1.4 miles) is made more challenging by stretches of coarse gravel. The view from the lookout is expansive. The return descent is steep and degraded.

General location: Begins near Parker Meadows Campground, approximately 25 miles northeast of Butte Falls, Oregon.

Elevation change: The ride begins at 5,100′, climbs 40′, and then drops quickly to 4,980′ at the turn for Forest Service Road 640. From here, FS 640 climbs steadily to 6,208′ atop Rustler Peak. Undulations in the topography add about 200′ of climbing to the circuit. Total elevation gain: 1,468′.

Season: These roads are usually free of snow by late June. Avoid riding here during hunting season.

Riding with John McBurney.

Services: Water can be obtained seasonally at Parker Meadows Campground. Food, lodging, gas, and groceries are available in Butte Falls.

Hazards: Although traffic is usually light, you may share these roads with motorists. Control your speed while descending and watch for obstacles like gravel, washboarding, ruts, rocks, and loose soil.

Rescue index: Help can be found in Butte Falls.

Land status: Rogue River National Forest.

Maps: The district map of the Butte Falls Ranger District is a good guide to this trip. USGS 7.5 minute quad: Rustler Peak.

Finding the trail: From the community of Butte Falls, follow Butte Falls Road east for .9 miles and turn left onto Butte Falls–Prospect Road. Stay on Butte Falls–Prospect Road for 9 miles to Lodgepole Road/FS 34. Turn right onto FS 34. In 7.7 miles you will pass South Fork Campground, then cross the South Fork of the Rogue River. After the river you come to FS 3775, on the left—which leads to Nichols Creek Picnic Area—and then to Parker Meadows

Road/FS 37. Turn right to follow FS 37 south for 7.4 miles. This road brings you to FS 660, on the right, which leads into Parker Meadows Campground. Continue on FS 37 for .3 miles to a closed road on the right. There is room to park one vehicle here. Additional parking can be found farther up FS 37 on the left.

Sources of additional information:

Butte Falls Ranger District
P.O. Box 227
Butte Falls, OR 97522
(503) 865-3581

Notes on the trail: Ride south on FS 37. After a short, gentle climb you will begin a fast descent. From this crest, it is .4 miles to FS 640, on the right. (Watch carefully; this road is easy to miss.) Turn right onto FS 640 and stay on this main road to reach Rustler Peak. Return down FS 640 for 1.4 miles to FS 660. Turn left onto FS 660 and drop to Parker Meadows Campground. Stay to the right, on FS 660, through the campground. Turn right onto FS 37 and ride to your vehicle.

RIDE 9   *MINNEHAHA LOOP*

This is an easy seven-mile loop that you can start from your campsite in Hamaker Campground. Half of the ride is on gravel roads in good condition; the other half is on a single-track in fair condition, with some tree roots, windfalls, and several pummy sections of trail. The circuit passes through lovely meadows and a forest of lodgepole pine, western white pine, and old-growth Douglas fir.

General location: Hamaker Campground is approximately 25 miles north of Prospect, Oregon.
Elevation change: The ride begins at 4,000', and a high point of 4,400' is attained at the footbridge at Soda Springs. Total elevation gain: 400'.
Season: The trail is fragile and should be avoided when wet. The driest time of year is generally June through October.
Services: Water can be obtained seasonally at Hamaker Campground. Food, lodging, gas, and groceries are available in Prospect and at Diamond Lake.
Hazards: Stay alert for traffic on the roads in the forest. The Minnehaha Trail is eroded in places and contains some exposed tree roots. Control your speed and anticipate other trail users.
Rescue index: Help is available in Prospect and at Diamond Lake.

RIDE 9 *MINNEHAHA LOOP*

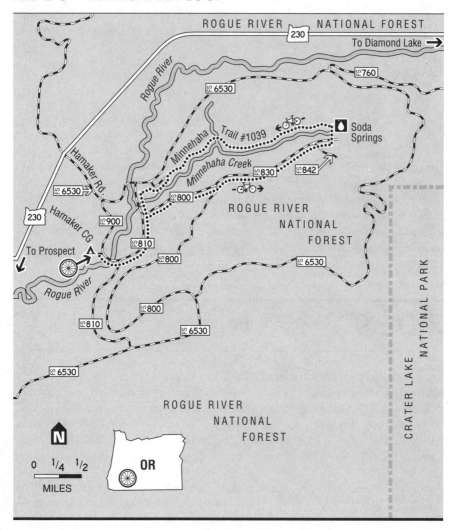

Land status: Rogue River National Forest.

Maps: The district map of the Prospect Ranger District is a good guide to this trip. The Rogue River National Forest map also shows this trail adequately. USGS 7.5 minute quad: Hamaker Butte.

Finding the trail: From Prospect, follow OR 62 north for 11 miles, to the junction with OR 230. Stay left to follow OR 230 for approximately 12 miles, to Hamaker Road/Forest Service Road 6530 (on the right). From Diamond Lake, drive southwest on OR 230 for about 11 miles to Hamaker Road/FS 6530 (on the left). Turn onto Hamaker Road and proceed in a southeasterly direction for

Minnehaha Trail.

.6 miles to FS 900. Turn right onto FS 900 and follow it for .8 miles to FS 930 (on the right). FS 930 leads into Hamaker Campground. Turn right and park in the campground if you intend to camp; otherwise, park along FS 900.

Sources of additional information:

Prospect Ranger District
47201 Highway 62
Prospect, OR 97536
(503) 560-3623

Notes on the trail: Cross the bridge over the Rogue River and pass your bike under the gate on the other side. Follow the double-track and turn left at the first intersection (a sign points left toward OR 230). Turn right at the next intersection (a sign points both left and right toward OR 230). You are now on unsigned FS 800. Follow this road for .9 miles, then turn left onto FS 830. The road narrows to an overgrown double-track after 1.5 miles. This double-track leads to Soda Springs Trail #1039. Turn left onto the trail. The trail becomes unsigned Minnehaha Trail #1039 after passing Soda Springs. This single-track follows Minnehaha Creek downstream for about 1.5 miles and then becomes more roadlike. In .25 miles, the road goes right and uphill; continue straight instead, following the trail into the woods. Turn left upon reaching unsigned FS 800. Pedal .25 miles, and turn right onto unsigned FS 810 to backtrack to your vehicle.

RIDE 10   *SHERWOOD BUTTE*

Sherwood Butte Loop is 31 miles long and mostly follows moderately difficult terrain. The gravel and dirt roads traveled on this route are in good condition. There is some steep climbing, and the length of the ride makes this a taxing trip.

Typical of forests throughout the Pacific Northwest, the Rogue River and Umpqua national forests are loaded with logging roads. A spirit of adventure and a good map will make finding mountain bike routes as simple as getting out there and going for it. The Hamaker Campground makes a nice base of operations for exploring the region.

General location: Hamaker Campground is approximately 25 miles north of Prospect, Oregon.

Elevation change: The ride starts at 4,000′ at Hamaker Campground and ascends to 5,100′ at Lake West. Beyond the lake, over rolling terrain, the route gains elevation to 5,420′ before reaching OR 230. From the highway, the ride climbs on Forest Service Road 3703 for 4 miles, to 6,100′, and then drops for about 1 mile, to 5,880′. The trip reaches 6,080′ near Three Lakes and then begins a long descent. This downhill stretch starts out gradually and becomes increasingly steep. The turn onto FS 100 lies at 4,880′. This road leads to FS 37, at 4,480′. The riding is uphill on FS 37 for 2.3 miles, to the Rogue-Umpqua Divide, at 5,040′. A long drop ensues from the divide to OR 230, at 4,140′. Pedaling from the highway to the campground is mostly level and downhill. Rolling topography and shorter hills over the course of the ride add an additional 500′ of climbing to the circuit. Total elevation gain: 3,360′.

Season: These roads are usually free of snow from June through October.

Services: Water is available seasonally at Hamaker Campground. Food, lodging, gas, and limited groceries are available in Prospect and at Diamond Lake.

Hazards: Expect logging trucks and loose gravel on the roads.

Rescue index: Help is available in Prospect and at Diamond Lake.

Land status: Rogue River National Forest and Umpqua National Forest.

Maps: The district map of the Prospect Ranger District of the Rogue River

RIDE 10 · *SHERWOOD BUTTE*

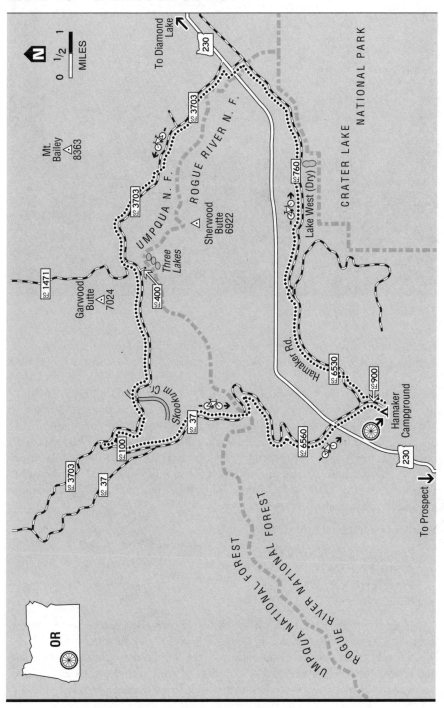

Road riding in the Rogue River.

National Forest is an excellent guide to the forest roads of this region. USGS 7.5 minute quads: Pumice Desert West, Hamaker Butte, Diamond Lake, and Garwood Butte.

Finding the trail: From Prospect, follow OR 62 north for 11 miles, to the junction with OR 230. Stay left, following OR 230 for approximately 12 miles to Hamaker Road/FS 6530 (on the right). From Diamond Lake, drive southwest on OR 230 for about 11 miles to Hamaker Road/FS 6530 (on the left). Turn onto Hamaker Road and proceed in a southeasterly direction for .6 miles to FS 900. Turn right onto FS 900 and follow it for .8 miles to FS 930, on the right. FS 930 leads into Hamaker Campground. Turn right and park in the campground if you intend to camp; otherwise, park along FS 900.

Sources of additional information:

Prospect Ranger District
47201 Highway 62
Prospect, OR 97536
(503) 560-3623

Notes on the trail: Ride back out FS 900 and turn right onto FS 6530 at the stop sign. After 4 miles of riding, turn left onto FS 760, heading toward Lake West. Cycle past Lake West and continue to a sign on the right that points left and reads, "State Highway 230—.25 miles." Turn left at this intersection and proceed to the highway. Turn right onto OR 230. In .3 miles, turn left at a sign for South Umpqua Road/FS 3703. You will pass a spur road to Three Lakes (FS 400) after 6 miles of cycling on FS 3703. You will cross over Skookum Creek after 3 more miles and then start losing elevation rapidly. Approximately 2 miles past Skookum Creek, turn left onto Three Lakes Connector Road/FS 100. Arrive at signed Fish Creek Road/FS 37 after 1.7 miles on FS 100. Turn left and uphill onto FS 37. Continue straight at the top of the Rogue-Umpqua Divide as the Fish Creek Road designation changes from FS 37 to FS 6560. The long descent on FS 6560 ends as you cross Muir Creek. It is .5 miles from Muir Creek to OR 230. Cross the highway and follow FS 6530 to signed FS 900. Turn right and follow FS 900 to your vehicle.

RIDE 11 *NORTH CRATER TRAIL / CRATER TRAIL LOOP*

This is a moderately difficult 21-mile loop near Diamond Lake. The circuit follows trails and roads that are in mostly good condition. North Crater Trail is a single-track that rolls up and down for several miles. Then it commences an easy to moderately difficult six-mile climb to the North Crater Trailhead. Next, the ride follows OR 138 for 1.5 miles. This highway leads to an abandoned fire road known as Crater Trail. Crater Trail includes a pleasant four-mile descent, several miles of easy riding, and some short, moderately difficult climbs.

North Crater Trail is well maintained and just challenging enough to make your ride exciting. The path travels through a forest of fir and lodgepole pine, and passes a few open meadows with good wildflowers in the spring. A spur road leads to a viewpoint at Summit Rock, where you can see Mt. Thielsen and Mt. Bailey in the distance.

General location: This ride begins at the Howlock Mountain Trailhead, near Diamond Lake Resort. Diamond Lake lies within the Umpqua National Forest, just north of Crater Lake National Park on OR 138.

Elevation change: The ride starts at 5,360′ and follows North Crater Trail to 5,860′, at the North Crater Trailhead. The high point is 6,060′, at Summit Rock. Undulations in the trails and roads add about 500′ of climbing to the loop. Total elevation gain: 1,200′.

Season: It may be late spring before the snow has melted and the trails are dry around Diamond Lake. Phone the forest service for current conditions. Arrive before Memorial Day or after Labor Day to avoid the busy season.

Services: Water is available seasonally at the Forest Service campgrounds on Diamond Lake. Food, lodging, gas, limited groceries, and mountain bike rentals can be found at Diamond Lake Resort.

Hazards: The trails around Diamond Lake are popular with hikers and equestrians. There are several highway crossings and 1.5 miles of cycling along the

RIDE 11 NORTH CRATER TRAIL / CRATER TRAIL LOOP

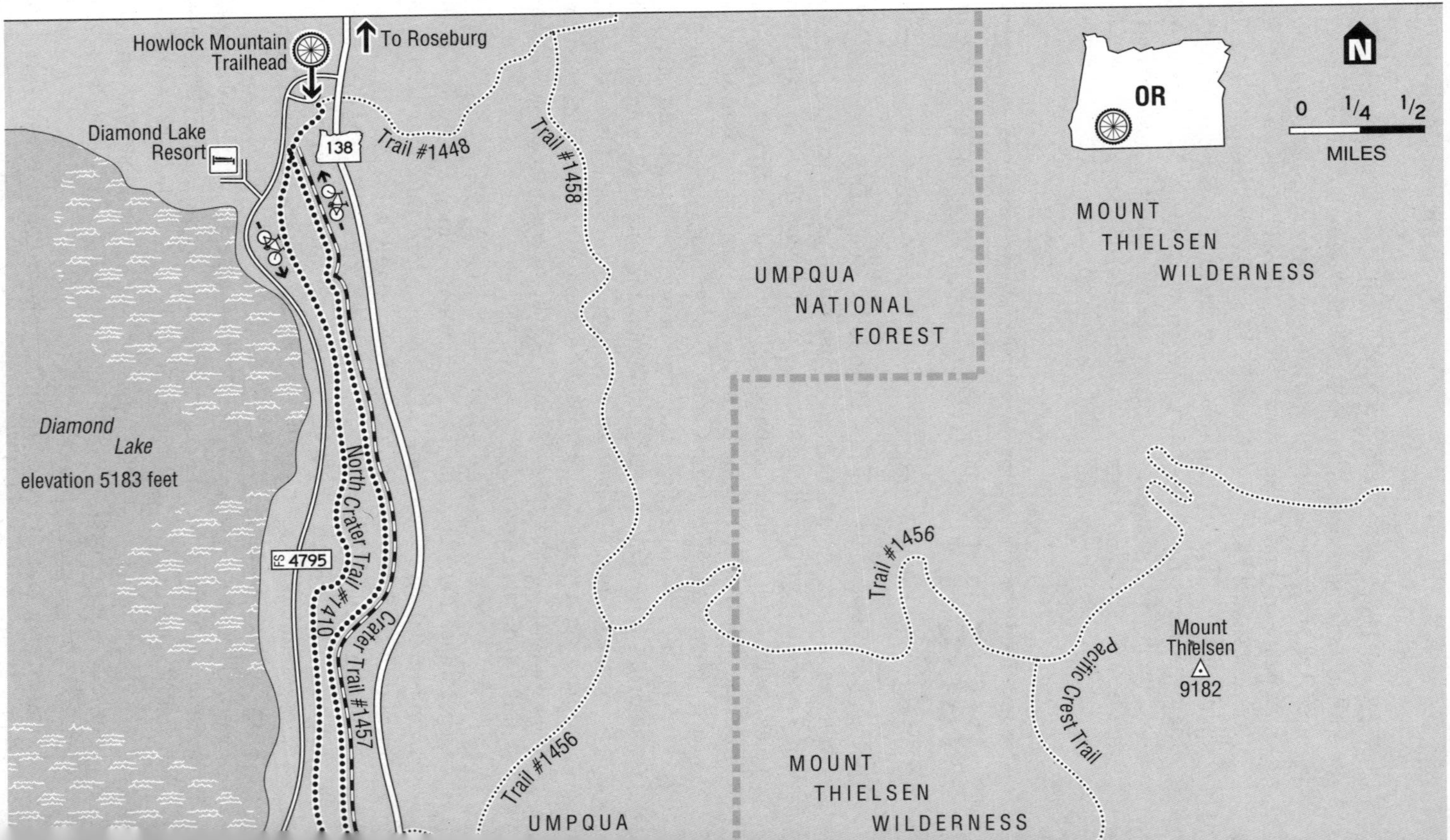

N

0   1/4   1/2
MILES

OR

MOUNT
THIELSEN
WILDERNESS

Mount
Thielsen
9182

Pacific Crest Trail

UMPQUA
NATIONAL
FOREST

Trail #1456

MOUNT
THIELSEN
WILDERNESS

Trail #1458

UMPQUA

Trail #1456

To Roseburg

Trail #1448

Howlock Mountain
Trailhead

138

Crater Trail #1457

North Crater Trail #1410

4795
FS

Diamond Lake
Resort

Diamond
Lake
elevation 5183 feet

46

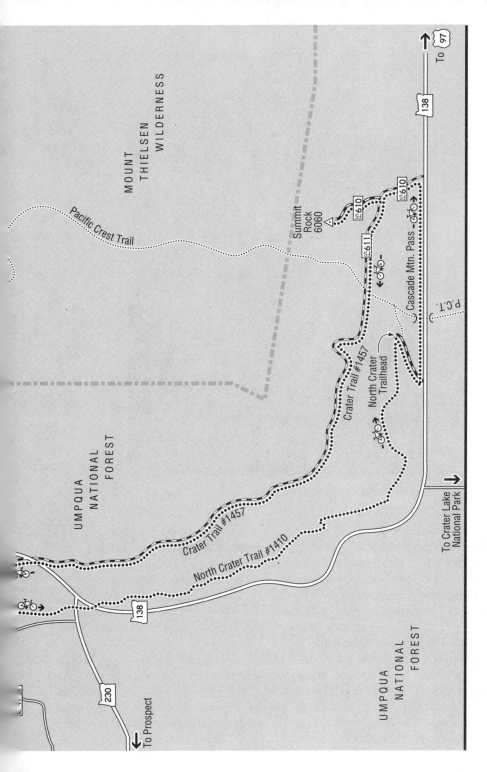

View of Mt. Thielsen from Summit Rock.

narrow shoulder of OR 138.

Rescue index: Help is available at Diamond Lake Resort or at the Forest Service's Information Center on the east shore of Diamond Lake. The Information Center is open seasonally and during regular business hours.

Land status: Umpqua National Forest.

Maps: The district map of the Diamond Lake Ranger District is a good guide to this ride. USGS 7.5 minute quads: Pumice Desert East, Pumice Desert West, Mount Thielsen, and Diamond Lake.

Finding the trail: From US 97 at Diamond Lake Junction, travel west on OR 138. Follow OR 138 for 23 miles to the northern entrance of Diamond Lake Recreation Area, on the left (west) side of the highway. From Interstate 5 in Roseburg, take OR 138 east for 76 miles to the northern entrance of Diamond Lake Recreation Area, on the right (west) side of the highway. At the northern entrance to the recreation area, turn west onto Forest Service Road 4795. Drive

.3 miles on FS 4795 and turn left into the Howlock Mountain Trailhead. Proceed past the corrals to the farthest parking area.

Sources of additional information:

Diamond Lake Ranger District
HC 60, Box 101
Idleyld Park, OR 97447
(503) 498-2531

Diamond Lake Resort
Diamond Lake, OR 97731
(503) 793-3333

Notes on the trail: From the Howlock Mountain Trailhead, bear right onto North Crater Trail #1410. Continue in a southerly direction on North Crater Trail as it passes behind the corrals. Follow the signs toward South Shore. Take note of the blue diamond-shaped markers that have been placed at intervals on the trees that border the trail. Follow the blue diamonds to remain on North Crater Trail. The trail crosses OR 230 after about 5 miles of pedaling. It crosses OR 138 in another .3 miles. From this highway crossing it is 1.5 miles to a point where the single-track meets an abandoned dirt road. Turn left onto this double-track road. It climbs gently for .8 miles and then switchbacks hard to the left. Look to the right at this switchback for an easy-to-miss single-track that is marked with blue diamonds. Turn right and follow this trail. It climbs steeply at first and then deposits you at another abandoned road. Ride across the road to continue on the trail marked by the blue diamonds. The trail rolls up and down and widens to a double-track. This portion of the route is marked by orange and blue diamonds. It is .4 miles from the last road crossing to a single-track that breaks off to the right (marked by blue diamonds). Turn right and follow this trail to a horse camp and a gravel road at the North Crater Trailhead. Follow the gravel road to OR 138 and turn left. You will reach signed Cascade Mountain Pass after .5 miles on OR 138, then you will begin a gentle descent. Turn left onto unmarked FS 610—1 mile past the summit and the first road on the left. FS 610 brings you to FS 611. Continue straight on FS 610, following the sign for Summit Rock. The road enters a clearing and then climbs steeply up to the viewpoint.

Return the way you came to the intersection of FS 610 and FS 611. Turn right onto FS 611. Shortly, the road crosses the Pacific Crest Trail and begins a long descent. At this point the road's designation changes from FS 611 to Crater Trail #1457. Stay on Crater Trail and follow the signs for Diamond Lake. You will arrive at OR 138 after descending for approximately 4 miles. Cross the highway and continue on Crater Trail for another 4 miles to your parked vehicle at the Howlock Mountain Trailhead.

You may wish to check out the Diamond Lake Bicycle Path while visiting the area. Linking this trail with FS 4795 creates a pleasant 11-mile loop around the lake. A handout describing the path's points of interest can be obtained at the Diamond Lake Visitor Information Center.

RIDE 12 *UMPQUA HOT SPRINGS*

This easy loop (with an out-and-back spur) is 6.5 miles long. There is a moderately difficult one-half-mile stretch of paved cycling on Forest Service Road 34, and there are some moderately difficult rolling hills on the North Umpqua Trail #1414. The hike to the springs is short but steep. The ride begins with about 1-mile of pavement, then travels over a gravel road in good condition for 3.5 miles. The rest of the trip is on a single-track trail in fair to good condition.

Umpqua Hot Springs is a small "tub" that has been carved out of the travertine that surrounds the springs. This soaking hole is very popular, and nudity is common. The single-track cycling is on the Hot Springs segment of the North Umpqua Trail. Rolling hills along this trail add a touch of excitement to the circuit.

General location: This ride starts at Toketee Lake Campground near Clearwater, Oregon. Clearwater is approximately 60 miles east of Roseburg.

Elevation change: From 2,440′ at Toketee Lake Campground, the ride ascends to 2,680′ at the parking area and trailhead for the springs. The hiking trail to the springs climbs about 150′. The route returns from the hot springs parking area to the North Umpqua Trail, at 2,600′. There are many small hills on this trail. Ups and downs add an estimated 100′ of climbing to the trip. Total elevation gain: 340′ (hike not included).

Season: The hot springs can be enjoyed year-round. In general, the region sees the most precipitation in the winter and the spring. Portions of the North Umpqua Trail are vulnerable to erosion. If the single-track appears to be wet, please return on the roads.

Services: There is no water on this ride, nor at Toketee Lake Campground. The nearby community of Clearwater has limited services. All services can be obtained in Glide, which is about 40 miles west of Clearwater on OR 138.

Hazards: Part of the route is on paved and gravel roads that see fair amounts of traffic. The water in the hot springs can be very hot (typically 108 degrees). The twisting and rolling nature of the North Umpqua Trail creates some blind spots; anticipate others approaching from the opposite direction. Walk your bike over degraded sections of the trail.

Rescue index: Help can be found at the Toketee Ranger Station in Clearwater during regular business hours. Emergency services are located in Glide.

RIDE 12 *UMPQUA HOT SPRINGS*

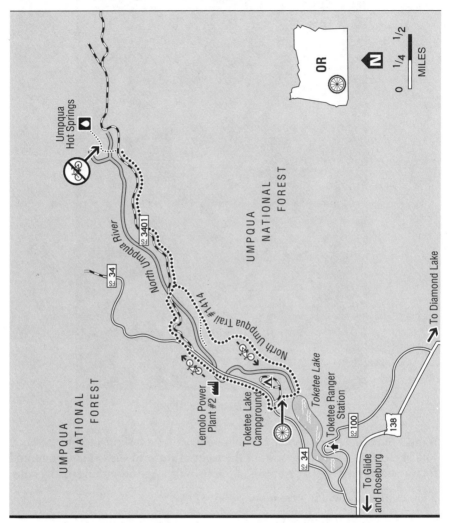

Land status: Umpqua National Forest.

Maps: The district map of the Diamond Lake Ranger District is a good guide to this ride. USGS 7.5 minute quads: Potter Mountain and Toketee Falls.

Finding the trail: From Roseburg, travel east on OR 138 for approximately 60 miles to FS 34 (on the left). From Diamond Lake, follow OR 138 west for about 20 miles to FS 34 (on the right). Turn north onto FS 34 (the west entrance to Toketee Ranger Station). At the bottom of the hill, turn left and cross two concrete bridges, staying on FS 34 where FS 100 goes right toward the Toketee

Footbridge over the North Umpqua River.

Ranger Station. Drive another 1.2 miles (along the west shore of Toketee Lake) to Toketee Lake Campground on the right. Turn into the campground and follow the entrance road past the boat ramp to the day-use parking on the right.

Sources of additional information:

Diamond Lake Ranger District
HC 60, Box 101
Idleyld Park, OR 97447
(503) 498-2531

Notes on the trail: Exit Toketee Lake Campground and turn right onto paved FS 34. Continue on FS 34 as it passes Lemolo Power Plant No. 2 and crosses a bridge over the North Umpqua River. After the bridge, the road climbs moderately to FS 3401 (Thorn Prairie Road). Turn right onto FS 3401. Go over the next bridge. Note that the North Umpqua Trail crosses FS 3401 here; you will pick up the North Umpqua Trail at this point on your return from the springs. Cycle another 1.4 miles on FS 3401 to an unsigned parking area for the Umpqua Hot Springs on the left. Lock your bike and cross the footbridge. Turn right after the bridge and follow the trail to the hot springs. After your soak, return the way you came on FS 3401. Turn left onto North Umpqua Trail #1414. In about 1 mile, turn left, following signed North Umpqua Trail. In another mile you will come to an intersection where the dirt single-track meets a gravel path. Turn right onto this gravel path and stay to the right; you will then reach a footbridge over the North Umpqua River. Cross the bridge into the day-use parking area of Toketee Lake Campground.

RIDE 13   *NORTH UMPQUA TRAIL / TIOGA AND FOX SECTIONS*

The North Umpqua Trail parallels the North Umpqua River for approximately 80 miles. Our route covers the Tioga and Fox sections of the trail and returns to the trailhead on OR 138. It is a strenuous 28-mile loop and requires good bike handling skills. The most challenging climb is a switchbacking ascent around Bob Butte, which you will encounter about three miles into the ride. In general, the route is well maintained. Some of the trail's steeper sections are degraded and rocky. There may also be some windfalls blocking the single-track.

The Tioga section of the trail has recently seen many improvements. New wooden footbridges span small waterfalls and creeks. An interpretive display near the start of the ride offers visitors a scenic spot for watching migrating salmon. The North Umpqua is famous for its steelhead and trout fishing.

General location: This trip begins at the Swiftwater County Park, 6 miles east of Glide, Oregon. This trailhead is the western terminus of the North Umpqua Trail.
Elevation change: The trip begins at 1,200′ and reaches a high point of 2,000′ near Bob Butte. The undulating character of the loop adds about 1,500′ of climbing to the ride. Total elevation gain: 2,300′.
Season: Wet weather may preclude traveling on this loop in the winter and spring. The river is popular for both summer and winter steelhead fishing. You can see chinook salmon spawning in September and October.
Services: There is no water available on this ride. Water, food, lodging, groceries, and gas can be obtained in Glide.
Hazards: This narrow trail sees traffic from pack and saddle stock, hikers, fishermen, and mountain bikers. The descent from Bob Butte involves a series of steep, rocky switchbacks. Some of the cycling is along sections of trail that

RIDE 13   *NORTH UMPQUA TRAIL / TIOGA AND FOX SECTIONS*

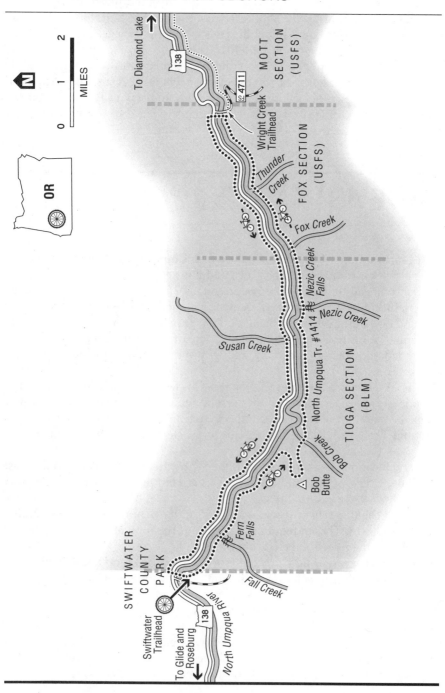

To Diamond Lake

138

FS 4711

MOTT SECTION (USFS)

Wright Creek Trailhead

Thunder Creek

FOX SECTION (USFS)

Fox Creek

Nezic Creek Falls

Nezic Creek

North Umpqua Tr. #1414

Susan Creek

TIOGA SECTION (BLM)

Bob Creek

Bob Butte

Fern Falls

Fall Creek

SWIFTWATER COUNTY PARK

Swiftwater Trailhead

138

To Glide and Roseburg

North Umpqua River

N

0   1   2
MILES

OR

One of many bridges on the North Umpqua Trail.

drop off steeply to the river. Walk your bike where you encounter dangerous conditions. Rattlesnakes may be present in the rocky, drier areas. Poison oak borders the trail in places. The return to the trailhead is via OR 138. This two-lane highway has no shoulder and can see heavy traffic from logging trucks and recreational vehicles.

Rescue index: Help can be found in Glide. There are no bail-out points on the 15-mile stretch of single-track. If an emergency presents itself, you will need to consider how best to exit the trail. Once you are past Bob Butte, backtracking becomes more difficult.

Land status: Lands administered by the Bureau of Land Management, Umpqua National Forest, and county government.

Maps: A pamphlet called "North Umpqua Trail" contains a passable map of the route as well as interesting interpretive information. It is available at the North Umpqua Ranger Station in Glide; you can also get a copy by writing the Bureau of Land Management Office in Roseburg. USGS 7.5 minute quads:

The North Umpqua River and Highway 138.

Glide, Mace Mountain, and Old Fairview.

Finding the trail: From Interstate 5 in Roseburg, drive east on OR 138 for 23 miles (6 miles east of Glide) to the Swiftwater County Park, on the right side of the highway. Turn and proceed over the bridge that spans the North Umpqua River. Immediately after crossing the bridge, turn left into the parking area for the North Umpqua Trail.

Sources of additional information:

Bureau of Land Management
Roseburg District
777 N.W. Garden Valley Boulevard
Roseburg, OR 97470
(503) 672-4491

Umpqua National Forest
North Umpqua Ranger District
Glide, OR 97443
(503) 496-3532

Notes on the trail: Ride upstream on the North Umpqua Trail. You will follow this trail for 15.3 miles to Forest Service Road 4711 at Wright Creek. Turn left onto FS 4711 and cross the bridge over the North Umpqua River. Turn left onto OR 138. Ride west on OR 138 for 12.4 miles to the entrance road for the Swiftwater County Park (on the left).

An easier option is to ride up the North Umpqua Trail and turn around when the riding gets too difficult. The first few miles of the trail roll up and down and are very scenic.

Southeast Oregon Area Rides

The Oregon Desert dominates southeastern Oregon. This huge sagebrush plateau, which covers roughly 45,000 square miles, accounts for approximately one-quarter of the state's area. Most of the land is owned by the government and administered by the Bureau of Land Management. The desert is bordered by national forests.

Lakeview, on the southwestern fringes of the desert, is surrounded by the Fremont National Forest. Hunting and fishing are the most popular recreational pursuits in the forest. Increasingly, however, active sports are emerging as major draws to the area. You can look at the traffic on the highway and tell what sports people are into. Nearly as common as motor homes are vehicles filled with grinning passengers and topped by roof racks laden with hang gliders, kayaks, windsurfers, and mountain bikes.

The Hart Mountain National Antelope Refuge, to the northeast of Lakeview, is a vast haven for pronghorn antelope, California bighorn sheep, mule deer, jackrabbits, golden eagles, and many other species of mammals and birds. Traveling through this remote region has been likened to going on safari. Lovers of starkness and spaciousness will delight in riding over the quiet roads of the refuge.

Farther to the northeast (near 9,773-foot Steens Mountain) is Diamond Craters. Geologists marvel at the diverse volcanic features found here. To most visitors, Diamond Craters is acres of sagebrush and some lava flows. Mountain bikers see good early-season bike rides.

Austere beauty and spaciousness abound in southeastern Oregon. The climate is dry, with an abundance of sunny days throughout the year. Services are a long way apart in this part of the country—you will want to come prepared. Get the car tuned up, fill about a hundred water bottles, and set out for the openness and freedom found only in great desert spaces.

RIDE 14   *BULLARD CANYON AND BLACK CAP*

This 11-mile ride combines an out-and-back trip with a loop. The entire circuit is on gravel roads in mostly good condition. The first two miles are an easy climb up Bullard Canyon. The next two miles are moderately difficult to steep. This ascent is followed by 2.5 miles of gradual to moderate climbing to Black Cap.

RIDE 14 *BULLARD CANYON AND BLACK CAP*

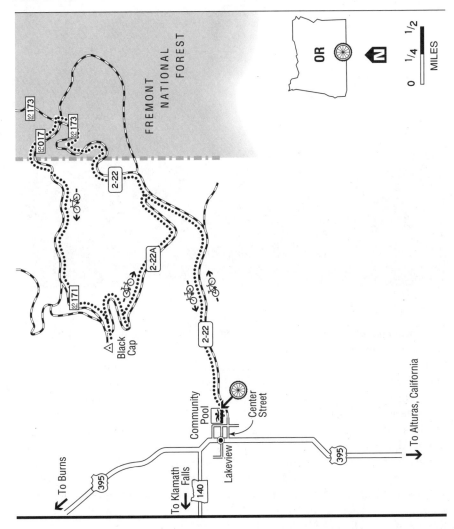

From Black Cap, you get an expansive view of Drews Valley to the west and Goose Lake to the south. If you are lucky, you can watch hang gliders soaring on the thermals above Lakeview. The developed launch site on Black Cap is becoming increasingly popular. The loop ends with 4.5 miles of downhill cycling. It starts out furiously, then mellows to a pleasant cruise through Bullard Canyon.

General location: This ride begins in Lakeview, Oregon, a community on US 395, 15 miles north of the California border.

Drews Valley.

Elevation change: The trip starts at 4,880′ and climbs to 6,400′ at Black Cap. Total elevation gain: 1,520′.

Season: If you are interested in watching the hang gliders take off and soar, plan on a summer visit: hot afternoons produce the conditions that the pilots seek. The roads are generally free from snow and mud by late May and remain passable through October.

Services: Water can be obtained seasonally at the community pool near the trailhead. All services are available in Lakeview.

Hazards: There is some traffic through Bullard Canyon. There are homes in the hills above Lakeview, and sportsmen use these roads to access the forest. The descent from Black Cap is steep. The road contains patches of loose gravel, especially in corners.

Rescue index: Help can be found in Lakeview.

Land status: Fremont National Forest and state forest lands.

Maps: The district map of the Lakeview Ranger District is a good guide to this ride. USGS 7.5 minute quad: Lakeview NE.

Finding the trail: From the intersection of US 395 and OR 140 in Lakeview, follow US 395 south. In .3 miles, turn left on Center Street. Follow the signs to the community pool. Stay on Center Street, drive just beyond the pool, and park on the left near the start of Bullard Canyon.

Sources of additional information:

> Fremont National Forest
> Supervisor's Office
> 524 North G Street
> Lakeview, OR 97630
> (503) 947-2151

> Lakeview Ranger District
> HC 64, Box 60
> Lakeview, OR 97630
> (503) 947-3334

Notes on the trail: Head east up the canyon on unsigned County Road 2-22. Turn left at the first intersection of roads, staying on CR 2-22. It is just over .5 miles from this turn to the next intersection, near some power lines; here, continue straight. In another mile you will enter the national forest and the road designation will change to Forest Service Road 173. Ride .5 miles farther on FS 173 to a hub of roads. Turn hard to the left here, onto FS 017, where FS 173 continues straight. Stay on the main road and ride for close to 2 miles, until you see an open area and FS 171 on the left. Turn left onto FS 171. Some radio towers will come into view after about .4 miles on this rougher, steeper road. Just before you arrive at the base of these towers, turn to the right and follow a double-track toward Black Cap and some distant radio towers. Shortly before you get to Black Cap, notice a road that goes left and downhill steeply. This is unsigned CR 2-22A. You will descend from Black Cap on this road. Check out the vista and descend on CR 2-22A for 2 miles to unsigned CR 2-22. Turn right onto CR 2-22 to continue your descent and return to your vehicle.

RIDE 15 *HART MOUNTAIN / GUANO CREEK LOOP*

This trip is a 22.5-mile loop through a portion of the Hart Mountain National Antelope Refuge. The ride is long and exposed and lies at a relatively high elevation. There is a lot of climbing, but it is all easy to moderately difficult. The first 15.5 miles are over two-wheel-drive gravel roads in mostly good condition. These roads contain some loose gravel and washboarding. The remaining seven miles are on four-wheel-drive roads in fair condition, with some deep ruts and large rocks. The most degraded section of road occurs on the final descent.

Pedaling through this sagebrush desert is a treat for those seeking a more remote riding experience—you may even find yourself humming "Home on the Range." Bands of pronghorn antelope are a common sight, as are mule deer and coyotes. Aspen thickets dot the hillsides of Hart Mountain and add a splash of

RIDE 15 *HART MOUNTAIN / GUANO CREEK LOOP*

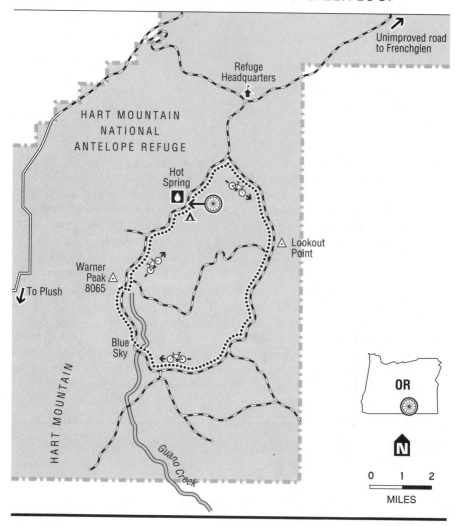

fall color to the landscape along Guano Creek. A soak in the hot spring (at the trailhead) caps off a nice day of cycling.

General location: This ride begins near Hot Springs Camp in the Hart Mountain National Antelope Refuge (approximately 70 miles northeast of Lakeview, Oregon).

Elevation change: The loop starts at 5,600´ and rolls up and down to reach 6,185´ at Lookout Point. The ride's high point—6,860´—is attained near the

Hart Mountain National Antelope Refuge.

end of the trip. Undulations add about 700′ of climbing to the circuit. Total elevation gain: 1,960′.

Season: The best time to ride here is from August 1 through October. The main roads are closed from November through Memorial Day, and the four-wheel-drive roads are closed until August 1. Road conditions and wildlife protection practices may limit access to parts of the area at any time; call ahead to check on closures.

Services: Water can be obtained at the refuge headquarters. Gas, limited groceries, and a pay phone can be found in the town of Plush (approximately 28 miles from the campground). All services are available in Lakeview.

Hazards: Watch for motorists. Some of the descents go over coarse gravel, ruts, and large rocks. The route crosses several cattle guards.

Rescue index: Help can be obtained at the refuge headquarters or in the town of Plush.

Land status: Public lands administered by the Department of the Interior.

Maps: A Hart Mountain Refuge brochure, which can be obtained at the refuge headquarters, is an adequate guide to this outing. USGS 7.5 minute quads: Campbell Lake, Flook Lake, Swede Knoll, and Warner Peak.

Finding the trail: From Lakeview, follow US 395 north for 4.5 miles to its junction with OR 140. Turn right onto OR 140 and drive 16 miles to the intersection of County Road 313/Plush Cutoff Road (a sign points left toward Plush and Hart Mountain Refuge). Turn left and follow CR 313 for 19 miles. Follow the road through Plush and turn right onto Hart Mountain Road (where a sign for Hart Mountain Refuge points right). This paved road changes to dirt after winding through farmlands for 13.6 miles. Continue on the dirt road for another 10 miles, until you reach the refuge headquarters. From the headquarters, drive south for 1.7 miles to a Y intersection. Bear right and travel 2.5 miles to the hot spring on the right. Turn right toward the hot spring and park your vehicle.

Sources of additional information:

Hart Mountain National Antelope Refuge
P.O. Box 111
Lakeview, OR 97630
(503) 947-3315

Notes on the trail: Turn left out of the hot spring parking area and follow the road back toward the refuge headquarters. Turn right at the next intersection. A sign here reads "Road Closed November 1–May 25 due to Hazardous Conditions and to Reduce Wildlife Disturbance." After pedaling 4.2 miles on this road you will come to a sign that directs you left toward Lookout Point. Turn left and ride .1 miles to the viewpoint. Return to the main road and turn left to continue on the loop. Several jeep trails branch off from the route; be careful to stay on the main road. It is 8.4 miles from the lookout to a culvert where Guano Creek passes under the road. Soon after passing over the creek, you will come to a road that leads left toward Blue Sky (a private hunting camp); stay to the right, on the main road. After this intersection the route begins to climb more steeply and changes from a two-wheel-drive to a four-wheel-drive road. This climb tops out at a gate. Go through the gate and descend. The road rolls up and down and crosses two shallow creeks. This leg is followed by an easy climb that crests at a Y intersection. Here, continue straight on the main road as a lesser road goes left and uphill. Descend to your vehicle.

RIDE 16 *DIAMOND CRATERS*

This is an easy 9.4-mile out-and-back ride. Diamond Craters is said to have the "best and most diverse basaltic volcanic features in the United States." We enjoyed the area most for its remoteness. The surrounding sage and rock desert is stark but beautiful. The view to the south is filled by broad-shouldered, mile-high Steens Mountain.

You probably need to be a geologist to fully appreciate the region's volcanic diversity, but a mountain biker can have a good time here too. When the snow

RIDE 16 *DIAMOND CRATERS*

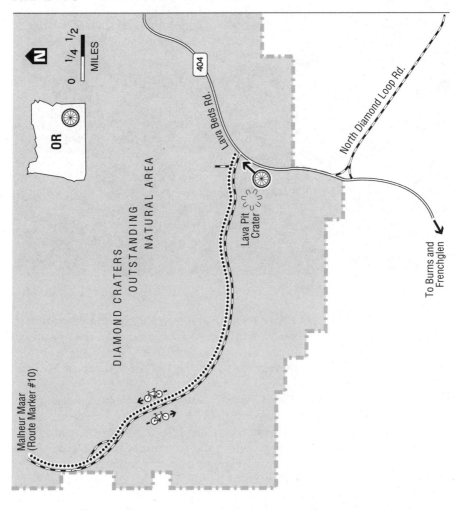

is still deep on the mountain trails, this isolated route will be dry and rideable. The cycling is on a four-wheel-drive cinder road. The road is rough and impassable to low-clearance vehicles for the first mile. The road improves, but it contains some pockets of loose cinders.

General location: Diamond Craters is located about 55 miles southeast of Burns, Oregon.

Elevation change: The ride begins at 4,300′ and climbs to a high point of

Lava Pit Crater.

4,420′ in the first mile. The road rolls up and down to reach a low point of 4,220′. Undulations in the terrain add about 50′ of climbing to the ride. Total elevation gain: 370′.

Season: The best times to ride here are the spring and fall. Temperatures in the summer can soar.

Services: No water is available on this ride. Water, food, lodging, groceries, and gas can be obtained in Burns.

Hazards: The first mile of road is rutted; be careful on the return descent. Wide tires are recommended for negotiating the sometimes loose roadbed. Be prepared for any emergency. Rattlesnakes reside in this natural area.

Rescue index: Help can be found in Burns. The nearest pay phone is in Frenchglen (27 miles south).

Land status: Lands administered by the Bureau of Land Management.

Maps: The BLM pamphlet "Self-Guided Auto Tour of Diamond Craters" contains a useful map. The brochure gives a detailed description of the area's geology and makes the trip much more interesting. USGS 7.5 minute quads: Diamond and Diamond Swamp.

Finding the trail: From Burns, follow OR 78 east for 1.6 miles and turn right onto OR 205. A sign here reads "Frenchglen 59, Fields 111, Denio 132." Drive 40 miles on OR 205 to Diamond Junction. Turn left at Diamond Junction onto Diamond Grain Camp Road/County Road 409. Follow this road for 6.7 miles, then turn left onto Lava Beds Road/CR 404. Drive 1.8 miles on Lava Beds Road; you will pass a large sign on the left announcing the Diamond Craters

Outstanding Natural Area. Turn left in another 1.4 miles onto a hard-packed cinder pullout. The route heads east from this parking area.

Sources of additional information:

Bureau of Land Management
Burns District
HC 74-12533 Highway 20 West
Hines, OR 97738
(503) 573-5241

Notes on the trail: From the parking area, follow the rough cinder road uphill. Stay left to remain on the main road. The route is well marked with numbered signs and arrows for the interpretive auto tour. Follow the markers to #10. Turn around, and in .3 miles, take the road to the right and return to your vehicle.

Northeast Oregon Area Rides

Most of the recreational lands in northeastern Oregon are in the 2.4-million-acre Wallowa-Whitman National Forest. Although the forest includes four wilderness areas that are off-limits to bikes, you should have little difficulty finding places to ride. There are 9,000 miles of dirt roads and 750 miles of trails open to two-wheel travel.

Varied terrain is the hallmark of northeastern Oregon. The Blue Mountains parade through the region, with many peaks reaching upward of 10,000 feet. Some of the individual mountain groups within this range are extremely rugged, especially the Wallowas.

The Blue Mountains contain not only lofty peaks but also Hells Canyon, the deepest canyon in the United States. This 6,000-foot-deep gorge on the Snake River separates the Wallowas from the Seven Devils Mountain Range of northern Idaho. The size and scale of the canyon is awe-inspiring.

The region that includes Enterprise, Joseph, and Imnaha was the land of Chief Joseph and the Nez Perce Indians (the Nee-Me-Poo people). The tribe spent their summers beside Wallowa Lake and wintered near the mouth of Joseph Creek at the Snake River. Hostilities between the Nez Perce and whites reached a fever pitch when gold was discovered in Orofino, Idaho. Now adding to the trespasses of cattlemen and settlers were 10,000 miners searching for gold.

After years of broken treaties, misunderstandings, and conflicts, the U.S. government forced the Nez Perce to leave their homeland and move to a reservation in Idaho. As the displaced Indians neared their new home, a small band of young warriors turned back and raided a white settlement. The cavalry was sent to bring in the Nez Perce.

Like Sitting Bull after defeating Custer, the Nez Perce decided to flee to Canada. The retreat, led by Chief Joseph, was an incredible march; every mile was filled with danger. After several horrible battles, and a flight of 2,000 miles in four months, the Indians were defeated—just 40 miles from the Canadian border.

The Nee-Me-Poo National Recreation Trail in Hells Canyon offers hikers a chance to walk in the footsteps of the Nez Perce. You can obtain an informative brochure about the trail at the Wallowa Mountains Visitor Center in Enterprise. The center's interpretive displays alone are worth a stop. The place is sure to please history buffs and windshield naturalists. The rangers at the center are very helpful and are armed with maps and handouts.

Towns throughout the region are home to district ranger stations. Take the opportunity to visit these posts; information on mountain biking is often available for the asking. There is great cycling near LaGrande, near Baker, and in the mountains between Joseph and Halfway. Explorations in these areas are easy in a four-wheel-drive vehicle, but a high-clearance, two-wheel-drive car will do the trick too.

Winters in northeastern Oregon are generally cold and damp; rain and snow are common. The spring and fall tend to be mild, while summers are hot and dry. Hells Canyon experiences temperate winters and hot summers.

RIDE 17 *PHILLIPS RESERVOIR LOOP*

Phillips Reservoir Loop is a 16-mile ride suitable for strong beginners. Ten miles of mellow single-track cycling on Shoreline Trail highlight the trip. The trail runs along the lakeshore contours and offers views of Elkhorn Crest and of boats bobbing on the water.

The riding is easy but not totally free of obstacles. A couple of rocky and sandy sections help keep the trail interesting. Ups and downs on the route are nicely graded and easy to handle. There are 3.2 miles of pedaling on paved and dirt forest roads in good condition. A downside to the loop is a 2.8-mile stretch on OR 7.

General location: The trailhead is located approximately 20 miles southwest of Baker City, Oregon.
Elevation change: The ride begins at 4,100′ and varies little over the course of the outing. Ups and downs on the route add up to about 500′ of climbing.
Season: Pedal around the lake on a fall weekday and you'll have the place to yourself—or nearly so. The reservoir is a popular summer destination, and the trail may be busy with hikers (especially on weekends).
Services: Water can be found seasonally at Union Creek Campground. There is a pay phone near the entrance to the campground. All services are available in Baker City.
Hazards: Ride with care on OR 7; the shoulder width varies from 0 to 3 feet, and traffic moves rapidly. Watch for loose rocks, sandy spots, and other trail users on Shoreline Trail.
Rescue index: You may be able to obtain emergency assistance at Union Creek Campground during the summer. Emergency services are located in Baker City.
Land status: Wallowa-Whitman National Forest.

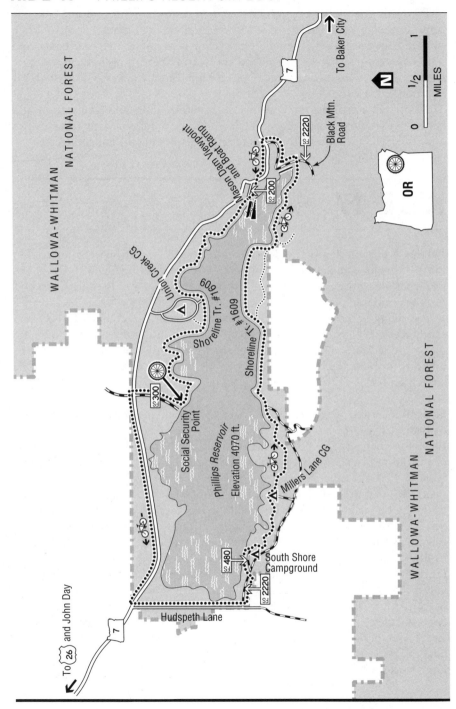

Shoreline Trail.

Maps: The district map for the Baker Ranger District is a good guide to this route. USGS 7.5 minute quads: Phillips Lake and Blue Canyon.

Finding the trail: From Interstate 84, take Exit 304 and follow the signs to Baker City. In 1.1 miles turn left onto Main Street/OR 7. Follow OR 7 south for approximately 20 miles to the Union Creek Recreation Area Campground, on the left. Continue west past the campground for .9 miles, to Forest Service Road 300. Turn left onto FS 300 toward Social Security Point. Drive down the road .4 miles to a parking area on the left.

Sources of additional information:

Baker Ranger District
3165 10th Street
Baker City, OR 97814
(503) 523-6391

Notes on the trail: Ride back up the gravel road and turn left onto OR 7. Follow OR 7 for 2.3 miles, then turn left onto Hudspeth Lane. In 1.2 miles, turn left onto gravel FS 2220 toward South Shore Campground. Follow FS 2220 for about .5 miles; turn left onto FS 480 to enter the campground. Follow the campground road east to the end of a cul-de-sac and the trail. Turn right onto the single-track. Stay on Shoreline Trail where side trails go right.

You will pass a ditch as you near the east end of the lake. Then turn left to cross a footbridge, and then left again to regain the trail. When you reach the gravel road at Mason Dam, turn left. Pedal over the dam and out to OR 7. Turn left onto the highway. In .5 miles, turn left into the Mason Dam Viewpoint and Boat Ramp (FS 200). Ride down toward the water, and turn right onto the trail near the parking area. Shoreline Trail changes to a paved surface as it passes through Union Creek Campground. Continue straight across the large boat ramp to pick up the trail on the other side. In another .4 miles, bear left onto a dirt single-track. The paved path will lead up to day-use parking if you miss the turn onto the dirt trail. Continue around the lakeshore (crossing several bridges and catwalks) to arrive back at your vehicle.

RIDE 18 *HORSE LAKE / BUCK'S CROSSING*

This is a 13-mile loop for intermediate and advanced cyclists. It is not a scenic trip, but it is a good workout. Horse Lake and Buck's Crossing trails are hoof-worn double-tracks used mostly by cattle and equestrians. Gravel roads account for about one-third of the circuit, and they are in good shape. Finding your way on this route is a challenge; at one point the trail fades away completely. The loop includes steep climbs and descents.

General location: This ride starts at Fish Lake, approximately 20 miles north of Halfway, Oregon.

Elevation change: The ride begins at 6,660′ and climbs to a high point of 6,960′ at the intersection of Forest Service Road 66 and FS 450. From here, the route descends to a low point of 5,600′ at Lake Fork Creek. The route then climbs back to 6,720′. Undulations on the trip add about 300′ of climbing to the excursion. Total elevation gain: 1,720′.

Season: It is possible to ride here from the late spring through the fall. The trails are less dusty early in the riding season.

Services: There is no water on the ride. Water, food, gas, lodging, pay phones, and groceries are available in Halfway.

Hazards: Loose rocks and soft soil are common on the double-track and single-track trails. There are some steep descents that are very rocky—walk your bike down. Watch for cars on the forest roads.

Rescue index: Help is available in Halfway.

Land status: Wallowa-Whitman National Forest.

Maps: The district map for the Pine Ranger District is a good guide to this route. USGS 7.5 minute quad: Deadman Point.

RIDE 18 *HORSE LAKE / BUCK'S CROSSING*

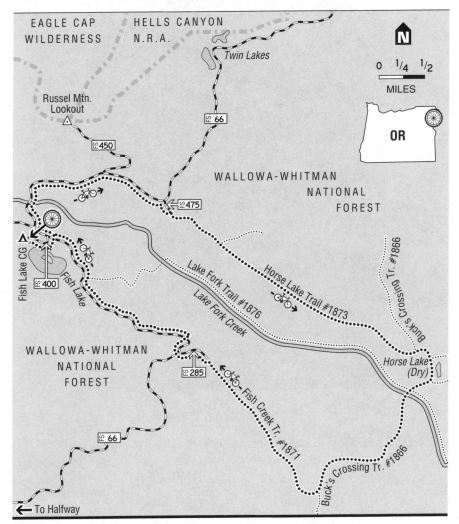

Finding the trail: From the main intersection in downtown Halfway, follow OR 413 (East Pine Road) north through town. Turn right in .4 miles onto County Road 1009 (the sign points right to Fish Lake). Turn left onto gravel CR 999 after 3.2 miles (a sign points left to Fish Lake). Follow this road for 16.2 miles to Fish Lake Campground, on the left. (The road's designation changes to FS 66 where it enters the national forest.) Turn left into the campground. Park on the left side of the entrance road, across from the vault toilets.

Horse Lake Trail.

Sources of additional information:

Pine Ranger District
General Delivery
Halfway, OR 97834
(503) 742-7511

Notes on the trail: Due to the number of unsigned intersections found on this loop, a bicycle odometer is recommended for this ride. All mileage notes in the description below are cumulative. Cyclists proficient at route finding may decide that the recommended topo maps and a compass are sufficient directional aids.

Ride out of the campground and turn left onto FS 66. In 2.4 miles, turn right onto FS 475. Follow this rough new road a short distance to its end at a blazed trail. Follow this trail into the woods and to the right. Turn left when the trail ends at an old double-track (2.6 miles). You are now on unsigned Horse Lake Trail #1873. Stay to the right at the next Y intersection (3.6 miles). Continue straight and downhill at the signs for Horse Lake and Buck's Crossing trails (5.8 miles). You will soon come upon Horse Lake Cow Camp, where you will see a couple of log structures. If you ride into the center of camp you have gone too far. As you approach the buildings, look to the right for the trail—it passes between two halves of a sawn log at 6.1 miles. Bear right and follow this trail south along dry Horse Lake. At the south end of the lake, the trail gets very rocky and starts to veer to the left. Look for a faint trail to the right at 6.3 miles. Turn onto this trail and descend through a boulder field. Walk your bike down a couple of steep rocky pitches and out onto a hillside where several cow paths branch off. Below you is a large open area with two signs on a post. Choose whichever cow path looks most desirable and descend to the signpost. The signs are at 6.5 miles and mark Buck's Crossing and Lake Fork Trails. Continue straight (toward Little Elk Road) and cross Lake Fork Creek. The trail fades out on the other side of the creek. Climb the hillside, bearing left on a faint cow path. You reenter open woods as you ascend higher, then you arrive at a canal at 6.6 miles. Get your feet wet crossing the canal and continue to push your bike up the pathless hillside. Go up steeply, bearing left a little. You will come to a double-track at 6.8 miles; turn left onto it. This double-track passes through heavier woods and through open areas and crosses several creeks. Buck's Crossing Trail is signed at 7.5 miles. Continue on the now faint double-track; soon the trail begins to climb and crosses more creeks. At the next open area (8.2 miles), you will pass another sign for Buck's Crossing Trail. Bear to the right and go through a gate in a barbed-wire fence. Go left and steeply uphill after passing through the gate, until you reach a double-track. A sign at this road denotes Fish Creek Trail #1871 and points right for FS 66. Turn right and climb. The riding gets more demanding and the scenery gets prettier. Go through many more barbed-wire gates, following the main road. Turn left at 9.9 miles onto a more traveled double-track. Cross a crude bridge over a creek at 10.4 miles, then follow the main road through an open area. Turn right onto FS 66 at 10.6 miles. Turn left at 12.9 miles into Fish Lake Campground.

RIDE 19 *SUGARLOAF / DEADMAN TRAILS*

We nicknamed this 6.7-mile ride "Cow Poop Loop." Much of the route follows dusty, hoof-worn cow paths through woods and grassy meadows. Technical, rocky ups and downs will have all but superheroes dabbing.

The trip begins with three miles of gravel roads. A quick descent leads into

RIDE 19 *SUGARLOAF / DEADMAN TRAILS*

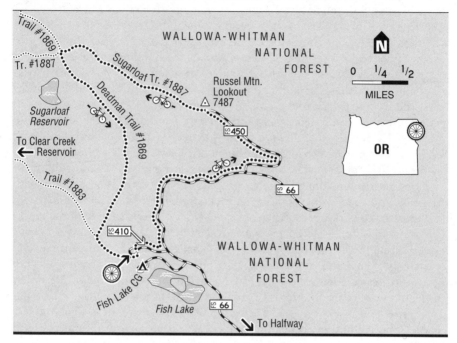

an easy to moderately difficult climb on Forest Service Road 66—the road is in good condition. The climbing becomes moderately difficult to steep on degraded FS 450. This pull lasts for 1.2 miles and ends at the Russel Mountain Lookout. Climb up the tower for a panoramic view of the surrounding countryside. Prominent to the north are snow-capped peaks in the Eagle Cap Wilderness. To the east are Hells Canyon and the distant Seven Devils. Badlands-like scenery stretches out to the south. Fish Lake lies to the southwest, the Wallowa Mountains to the west.

General location: The ride begins near Fish Lake, approximately 20 miles north of Halfway, Oregon.
Elevation gain: The loop starts at 6,800′ and quickly drops to the low point of the ride—6,720′. Russel Mountain, at 7,487′, is the high point of the trip. Undulations on the circuit add about 100′ of climbing to the loop. Total elevation gain: 867′.
Season: Snow may linger at higher elevations into the late spring. The meadows often remain boggy until later in the summer. The fall is an excellent time for visiting the region.
Services: There is no water on this ride. Water, food, gas, lodging, pay

Cow Poop Loop.

phones, and groceries are available in Halfway.

Hazards: Treacherous rocks and roots are encountered on this ride. Control your speed and watch for loose gravel and rocks while descending. You may encounter traffic on the roads.

Rescue index: Help is available in Halfway.

Land status: Wallowa-Whitman National Forest.

Maps: The district map of the Pine Ranger District is a good guide to this ride. USGS 7.5 minute quads: Deadman and Cornucopia.

Finding the trail: From the main intersection in downtown Halfway, follow OR 413 (East Pine Road) north through town. Turn right in .4 miles onto County Road 1009 (the sign points right to Fish Lake). Turn left onto gravel CR 999 after 3.2 miles (a sign points left to Fish Lake). Follow this road (FS 66, once it enters the national forest) for 16.2 miles; you will pass Fish Lake Campground on the left. Drive .1 miles past the entrance to Fish Lake Campground and turn left onto FS 410. Proceed to the end of the road, where there is a parking area for Deadman Canyon.

Sources of additional information:

Pine Ranger District
General Delivery
Halfway, OR 97834
(503) 742-7511

Notes on the trail: Ride back down the road and turn left onto FS 66. Follow this main road to the crest of a hill and turn left onto FS 450. The Russel Mountain Lookout Tower stands at the end of FS 450. Continue straight onto the single-track (unsigned Sugarloaf Trail #1887). The trail descends to a large alpine meadow. Continue in a northwesterly direction across the meadow. The path fades in and out—look for the wooden posts that mark the trail. The route becomes obvious again at the western end of the clearing. Climb up the hill to reenter the woods. Shortly, you arrive at another meadow and a T intersection with a sign for Sugarloaf Trail. Turn left and follow the cow path down the draw (you are now on unsigned Deadman Trail #1869). Stay downhill on the main trail. You will pass a couple of signs—one for Sugarloaf Trail and one for Sugarloaf Reservoir. Soon the path reenters the woods and takes you through more rocky areas and meadows. At the intersection where a trail goes right, toward Clear Creek Reservoir, continue straight (left). The trail becomes a rough road that drops steeply. Pass around the gate near the bottom of the hill, and turn left to reach your vehicle.

You can add 6 miles to your ride with a side trip to Clear Creek Reservoir.

RIDE 20 *POINT PROMINENCE*

Good mountain biking opportunities exist in the LaGrande Ranger District of the Wallowa-Whitman National Forest. While some of the riding is easily accessible, much of it is off the beaten track. If you have plenty of time, a reliable vehicle, and an adventurous spirit, you can find miles of dirt roads and trails here.

We spent a day cycling near Point Prominence and were lost for about half of the outing. Seems we missed a turn while on Indian Creek Trail #1917. Our mistake put us on a bootleg ORV route and then a horse trail. Things became more muddled as the day wore on. Eventually we reckoned our way out to the Indian Creek drainage. Unfortunately, logging operations had trees down all over the roads. In the end, we caught a ride back to our vehicle from a friendly forester.

The next morning we did what we should have done in the first place. We drove to the LaGrande Ranger Station and got some information. Mark Gomez, the district's recreation specialist and an avid mountain biker himself, supplied us with useful information and handouts on some popular rides. He recommended a ride called Mt. Fanny. It sounds like a scenic loop that is about half single-track and half forest roads.

We think we know where we went astray on the Point Prominence Loop. If you are feeling lucky, you can see if our "Notes on the Trail" information is

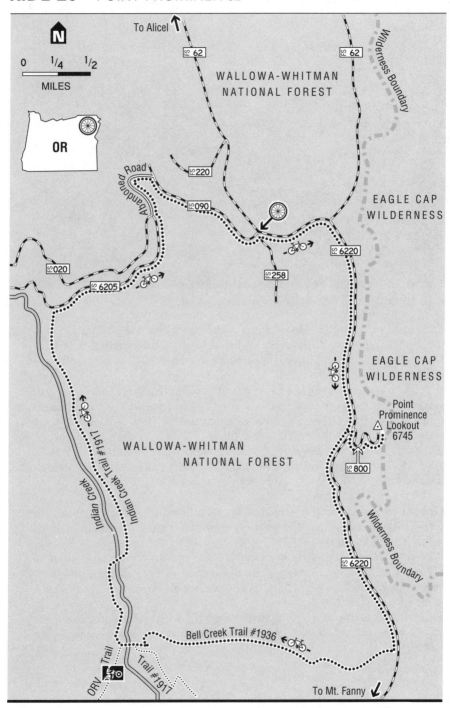

N

0   1/4   1/2
MILES

OR

To Alicel

FS 62   FS 62

Wilderness Boundary

WALLOWA-WHITMAN
NATIONAL FOREST

Abandoned Road

FS 220

EAGLE CAP
WILDERNESS

FS 090

FS 6220

FS 020

FS 6205   FS 258

EAGLE CAP
WILDERNESS

Point
Prominence
Lookout
6745

Indian Creek

Indian Creek Trail #1917

WALLOWA-WHITMAN
NATIONAL FOREST

FS 800

Bell Creek Trail #1936

FS 6220

Wilderness Boundary

ORV Trail

Trail #1917

To Mt. Fanny

Eagle Cap Wilderness from Point Prominence Lookout.

accurate. As for the difficulty of the trip and condition of the riding surfaces, we can only report on the portions of the ride that we completed. Reader feedback is encouraged. Find out if the intense logging is still under way before attempting the ride.

Point Prominence Loop is a 15-mile circuit, about half gravel roads and half single-track. Two of the road miles are built of coarse, fist-sized rock that is difficult to negotiate. These conditions exist near the start of the ride, where there is a lot of steep climbing. After Point Prominence, the roads improve. The trails are in good shape, with some ditchlike conditions, ruts, and rockiness. Most of the trail miles are downhill. We were exhausted after attempting this loop; you probably will be too.

General location: Point Prominence Lookout is on a high ridge above the Grande Ronde Valley in northeastern Oregon. The trailhead is about 30 miles northeast of LaGrande.

Elevation change: The ride begins at 5,800′ and reaches a high point of 6,745′ at the lookout. The low point of the loop, 4,800′, comes at the intersection of Indian Creek Trail and Forest Service Road 6205. Total elevation gain: 1,945′.

Season: This ride is relatively difficult to get to. When other parts of the forest are busy with vacationers, this area is quiet. It makes a good summertime destination.

Services: There is no water available on the ride—bring all you will need with you. All services are available in LaGrande.

Hazards: Some segments of the roads are extremely rough and contain patches of sand. The trails are eroded in places and have some rocky areas. Watch for pack stock, hikers, ORVs, and logging trucks. Timber operations may create impassable conditions and force a long rerouting for a return to your vehicle. Our description of the ride may be somewhat inaccurate, and trails may not be marked, so getting lost is a distinct possibility.

Rescue index: The nearest help is in LaGrande.

Land status: Wallowa-Whitman National Forest.

Maps: We used the district map for the LaGrande Ranger District of the Wallowa-Whitman National Forest. It shows some of the trails and roads we wandered around on. Find out if an updated map is available. USGS 7.5 minute quads: Gasset Bluff, Mt. Moriah, Cove, and Mt. Fanny.

Finding the trail: From Interstate 84, take Exit 261 in LaGrande. Follow OR 82 northeast for about 9 miles to Alicel. The town of Alicel is little more than a sawmill and a grain elevator next to the highway. Turn right onto Alicel Lane and proceed down it for .5 miles to a T intersection. Turn left, remaining on Alicel Lane. In another 3.2 miles you will arrive at the intersection with Grays Corner Road. Turn right here, following the sign that points toward Mt. Harris Lookout. Travel another mile to a sign that points left for Mt. Harris Loop. Turn left here onto a very rough and steep gravel road; Grays Corner Road continues straight. The steepness of the road eases and the surface improves after about 2.5 miles. Then you come to an intersection where Mt. Harris Loop goes left and FS 62 goes right, toward Point Prominence. Stay to the right, on FS 62. Follow the road signs to stay on FS 62 for 11 more miles to FS 090 and FS 258 (on the right). Park on the side of FS 62.

Sources of additional information:

LaGrande Ranger District
3502 Highway 30
LaGrande, OR 97850
(503) 963-7186

Notes on the trail: Continue east on FS 62 for .6 miles to FS 6220. Turn right onto FS 6220, following the sign for Point Prominence. Stay on this rough road for 1.8 miles to FS 800, on the left. Park your bike and walk up FS 800 to visit Point Prominence Lookout. (You can ride up instead if you feel like a little extra punishment.) There is a sign posted at the lookout asking you not to climb the tower. Announce your presence to the person manning the lookout—you may be invited up. Return down FS 800 to FS 6220 and turn left. Pedal 2 miles to Bell Creek Trail #1936. Turn right onto this single-track and ride 2.3 miles to a T intersection and unsigned Indian Creek Trail #1917. Turn right and ride a short distance to signed Indian Creek. This is where we made a wrong turn and got lost. We crossed the creek and went to the left onto a single-track. This trail connected us with a bootleg ORV trail known locally as Breashears Trail. Breashears Trail travels through an elk calving area, so the Forest Service discourages use of this trail and does not show it on their maps.

The following directions are what we have been told we should have done to complete the loop. They have not been checked in the field, and mileages are only approximate. Cross Indian Creek and bear right to pick up Indian Creek Trail #1917. The trail heads north and follows Indian Creek. The trail meets FS 6205 in 3.5 miles. Turn right onto FS 6205 and follow it for 1 mile, to a four-wheel-drive road. Turn right onto this road and ride for 1 mile to FS 090. Turn right onto FS 090 and follow it back to your vehicle. Good luck!

RIDE 21   *TENDERFOOT WAGON TRAIL*

This 10.5-mile loop is moderately difficult. Tenderfoot Wagon Trail climbs steeply at first but gets easier as it contours up the hillside. The trail contains some bumpy, hoof-damaged segments. The circuit drops rapidly for .4 miles on Big Sheep Cutoff Trail, then continues to descend for 2.4 miles on a rough gravel road. Next, a short pedal on pavement brings you to Forest Service Road 023. This double-track climbs (at times steeply) back to the trailhead at Salt Creek Summit. FS 023 is in poor condition, with rocky and pummy stretches.

This ride follows a 3.6-mile segment of the Tenderfoot Wagon Trail; it is well maintained and amply signed. The trail travels through an area devastated by the 1989 Canal Burn, a lightning-caused fire that ravaged a huge portion of the Wallowa-Whitman Forest. There are good views from the path of the Seven Devils Mountains in Idaho. Early pioneers used this route and installed more than three miles of "corduroy"—logs laid side by side to span boggy areas. Remnants of this wooden roadbed can still be seen today.

General location: Salt Creek Summit is located approximately 18 miles southeast of Joseph, Oregon.
Elevation change: The loop begins at 6,000′ and climbs to a high point of 6,400′ in the first 3 miles. A low point of 5,400′ occurs where FS 023 crosses Big Sheep Creek. Ups and downs add an estimated 300′ of climbing to the ride. Total elevation gain: 1,300′.
Season: The route is generally free of snow from June through October. Parts of Tenderfoot Wagon Trail may be boggy, especially in the spring.

Riding through the Canal Burn.

Services: There is no water on the ride. All services are available in Joseph.
Hazards: Portions of Tenderfoot Wagon Trail are obscured by tall grasses. Ruts and remnants of the corduroy are hidden from view; these obstacles can launch an unsuspecting cyclist right off the bike. Watch for traffic on the roads. The left turn onto FS 140 from paved FS 39 should be approached with caution—oncoming traffic has a restricted view.
Rescue index: Help is available in Joseph.
Land status: Wallowa-Whitman National Forest.
Maps: The district map for the Wallowa Valley Ranger District is a good guide to this ride. USGS 7.5 minute quad: Lick Creek.
Finding the trail: From Joseph, head east on OR 350. Turn right after 8 miles onto FS 39/Wallowa Mountain Road. Drive 9.5 miles to Salt Creek Summit and turn right onto FS 3920/Canal Road. Park on the left.

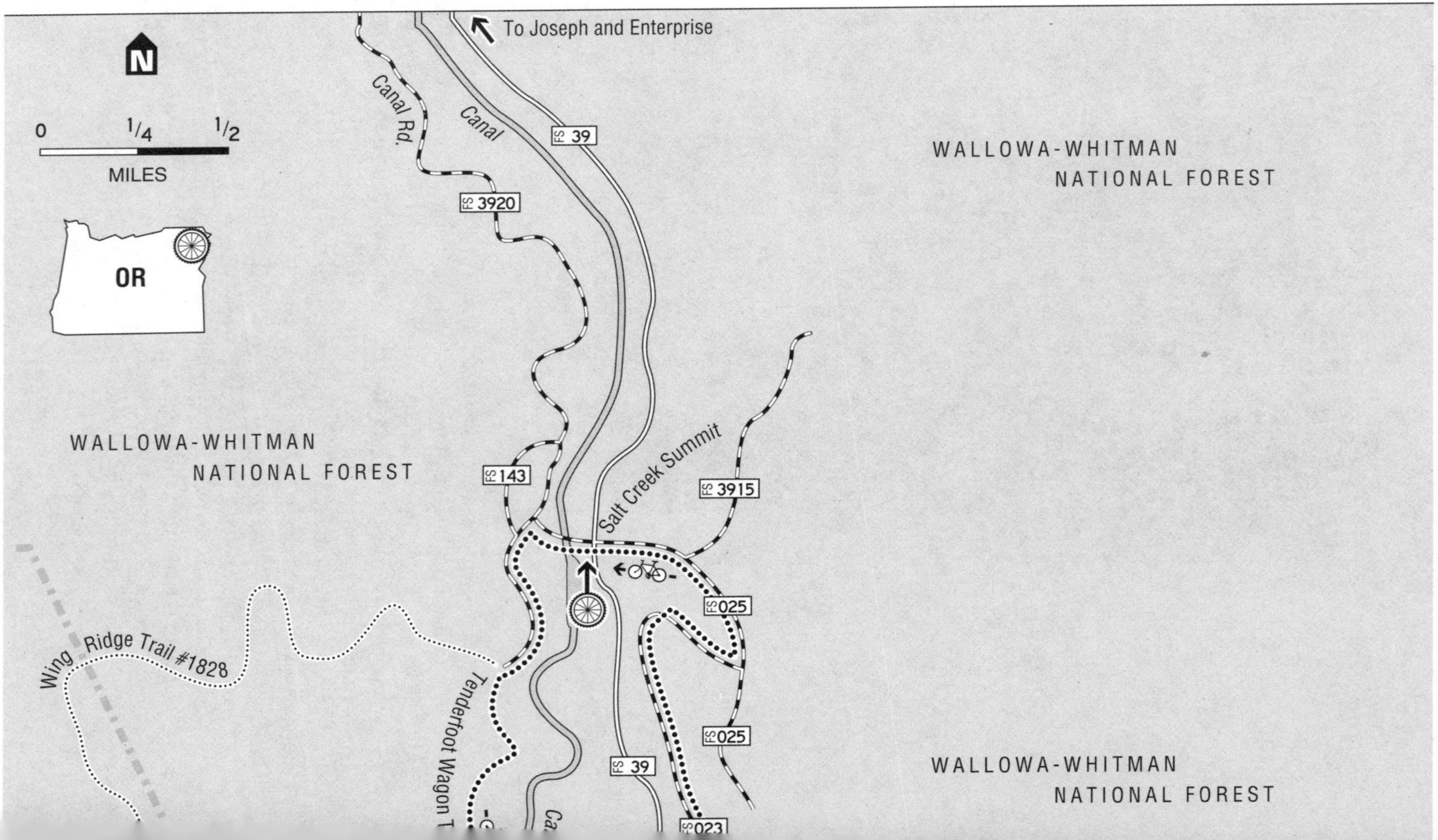

RIDE 21 *TENDERFOOT WAGON TRAIL*

N

0   1/4   1/2

MILES

OR

To Joseph and Enterprise

Canal

Canal Rd.

FS 39

FS 3920

FS 143

FS 3915

Salt Creek Summit

FS 025

FS 025

FS 023

FS 39

Canal

Tenderfoot Wagon Trail

WALLOWA-WHITMAN
NATIONAL FOREST

WALLOWA-WHITMAN
NATIONAL FOREST

WALLOWA-WHITMAN
NATIONAL FOREST

Wing Ridge Trail #1828

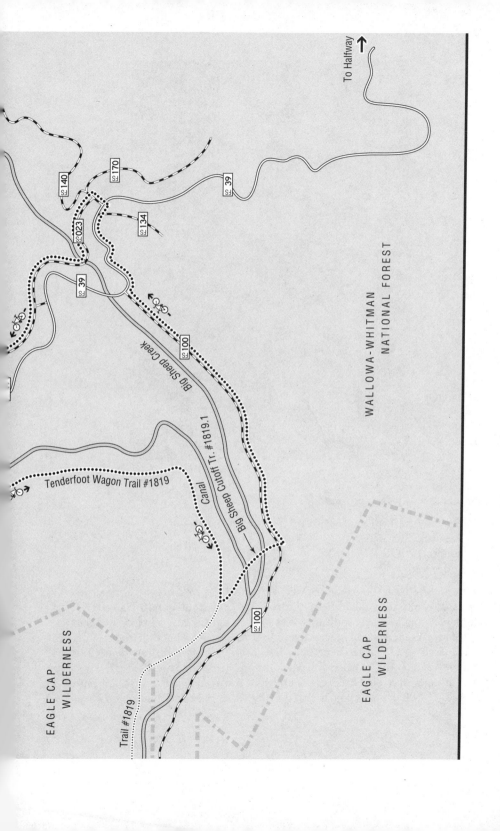

Tenderfoot.

Sources of additional information:

Wallowa Valley Ranger District
Route 1, Box 270A
Enterprise, OR 97828
(503) 426-4978

Notes on the trail: From the parking area, turn left to cross the bridge over the canal. Continue straight (left) up road-like Tenderfoot Wagon Trail #1819. Continue straight where indistinct FS 143 goes right. Cross a boggy area and arrive at a Y intersection where Tenderfoot Wagon Road goes left and Wing Ridge Trail #1828 goes right. Turn left, following the sign for Tenderfoot Wagon Road. Turn left when you reach Big Sheep Cutoff Trail #1819.1. Cross three bridges over Big Sheep Creek and pass a corral before turning left onto FS 100. FS 100 deposits you at paved FS 39. Turn right and descend on FS 39 for .5 miles to FS 140, a dangerous intersection on the left. FS 140 is hard to see—look for it after passing FS 134 (on the right). Turn left onto FS 140 and immediately turn left onto FS 023. (FS 023 is easy to miss; you have gone too far if you come to FS 170 on the right.) Follow the rough road past the boulders that block access to this portion of the road. Descend and then swing hard to the right; crossing the bridge over Big Sheep Creek. Push your bike across the clearing and turn right when you arrive at the road. Climb steeply to a road that comes in from the left (it accesses FS 39). Bear right to remain on FS 023. Stay on the main road where another road comes in from the left. You will come to a T intersection in 2.2 miles. Turn left onto FS 025. Follow the main road (stay left) to FS 39 at Salt Creek Summit. Cross the paved road to reach your vehicle.

RIDE 22   *WINDY RIDGE*

Windy Ridge is a 17.8-mile out-and-back trip suited to strong intermediate and advanced cyclists. It is a great ride, with wonderful views and good single-track cycling. The outing begins on the edge of Hells Canyon along Summit Ridge. There are some excellent vistas to the east. The Seven Devils feel close enough to touch, and there are glimpses of the Snake River far below. From Windy Ridge Trail, your view is to the west of Sleepy Ridge and the Wallowa Mountains. The scenery gets better as you head north. The grassy slopes at the turnaround offer sightings into the layered Imnaha River Canyon.

The first 1.6 miles twist and turn over Summit Ridge Trail. Summit Ridge Trail is a double-track that passes through a burned-out "matchstick forest." The road gets rougher and rockier as it rolls up and down along Summit Ridge. Next comes Windy Ridge Trail, an old road that is closed to motorized vehicles. The trail is about half single-track and half double-track. Trail conditions vary. Some stretches are rocky, hoof-worn, and rooty; some segments are great. There are some steep climbs, but the majority of the ascents are only moderately difficult. The return trip is more demanding.

The ride is hard to get to. Hat Point Road begins in Imnaha and climbs the cliffs of the Imnaha River Canyon. The road is steep—especially the first four miles. The roads are in good shape, except for the last few miles, where high clearance is recommended. The return drive down Hat Point Road is extremely hard on brakes.

At some point during your visit, climb the lookout at Hat Point—the view is top-drawer.

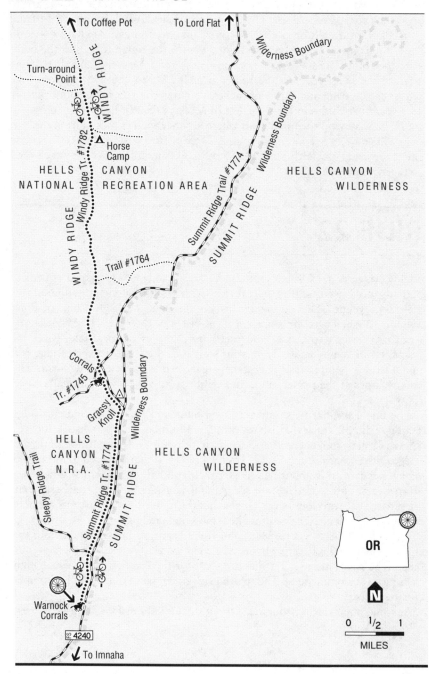

To Coffee Pot

To Lord Flat

Wilderness Boundary

Turn-around
Point

WINDY RIDGE

Wilderness Boundary

Horse
Camp

Windy Ridge Tr. #1782

Summit Ridge Trail #1774

HELLS   CANYON

NATIONAL   RECREATION   AREA

SUMMIT RIDGE

HELLS CANYON

WILDERNESS

Wilderness Boundary

WINDY RIDGE

Trail #1764

Corrals

Tr. #1745

Wilderness Boundary

Grassy
Knoll

HELLS
CANYON
N.R.A.

Summit Ridge Tr. #1774

SUMMIT RIDGE

HELLS CANYON

WILDERNESS

Sleepy Ridge Trail

Warnock
Corrals

FS 4240

To Imnaha

OR

N

0   1/2   1

MILES

Imnaha River Canyon from Windy Ridge Trail.

General location: Warnock Corrals are approximately 25 miles southeast of Imnaha, Oregon.

Elevation change: The ride begins at 6,720′ and rolls up and down to reach a low point of 5,840′ at the turnaround point. Undulations on the route add an estimated 800′ of climbing to the trip. Total elevation gain: 1,680′.

Season: The relatively high elevation and the remoteness of the ride make this a good summer trip. The early fall (before hunting season) is a quiet time on these ridges.

Services: There is no water on the ride. Bring all you will need for your stay in the Hells Canyon National Recreation Area. Imnaha has a tavern that sells limited supplies (no gas). All services are available in Joseph.

Hazards: Trail hazards include roots, rocks, soft spots, steep drop-offs, tall grass, and bumpy sections. The roads are pummy and contain areas of rocks and ruts. Watch for traffic on the roads.

Rescue index: There is a pay phone in Imnaha. Emergency services are available in Enterprise.

Land status: Hells Canyon National Recreation Area, Wallowa-Whitman National Forest.

Maps: The district map for the Hells Canyon National Recreation Area is a good guide to this ride. USGS 7.5 minute quad: Sleepy Ridge.

Finding the trail: In Imnaha, continue straight onto Forest Service Road 4240/Hat Point Road where Lower Imnaha Road goes left. Follow this main road for 20.9 miles to the intersection with FS 315 (the spur road to Hat Point Lookout) on the right. Stay to the left and drive another 4.2 miles on FS 4240 to Warnock Corrals. Proceed to the north end of the clearing, where the road reenters the woods and becomes a four-wheel-drive road. Park in a grassy area on the right or left.

Sources of additional information:

Hells Canyon National Recreation Area
Route 1, Box 270A
Enterprise, OR 97828
(503) 426-4978

Notes on the trail: Climb up the road to enter the woods. The road's designation changes here to Summit Ridge Trail #1774. Continue straight where Sleepy Ridge Trail goes left. Turn left toward Windy Ridge at the next intersection, where Summit Ridge Trail continues straight toward Lord Flat. You are now on Windy Ridge Trail #1782. Follow the double-track for .7 miles to the end of the road, at some corrals. The trail becomes single-track here. You will enter a campsite in another 1.9 miles. Continue straight where Trail #1764 goes right. The path is obvious for another 2.5 miles, then it fades out near a camp and some pine trees. Find the trail by continuing straight (north) along the grassy ridge. Look for a young pine tree. The trail passes just to the right of the tree. Proceed for about .5 miles to a small weathered sign on the left. It is illegible except for an arrow that points west. Park your bike and walk farther north for views of the Imnaha River Canyon. Return the way you came.

RIDE 23 _IMNAHA RIVER TRAIL_

Hells Canyon is an arid world of sun-baked, terraced rock and sagebrush. This area feels more like the Canyonlands of Utah than the Pacific Northwest. Imnaha River Trail winds through a beautiful high-walled gorge to the Snake River at Eureka Bar. Foundations and mine shafts are all that is left of the his-

RIDE 23   *IMNAHA RIVER TRAIL*

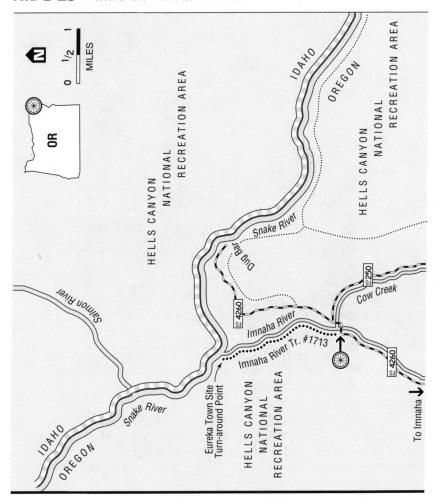

toric mining town of Eureka. Con artists created an elaborate scam to lure investors to the valueless mines. A stern-wheel riverboat was used to service the site; when you look at the Snake's treacherous waters, this fact seems amazing.

This is an 8.4-mile out-and-back single-track ride. The terrain is fairly level, but advanced technical skills are needed for the rocky ups and downs. There are some steep drop-offs, and brush (including lots of poison ivy) encroaches on the trail.

Imnaha River Trail.

The journey to reach the start of this trail is as much of an adventure as the ride itself. Forest Service Road 4260 is 13 miles of rugged one-lane gravel road. It is steep, rocky, twisty, and narrow, and has virtually no pullouts. Plan on camping—the trailhead at Cow Creek is a good location and offers excellent swimming in the Imnaha.

General location: Cow Creek Bridge is located approximately 20 miles north of Imnaha, Oregon.
Elevation change: The ride begins at 1,200' and reaches 900' at Eureka Bar. There are many lesser hills to climb on the way to and from the Snake River, adding about 500' of climbing to the trip. Total elevation gain: 800'.
Season: This is a good early and late season trip. Winters are generally mild, while summers are hot and dry. The access road to the ride should be avoided when it is wet.

Services: There is no water here—bring all you will need. Imnaha has a store/tavern with limited supplies. There is no gas in Imnaha; be sure to fill up in Joseph or Enterprise. All services are available in Joseph.

Hazards: Poison ivy thrives along the trail; there are times when touching it is unavoidable. The tread is narrow, and plant material obscures some obstacles. The trail is rocky and drops off steeply to the side in places. Thorns are a problem; use thorn-resistant tubes or a preferred antipuncture technology. Rattlesnakes are common in Hells Canyon.

Rescue index: Be prepared for any emergency—you are a long way from assistance. The nearest pay phone is in Imnaha. Emergency services are in Enterprise.

Land status: Hells Canyon National Recreation Area, Wallowa-Whitman National Forest.

Maps: USGS 7.5 minute quads: Cactus Mountain and Deadhorse Ridge.

Finding the trail: From Joseph, drive west and north on OR 350/Little Sheep Creek Highway to Imnaha (about 30 miles). In Imnaha, turn left onto Lower Imnaha Road. The pavement ends 6 miles outside of Imnaha. Follow the signs for Thorn Creek and Dug Bar (the road becomes Dug Bar Road/FS 4260 here). You will arrive at Cow Creek Bridge in 13 miles. Do not cross the bridge; instead, continue straight to reach the trail on the left. Park on the right.

Sources of additional information:

Hells Canyon National Recreation Area
Route 1, Box 270 A
Enterprise, OR 97828
(503) 426-4978

Notes on the trail: From the parking area, follow the path uphill to reach the signed trailhead for Imnaha River Trail #1713. Follow the single-track downstream to the confluence of the Snake and Imnaha Rivers. A rocky trail goes left toward the foundation of the Eureka Mill; you can see the mill on the hillside above the Snake. Return the way you came.

Bend and Central Oregon Area Rides

Bend, central Oregon's largest city, is the headliner for recreation in the region. People come here to ski, hike, shoot rapids, and take part in more fun-loving activities than you could imagine. The area's lineup of festivals, events, shindigs, and bazaars goes on and on. From rock hound powwows to bike races, snowboard championships to classical concerts: you name it, it's celebrated here with gusto.

Nestled at the foot of the Cascades, central Oregon is a playground surrounded by natural beauty. Volcanoes have played the largest role in the shaping of the region. The remnants of eruptions that occurred over 45 million years ago dominate the landscape. These cataclysmic events deposited layer upon layer of volcanic pumice and ash. We encounter these materials today as we ply the trails. When conditions are dry, the pumice in the soil gets ground into a fine powder. This material is deep like sand, but lighter. With practice, you can ride right through this thick dust. These soft conditions are less of a problem early in the season, before the soils become thoroughly dry.

Most of the riding around Bend (there's lots) is in the Deschutes National Forest. The rise in popularity of mountain biking has not gone unnoticed in the forest. Rangers in the Bend District have developed signed mountain bike routes, maps, and brochures on riding opportunities in the area.

Also tucked in along the eastern flank of the Cascades is Sisters, a community 21 miles northwest of Bend. Sisters entertains visitors with its western atmosphere, big summer events, and shopping. It is becoming increasingly popular with mountain bikers. Head in any direction from Sisters and you will find excellent riding.

Just north of Sisters is the tiny town of Camp Sherman. Nearby Green Ridge offers good gravel-road riding with views of Mt. Jefferson, Mt. Washington, and Three Sisters. Below the ridge is the Metolius River, famous for its year-round fly-fishing. The forest campgrounds along the river are very pleasant.

Traveling west from Sisters brings you into the McKenzie District of the Willamette National Forest. The area is home to some incredible single-track pedaling. The McKenzie River National Recreation Trail may be one of the finest riverside routes around. It parallels the tumultuous river for 27 miles, stumbles past waterfalls, and tests the mettle of hardened riders.

The loop around Waldo Lake (in the Oakridge District of the Willamette National Forest) is another excellent single-track outing. The water of this glacier-carved lake is pure and clean. Three large campgrounds on the eastern shore of the lake make good bases for extended travels in the forest. Primitive campsites on the western side of Waldo Lake make overnight outings an easy option.

Twenty miles to the east of Sisters is Redmond. Just a few miles north of Redmond is Smith Rock State Park. This park was created to preserve the towering red rock formations of the Crooked River Canyon. While you won't find much mountain biking in this state park, you will be mesmerized by its rocky spires and vertical faces. Climbers began to visit the area in the 1940s. In the last ten years, the park has gained an international reputation among rock climbers for its demanding routes. A short hike from the main parking area leads to an overlook of the beautiful canyon. At Smith Rock you can challenge the upper limits of the sport, scale your first ten-foot boulder, or simply marvel at the gymnastic feats of others.

If you go 20 miles east of Redmond you hit Prineville, the gateway to western portions of the Ochoco National Forest. Mountain bikers will find good gravel roads and single-tracks in this forest. A trip to the summit of Round Mountain gives you a nice perspective on the area. Descending from the mountain on Round Mountain National Recreation Trail is an exciting finish to this ride.

RIDE 24 *PHIL'S TRAIL*

This 11.2-mile loop near Bend is moderately difficult. The first 5.7 miles and the last 1.8 miles are on dirt roads and double-tracks in fair condition. The remainder is a fun 3.7-mile stretch of single-track. The trail twists and turns its way downhill through trees and rock outcroppings. The single-track is in good condition, with some pummy conditions in the corners.

It is easy to see why this ride is a local favorite. It is close to town, it's a quick workout, and it includes some fine single-track. Descending on Phil's Trail is bound to get you grinning.

General location: The trailhead is 3 miles west of Bend, Oregon.
Elevation change: The elevation at the start of the loop is 3,880′. The high point of the ride is 4,440′. Ups and downs add about 300′ of climbing to the trip. Total elevation gain: 860′.
Season: Because of soil conditions and the route's relatively low elevation, this is a good early season outing. Some of the best riding in this region is in the spring, before the area's pumice soils get too dry and soft.

RIDE 24 PHIL'S TRAIL

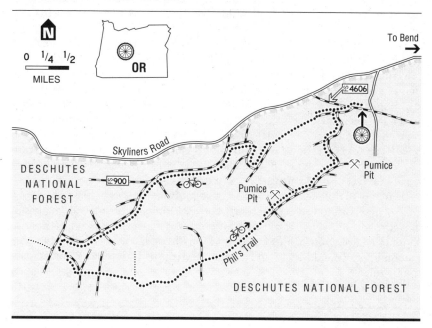

Services: There is no water on this ride. Water and all services are available in Bend.

Hazards: There are some rocky, pummy, and forest-littered areas on both the roads and the trail. Expect some downed trees. Control your speed on the single-track descent, and watch for others. Many of the roads are unsigned.

Rescue index: Help is available in Bend.

Land status: Deschutes National Forest.

Maps: At the time of our research, the route was not depicted thoroughly on any one map. Obtain the district map of the Bend Ranger District. Pick up a copy of their "Mountain Bike Route" guide as well. This ride is "Phil's Trail Loop—Route 24.5" in the brochure (described in a clockwise direction). USGS 7.5 minute quad: Bend.

Finding the trail: In downtown Bend, travel west on Franklin Street (follow the "Tour Route" signs). Shortly, Franklin becomes Galveston Street. Galveston winds past a park and crosses a bridge over the Deschutes River. Galveston becomes Tumalo Street after crossing the bridge. Then you arrive at a four-way stop at 14th Street (there is a Dairy Queen on the corner). Continue straight toward Tumalo Falls. The road soon becomes Skyliners Road. Proceed down this road for 2.7 miles to a paved road on the left (just

Basalt outcrops along Phil's Trail.

before a small "Entering Deschutes National Forest" sign on the right side of Skyliners Road). Turn left onto this unsigned road and drive .4 miles to a road crossing. Turn right onto the cinder road (unsigned Forest Service Road 4606) and park on the left side in a pullout. There is a small bicycle trailhead sign for Route 24.5 on FS 4606 (opposite the parking area).

Sources of additional information:

Bend Ranger District
1230 N.E. 3rd Street
Bend, OR 97701
(503) 388-5664

Bend Chamber of Commerce (Central Oregon Welcome Center)
63085 N. Highway 97
Bend, OR 97701-5765
(503) 382-3221; fax# (503) 385-9929

Notes on the trail: Phil's Trail Loop is designated Forest Service Mountain Bike Route 24.5. It is marked with brown fiberglass signposts. Follow the description in the Forest Service brochure (and the arrows on the signs) if you wish to climb on the single-track. We found the loop to be more fun in reverse (counterclockwise), riding the single-track as a descent. Following our direc-

Coasting down Phil's Trail.

tions, all Route 24.5 signs except for the first one will point back from where you came.

Head west on the cinder road. Turn left in .25 miles at the 24.5 sign. At the next Y intersection, go straight—do not go left to follow the 24.5 sign. Continue straight on the main road; you will soon enter a burn area. The route changes back and forth between double-track and single-track as it passes through the burn. You will come to an intersection and a 24.5 sign after 1.7 miles; turn right here and climb by a couple of rock outcrops. You will reach an intersection in another .3 miles. Go straight (right) where a road goes left. The route passes over some minor whoop-dee-doos, then heads out into an open area. Pedal over more small whoop-dee-doos as the double-track reenters the woods. Some side roads branch off to the right, but you should stay on the main double-track. Shortly you will arrive at a T intersection at a main road (marked by a 24.5/24.6 sign)—turn left. A major intersection of three roads occurs in another .8 miles. The first road goes left and is marked by a 24.6 sign. Go straight; you will immediately arrive at a Y where signed FS 900 goes right and an unsigned road veers left. Bear left onto the unsigned road. Stay on the main road for .4 miles to a Y intersection marked by a 24.6/24.5 sign. Turn left onto the double-track. In .5 miles, cross a road marked with a 24.5 sign. (Continue straight, remaining on the double-track.) In .7 miles, you will come to a T intersection at a 24.5 sign. Turn left onto the bumpy dirt road. A trail crosses this road in less than .2 miles. Turn left onto this single-track (marked with a 24.5 sign). This trail deposits you onto a road; follow the road around to the right. Soon you will come to a "No Vehicles" sign on the left. A double-track goes hard to the left here, and a single-track goes left. Turn left onto the single-track. Remain on this trail, cross a road, then turn right at a T intersection with a 24.5 sign. The trail crosses another road in about a mile. The route changes from single-track to double-track 1 mile beyond the last road crossing. The double-track crosses a road, then takes you past a pumice pit. Follow the light-colored road—also stay on this road where it changes to a dark cinder road. Soon a road goes hard left, but you should continue straight. Turn left onto the next double-track (at a low point in the road); it is marked by a 24.5 sign. Continue straight at the next intersection—this brings you into a clearing at a pumice pit. Immediately upon entering the clearing, turn left at a 24.5 sign and reenter the woods. Follow this double-track for .5 miles to another double-track marked with a 24.5 sign. Turn right and ride through an appliance graveyard. Turn right onto unsigned FS 4606 and pedal back to your vehicle.

RIDE 25 *TUMALO FALLS*

This easy five-mile out-and-back ride takes you to a beautiful waterfall. The route goes over several short, mellow hills and makes for a nice introductory mountain bike ride. The dirt road is in fair condition, with some sandy sections and some washboarding.

The road to Tumalo Falls goes through an area that burned in the 1980 Bridge Creek fire. To the north, over the young trees, are views of rimrock cliffs. A hiking trail at the end of the road goes up to a viewing platform beside the 90-foot falls.

General location: This ride starts about 12 miles west of Bend, Oregon.
Elevation change: From the trailhead, at 4,720', the road ascends to 4,960' at the turnaround point. Undulating terrain adds about 50' of climbing to the ride. The hike to the falls is approximately .3 miles long and climbs roughly 150'. Total elevation gain: 290' (hike not included).
Season: This ride can be enjoyed from early in the spring through the late fall. Ride here before Memorial Day or after Labor Day to avoid the heaviest traffic.
Services: There is no water on this trip. Water and all services are available in Bend.
Hazards: Expect to share the road with motorists. Watch for sandy spots in the road, particularly at the base of hills and in corners.
Rescue index: Help can be found in Bend.

RIDE 25   *TUMALO FALLS*

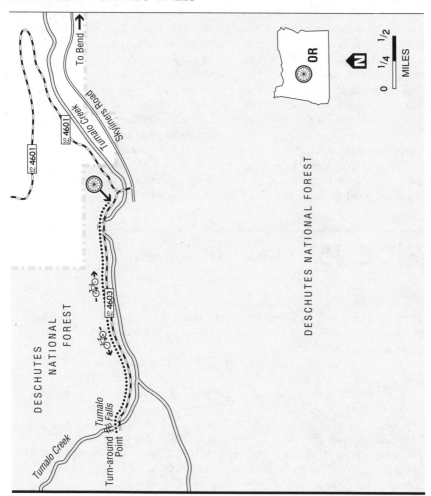

Land status: Deschutes National Forest.

Maps: The district map of the Bend Ranger District is a good guide to this ride. USGS 7.5 minute quads: Shevlin Park and Tumalo Falls.

Finding the trail: In Bend, travel west on Galveston. Galveston becomes Skyliners Road at 14th Street. Continue straight (west) onto Skyliners Road and follow it for 11.8 miles to signed Forest Service Road 4601. Turn right onto FS 4601 and cross a one-lane bridge over Tumalo Creek. Turn left onto

Lunch at Tumalo Falls.

signed FS 4603. Proceed through the open gate and immediately turn right into the parking area.

Sources of additional information:

Bend Ranger District
1230 N.E. 3rd Street
Bend, OR 97701
(503) 388-5664

Notes on the trail: Pedal west on FS 4603. After 2.5 miles you will cross a one-lane bridge over Tumalo Creek and reach the end of the road. No bikes are allowed on the hiking trail to the falls. Return the way you came.

RIDE 26 *DESCHUTES RIVER*

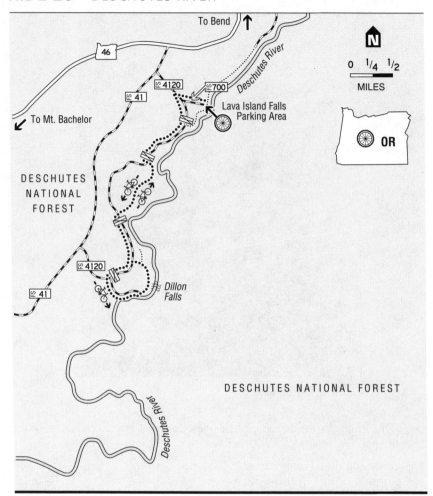

RIDE 26 *DESCHUTES RIVER*

Beginning mountain bikers will enjoy this 6.2-mile ride near the Deschutes River. The outing is a combination of a loop and an out-and-back trip. It follows four miles of good gravel roads and 2.2 miles of well-maintained single-

Dillon Falls.

track. Craggy lava rocks line the river and provide a great perch for viewing Dillon Falls. There is a fun, technical, twisting section of trail after the falls viewpoint.

General location: This ride begins at the Lava Island Falls parking area, approximately 8 miles southwest of Bend, Oregon.

Elevation change: The ride begins at 3,960′ and reaches a high point of 4,100′. Undulations add an estimated 100′ of climbing to the ride. Total elevation gain: 240′.

Season: The spring and fall are nice times of the year for a visit. The parking areas at the trailhead and viewpoint can be busy with pedestrian and motorized traffic in the summer.

Services: All services are available in Bend.

Hazards: Control your speed on the single-track; other trail users may be approaching.

Rescue index: Help can be found in Bend.

Land status: Deschutes National Forest.

Maps: A mountain biking handout is available from the Bend Ranger District. It includes a map and information about the ride. USGS 7.5 minute quad: Bend.

Finding the trail: From Bend, drive west on Highway 46 (also known as Century Drive and Cascade Lakes Highway). Turn left after about 7 miles

Deschutes River Trail.

onto Forest Service Road 41. Follow the signs to Lava Island Falls/Lava Island Rock Shelter (left onto FS 4120, then left onto FS 700). Park in the gravel lot at the end of FS 700.

Sources of additional information:

Bend Ranger District
1230 N.E. 3rd Street
Bend, OR 97701
(503) 388-5664

Notes on the trail: This is designated Forest Service Mountain Bike Route 2.3. The trail is well marked with signs and arrows. Start by riding up FS 700, then follow the signs. After about 3 miles, you will reach an unsigned Y intersection in a dispersed camp area. Bear to the left and ride through the camp on the dirt road. Soon you will arrive at a parking area and some trails that lead to overlooks of the river. Follow the signs for Bike Route 2.3.

RIDE 27 *TANGENT / QUARRY SITE 1041 LOOP*

This 13-mile loop is moderately difficult. It involves easy climbing and several uphills that will require a more concerted effort. The road conditions vary greatly over the course of the ride. Forest Service Road 4615 is in good condition. It is made of crushed volcanic cinders and compacted dirt. Most of the remaining miles are on dirt roads, and some stretches are very soft with volcanic pumice. These pummy sections are loose and make pedaling difficult; you may have to push your bike through some of these areas.

The view from Quarry Site 1041 is the highlight of this loop. A short scramble up a steep hillside reveals a lovely view of the surrounding forests and mountains. Broken Top and Mt. Bachelor are prominent in the west.

General location: This ride starts at the Virginia Meissner Sno-Park, approximately 13 miles west of Bend, Oregon.

Elevation change: From the trailhead, at 5,400′, you travel over rolling terrain to 5,540′ at the quarry site. Undulations on this portion of the loop add about 350′ of climbing to the ride. Descend rapidly from the quarry, to a low point of 4,720′, before pedaling back to the trailhead. Total elevation gain: 1,170′.

Season: Roads at these elevations may not be free of snow until late in the spring. This is a good summer ride.

Services: There is no water on the route. Water and all services can be obtained in Bend.

Hazards: Expect some traffic on the roads. Control your speed on the descent from the quarry, and watch for changing road conditions; soft spots can cause handling problems.

Rescue index: Help can be found in Bend.

Land status: Deschutes National Forest.

Maps: The district map of the Bend Ranger District is a good guide to this ride. USGS 7.5 minute quads: Benham Falls, Wanoga Butte, Shelvin Park, and Tumalo Falls.

Finding the trail: From Bend, drive west on OR 46 (Century Drive Highway/Cascade Lakes Highway) for 13 miles to signed FS 4615. Turn right and travel .1 miles on FS 4615; park in the Virginia Meissner Sno-Park, on the right.

Sources of additional information:

Bend Ranger District
1230 N.E. 3rd Street
Bend, OR 97701
(503) 388-5664

RIDE 27 *TANGENT / QUARRY SITE 1041 LOOP*

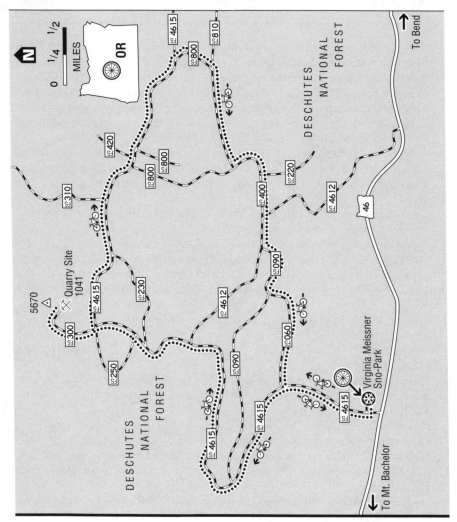

Notes on the trail: The Bend Ranger District has developed designated mountain bike routes throughout the forest. Pick up their "Mountain Bike Route Guide" at the ranger station. This particular route is marked with signs that show a bike symbol, a directional arrow, and the number 52.5.

Turn right out of the Sno-Park onto FS 4615. Stay on FS 4615 for 4.7 miles to the intersection with FS 300. Continue straight onto FS 300 and follow this road to its terminus at Quarry Site 1041. Park your bike and hike up the hill for good views. Cycle back down FS 300 to FS 4615 and turn left (east).

Broken Top from the hill above Quarry Site 1041.

Descend on FS 4615 for 2.9 miles to the third FS 800 entrance. This entrance for FS 800 is on the right; it comes just after the terrain levels out, climbs a bit, and levels out again. Turn right onto FS 800. After pedaling for 1.2 miles on FS 800, turn left onto FS 400. Continue straight on FS 400 where FS 220 goes left. In another .4 miles, you will reach an intersection where an unmarked road comes in from the left. Follow the mountain bike route sign that directs you straight, onto unsigned FS 4612. Proceed down FS 4612 for .2 miles to signed FS 090 on the left (where FS 4612 continues straight). Turn left onto FS 090. Cycle on FS 090 for .5 miles, then turn left onto signed FS 060. Stay on FS 060 for 1 mile to its intersection with signed FS 4615. Turn left onto FS 4615 to return to the Sno-Park.

RIDE 28 *SWAMPY LAKES / SOUTH FORK TRAIL*

The highlight of this 20-mile loop is a fun drop on South Fork Trail to Tumalo Falls—a switchbacking descent that contains some steep, technical sections. The ride's 5.2 miles of single-track are in fair to good condition. The route follows trails at the beginning of the trip, roads for the remaining miles. The

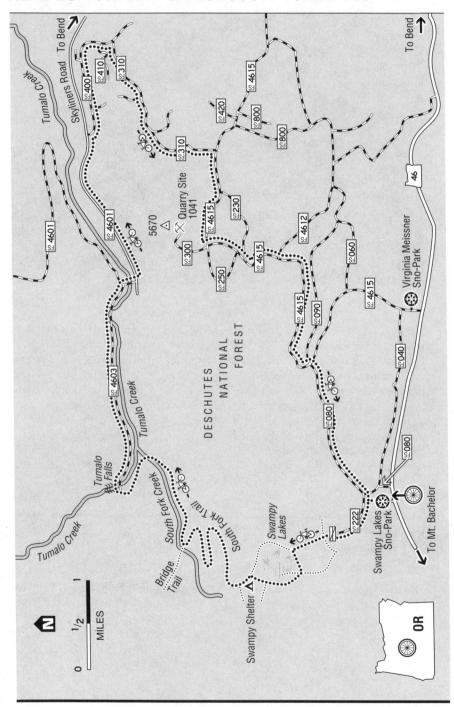

roads follow easy terrain at first, then get more demanding. The ascent back to the trailhead is long and moderately difficult, and ends with steep climbing. The gravel roads and dirt double-tracks are in fair condition (there are two miles of pavement). The trip is well suited to energetic intermediate cyclists and advanced cyclists.

General location: Swampy Lakes Sno-Park is approximately 15 miles west of Bend, Oregon.

Elevation change: The loop begins at 5,800′ and reaches a high point of 6,200′ within the first mile. The low point of the ride is 4,600′—it occurs on Forest Service Road 400. Ups and downs on the route add an estimated 300′ of climbing to the trip. Total elevation gain: 1,900′.

Season: This route is usually rideable from late June through October. The double-tracks and trails can become dusty later in the riding season.

Services: There is no water on this ride. Water and all services can be found in Bend.

Hazards: Control your speed on the single-track descent, and watch for other riders. On bright days, South Fork Trail is made more demanding by sun and shadow. Trees create patches of deep shade, which are followed by areas of blinding sunshine. Under these conditions, seeing becomes difficult—descend carefully. The trails contain rocks, roots, pummy spots, ruts, and sharp drop-offs. You will encounter deep sand in places on the double-tracks. Expect some traffic, especially on FS 4603 and Skyliners Road.

Rescue index: Help can be found in Bend.

Land status: Deschutes National Forest.

Maps: The district map of the Bend Ranger District is a good guide to this ride. Also, pick up a copy of the district's "Mountain Bike Route" guide. USGS 7.5 minute quads: Shevlin Park, Tumalo Falls, and Wanoga Butte.

Finding the trail: In downtown Bend, travel west on Franklin Street (follow the "Tour Route" signs). Shortly, Franklin becomes Galveston. Galveston winds past a park and crosses the Deschutes River. Galveston becomes Tumalo after crossing the bridge. Then you come to a four-way stop sign at 14th Street (there is a Dairy Queen on the corner). Turn left toward Mt. Bachelor Ski Area/Cascade Lakes. You are now on OR 46/Century Drive Highway/Cascade Lakes Highway. In 14.7 miles, turn right into the Swampy Lakes Sno-Park (2.1 miles beyond Virginia Meissner Sno-Park). The trailhead is at the north end of the large parking lot (across from the vault toilets).

Sources of additional information:

Bend Ranger District
1230 N.E. 3rd Street
Bend, OR 97701
(503) 388-5664

Juanita Edwards and Dan Smithey riding on the Swampy
Lakes trails.

Notes on the trail: This ride is a designated Forest Service Mountain Bike
Route; it is the "Rockless Ridge Ride—Route 52.3." This excursion (and
other such mountain bike routes) are marked in the field with brown fiberglass signposts. These signposts show a bike symbol, a directional arrow, and
a ride number. Follow the description in the Forest Service brochure if you
wish to climb on the single-track (i.e., to ride counterclockwise). We found the
loop to be more fun in reverse (clockwise), riding the single-track as a descent.

Take the trail that begins across from the toilets (marked as routes 52.1 and
52.2) to FS 222. Turn left onto the road, following the sign for Route 52.1.
At the end of the road, ride around the green gate onto the single-track.
Continue straight at the next intersection (follow the 52.1 sign). In another .5
miles, you will arrive at an intersection; here, turn left (again, follow the 52.1
sign). At the next junction of trails (.3 miles farther along), turn right where

the 52.1 route goes left. Immediately bear left at a Y intersection, following the sign "Easier Descent to Lake." The trail skirts the dry lake and comes to Flagline Trail, on the left, in .5 miles. Stay to the right toward Swampy Shelter. Turn left at the shelter, toward South Fork Trail. Bear right at the next intersection onto South Fork Trail; here you will be descending. When you get to Bridge Trail, turn right, remaining on South Fork Trail. Turn left onto the gravel road (unsigned FS 4603) to visit Tumalo Falls. Turn around at the falls and follow FS 4603 east for 2.5 miles to a stop sign. Turn right, cross Tumalo Creek, then turn left onto paved Skyliners Road/FS 4601. Stay on the pavement for 2 miles to FS 400, which is on the right at a 52.3 sign facing away from you. Turn right onto the double-track and follow it as it swings left, descends, and parallels Skyliners Road. You will pass two spur roads, then FS 400 swings right and begins to climb. Pass FS 410 (on the right), and turn right at the next intersection onto unsigned FS 310 (follow the 24.6 sign). The road gets very sandy in 1 mile. Then FS 310 meets an unsigned road on the right (where a 52.3 sign faces away from you). Continue straight through this open area. Shortly, you will arrive at another intersection where a road goes left at a 24.6 sign; here, continue straight. Turn right onto FS 4615 at the T intersection. Turn left in 1.3 miles, remaining on FS 4615. Stay on the main road for 2.8 miles to FS 080. Turn right onto FS 080 and follow the signs back to Swampy Lakes Sno-Park.

RIDE 29 *PETER SKENE OGDEN TRAIL*

This is one of those very satisfying rides that give you a lot for what you put in. The Peter Skene Ogden Trail parallels scenic Paulina Creek. The stream cascades into inviting pools and forms beautiful waterfalls. Once at Paulina Lake, you can muse on mountain peaks while enjoying refreshments at Paulina Lake Lodge. The dirt road descent is fast and exhilarating.

We recommend this 17.5-mile loop to strong intermediate cyclists and advanced cyclists. The trail climbs for eight miles, gaining over 2,000 feet of elevation. The surface is soft, pummy, and technically demanding. What would be a moderately difficult climb on a compacted dirt trail is challenging here. There are a few steep pitches and some intricate pedaling through rocky terrain, but most everything is rideable. The descent on forest roads contains some ruts, soft sections, and washboarding.

General location: The trailhead is approximately 25 miles south of Bend, Oregon.
Elevation change: The ride begins at 4,280′ and reaches a high point of

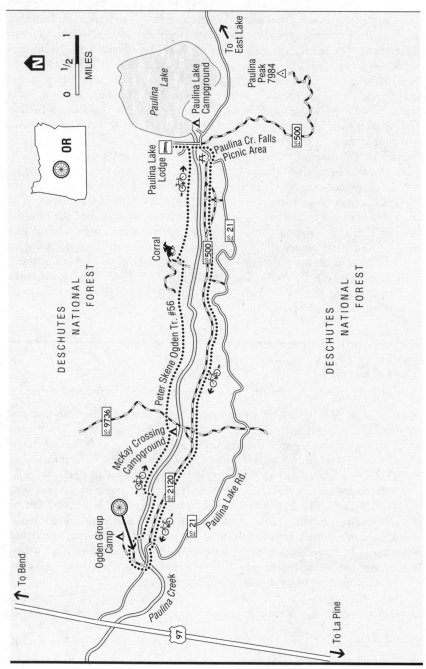

Paulina Creek.

6,340′ at Paulina Lake. Ups and downs add an estimated 200′ of climbing to the circuit. Total elevation gain: 2,260′.

Season: The route is generally free of snow from July through October.

Services: Water can be obtained seasonally at the Ogden Group Camp and Paulina Lake Campground. Food, lodging, limited groceries, and a pay phone can be found at the Paulina Lake Lodge. All services are available in Bend.

Hazards: Soft sections on the dirt roads make the descent somewhat dangerous; control your speed. Wide tires are recommended because of the pummy conditions encountered along the route. Watch for traffic on the roads.

Rescue index: Help can be found in Bend.

Land status: Deschutes National Forest.

Maps: The district map for the Bend Ranger District is a suitable guide to the route. Its only shortcoming—the trail is shown to cross the creek more than twice. USGS 7.5 minute quads: Paulina Peak and Finley Butte.

Finding the trail: From locations to the north, travel south from Bend on US 97 for approximately 22 miles to Forest Service Road 21/Paulina Lake Road (on the left). From locations to the south, drive north from La Pine on US 97 for about 6 miles to FS 21/Paulina Lake Road (on the right). Turn east onto FS 21, which is signed here for Newberry Crater, Paulina Lake, and East Lake. In 2.8 miles, turn left onto a gravel road at a sign for Ogden Group Camp. Bear right at the next intersection (at a trailhead sign) and park in the large gravel lot.

Paulina Falls.

Sources of additional information:

Fort Rock Ranger District
1230 N.E. 3rd Street
Bend, OR 97701
(503) 388-5664

Notes on the trail: Uncontrolled speed by mountain bikers descending on Peter Skene Ogden Trail has created safety concerns and erosion problems. The result is a Forest Service prohibition on downhill use of the trail by cyclists. This management decision is supported by local mountain bike groups and other forest users. Respect the policy—it is better than an outright ban on mountain bikes. Besides, riding the trail uphill gives you time to enjoy the beauty of Paulina Creek.

Walk your bike up the railroad tie steps at the National Recreation Trail sign and cross the log bridge to begin the trail. The beginning of the route is marked with horseshoe symbol signs on trees. You will arrive at a pummy double-track after pedaling .8 miles. Turn right onto the road to ride toward the boulders that close the road to most vehicles. At the boulders, turn left onto another road and ride .2 miles to a crossing of Paulina Creek. The bridge was out at the time of our visit, but a new bridge was scheduled to be constructed. Pass over to the north side of the creek and continue up the trail (on single-track again). The trail passes through McKay Crossing Campground in another 1.8 miles. Cross unsigned FS 9736 to continue on the trail. You will pass by an especially lovely series of waterfalls in another 2 miles, then arrive at a Y intersection. Continue straight (left) to follow the more rideable trail. You will come to another intersection in .5 miles. Continue straight where a path goes right to a footbridge over the creek. You will enter a horse camp and reach a road in .7 miles. Turn left onto the road and pedal a short distance to a trail on the right (just before a corral). Turn onto this trail. Continue straight onto a gravel road when you reach the eastern trailhead, near Paulina Lake. Pedal a short distance to a paved road and turn left. Follow the road to Paulina Lake Lodge. Turn around at the lodge and return the way you came. Cross the concrete bridge that spans the headwaters of Paulina Creek. This will bring you to FS 21. Turn right onto FS 21 and pedal .3 miles to the Paulina Creek Falls Picnic Area. Turn right and ride through the parking area to a faint trail at a small section of fence. Ride between the fenceposts to a sign pointing left for Paulina Falls Trail. Turn left to access unsigned FS 500. Follow the old roadbed and the telephone poles downhill. Stay on FS 500 where side roads branch off. Cross FS 9736. Bear left when you reach unsigned FS 2120 (a cinder road). FS 2120 takes you back to paved FS 21. Turn right onto the pavement and ride to the entrance of Ogden Group Camp. Turn right and pedal back to your vehicle.

RIDE 30 *GREEN RIDGE LOOP*

This 34.4-mile road loop includes a short out-and-back to a lookout tower. The ride is difficult due to its length and the long, steady climb to Green Ridge. Still, it is not technically demanding and could be tackled by determined intermediate cyclists. The trip follows gravel and dirt roads for 22.8 miles and pavement for 11.6 miles. Clear days allow good views of Mt. Washington, the Metolius River Basin, Three Sisters, and Three-Fingered Jack.

General location: This ride begins near the headwaters of the Metolius River, approximately 17 miles north of Sisters, Oregon.

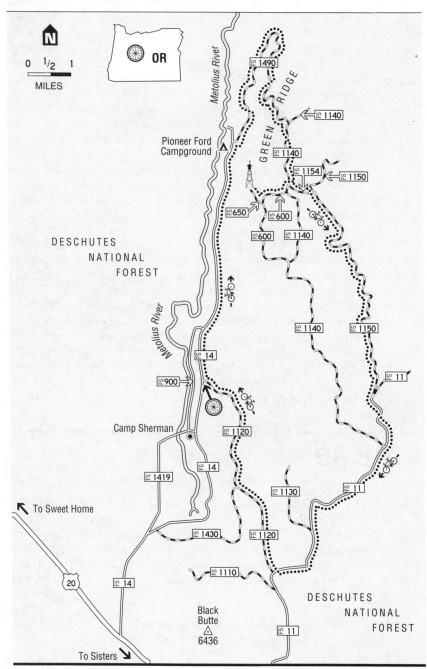

Climbing to Green Ridge.

Elevation change: The elevation at the start of the ride is 2,960´. The high point is on Forest Service Road 600, at 4,860´. Ups and downs contribute about 1,000´ of climbing to the tour. Total elevation gain: 2,900´.

Season: The roads are generally free of snow from late May through October.

Services: There is no water on this ride. Water is available seasonally at campgrounds along the Metolius River. A pay phone can be found in Camp Sherman. Food, lodging, groceries, and gas can be obtained in Sisters.

Hazards: Watch for traffic, and be especially careful while riding on the paved roads.

Rescue index: Help is available in Sisters.

Land status: Deschutes National Forest lands and public right-of-way through private property.

Maps: The district map of the Sisters Ranger District is a good guide to this ride. USGS 7.5 minute quads: Little Squaw Back, Black Butte, Prairie Farm Spring, and Candle Creek.

Finding the trail: From Sisters, drive north on US 20. After 9.8 miles, turn right onto unsigned FS 14. FS 14 is a paved two-lane road marked with a sign reading "Metolius River—5, Camp Sherman—5." Stay to the right in 2.7 miles, remaining on FS 14. (Follow the sign that directs you to the campgrounds.) Continue on FS 14 for another 4.6 miles and turn right onto FS 1120. Take the next right, onto a double-track. Park on the right.

Sources of additional information:

> Sisters Ranger District
> P.O. Box 249
> Sisters, OR 97759
> (503) 549-2111

Notes on the trail: Ride back to FS 14 and turn right. After nearly 6 miles of pavement, turn right onto red cinder FS 1490. (You come to this turn after passing Pioneer Ford Campground.) Remain on FS 1490 as spur roads branch off. After attaining the ridge, you will arrive at a T intersection. Turn right onto FS 1140. In another 1.5 miles, bear right, remaining on FS 1140 where FS 1154 goes left. (You will return to this intersection after visiting the lookout.) Ride .25 miles farther on FS 1140 and turn right onto FS 600. Stay on FS 600 for 1.3 miles to FS 650. Turn right onto FS 650 and descend to the lookout tower. Turn around at the lookout and return the way you came, to the intersection of FS 1140 and FS 1154. Turn right onto FS 1154 (toward Highway 20). Turn right onto FS 1150 (again, toward Highway 20) in .7 miles. Follow FS 1150 for 6.8 miles to a stop sign and paved FS 11. Continue straight onto FS 11. After 5.8 miles on FS 11, turn right onto cinder FS 1120. Remain on FS 1120 to reach your vehicle on the left.

RIDE 31 MCKENZIE RIVER NATIONAL RECREATION TRAIL

The upper McKenzie is a spectacular whitewater river originating in the high Cascades. The 27-mile long McKenzie River National Recreation Trail #3507 closely follows the river and passes through many contrasting environments. The northern end traverses an area of recent volcanic activity. The riding is extreme as the path crosses lava flows and skirts the eastern shore of beautiful Clear Lake. Beyond the lake, the trail passes two magnificent waterfalls before entering Tamolitch Valley. The river flows underground through much of the valley and then emerges from the base of a cliff (dry Tamolitch Falls), forming an azure, crystalline pool. The variety of environments is less dramatic

RIDE 31 *McKENZIE RIVER NATIONAL RECREATION TRAIL*

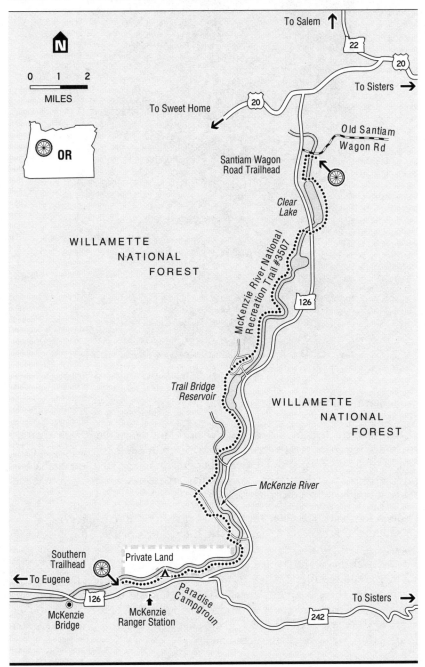

Log bridge on McKenzie River National Recreation Trail.

in the remaining miles of the ride—just more great single-track, lush forest, and tumbling water.

The northern half of the trail is technical and demanding, with narrow, twisty sections over razor-edged lava rock. Steep ups and downs near Sahalie and Koosah falls are real skill-testers. South of Tamolitch Falls, the riding gets progressively easier. Beginners may wish to start at Paradise Campground and ride out and back in either direction.

General location: The southern terminus of the trail is 1.5 miles east of the community of McKenzie Bridge, on OR 126 (approximately 50 miles east of Eugene).

Elevation change: The Santiam Wagon Road Trailhead is at 3,200'. The southern trailhead is at 1,450'. There are uphill stretches along the course of the descent. There is approximately 700' of climbing between the Santiam Wagon Road Trailhead and Trail Bridge Campground. There is about 400' of climbing between Trail Bridge and the southern trailhead. Total elevation gain: 1,100' (riding north to south only).

Season: Rhododendrons, dogwoods, and many species of wildflowers put on a good show of color in the spring and early summer. The trail is popular with hikers, and the highway can become busy with vacationers during the summer. Avoid the trail when it is wet; phone ahead to check on conditions.

Services: Water is available seasonally at Coldwater Cove, Trail Bridge, and Paradise campgrounds. Food, lodging, gas, and a pay phone can be found in McKenzie Bridge. All services are available in Springfield and Eugene.

Hazards: Creating a loop by using the highway is not recommended. Traffic travels at high speeds, and there are narrow bridges and blind corners to contend with. A possible exception is the stretch of highway from the southern trailhead to Paradise Campground—it has a wide shoulder. The trail crosses lava flows near Clear Lake and Tamolitch Falls. The tread is coarse and narrow, and pedaling over the lava requires good bike handling skills. A fall here can cause nasty cuts. The trail contains some steep drop-offs, especially near the waterfalls.

Rescue index: Help is available at the McKenzie Ranger Station during regular office hours. There is a pay phone at the intersection of Forest Service roads 730 and 655 (at the north end of Trail Bridge Reservoir). Assistance can also be found in McKenzie Bridge.

Land status: Willamette National Forest.

Maps: We highly recommend the Willamette National Forest color map/brochure of the McKenzie River National Recreation Trail. USGS 7.5 minute quads: McKenzie Bridge, Belknap Springs, Tamolitch Falls, Echo Mountain, Clear Lake, and Santiam Junction.

Finding the trail: From Interstate 5 in Eugene/Springfield, take Exit 194 and follow OR 126 east. Drive approximately 50 miles to the community of McKenzie Bridge. Continue east on OR 126 for another 1.8 miles to a parking area on the left for the trail's southernmost trailhead. Eleven parking areas dispersed along OR 126 provide additional access points to the trail. The northern terminus of the trail is at the Santiam Wagon Road Trailhead. To reach it, drive 21.3 miles north of McKenzie Bridge on OR 126 and turn right onto a gravel road marked with a large sign for the McKenzie River Trail. Proceed a short distance down the road to parking on the left and the trailhead on the right.

From locations to the east, follow either OR 126 or OR 242 from Sisters. Take OR 126 to access the Santiam Wagon Road Trailhead. Take OR 242 for a more direct route to the southern trailhead.

Sources of additional information:

McKenzie Ranger District
McKenzie Bridge, OR 97413
(503) 822-3381

Notes on the trail: Numerous access points along the trail create a myriad of opportunities for out-and-back or shuttle rides. Loops are possible, but they involve pedaling on the narrow highway. Because we had only one vehicle at our disposal, we rode on the highway to make a loop. From the southern trailhead, we rode uphill on the highway to Trail Bridge Campground and then back to our vehicle on the single-track. The next day, we formed another loop by riding up the highway from Trail Bridge to the northern trailhead at the Old Santiam Wagon Road. The climbing on the highway was easy but somewhat dangerous. The shoulder ends after Paradise Campground.

The Forest Service has recently reopened the upper portion of this trail to cyclists; however, they stress that the trail was designed as an easy, slow-paced recreational trail and that mountain bikers must practice trail etiquette and tread lightly—good advice. A high potential for user conflict exists from Trail Bridge Reservoir south. The area is popular with hikers, and there are some straight stretches of trail where cyclists tend to ride too fast. Slow down and anticipate others approaching from around the next bend. Be mindful that this trail is open to pedestrians and bicyclists only, so trail deterioration will be blamed on inappropriate bike handling. No skidding!

Most of the intersections on McKenzie River Trail are signed. You should have little difficulty finding your way, especially if you refer to your map. We came across a couple of unsigned intersections on the stretch from Trail Bridge Reservoir south. About 4 miles south of the reservoir you will cross a log bridge over signed Deer Creek, then the trail crosses a paved road. From this road crossing, it is 1.7 miles farther along the trail to an unsigned gravel spur road. Turn left onto the spur road and ride toward a locked gate. Go around the gate and immediately bear left onto the trail as it heads into the woods. The trail crosses another log bridge in 1.2 miles, then the trail splits at an unsigned Y intersection. Take either trail; both lead to a nearby unsigned road. Turn left onto the road and follow it over a bridge to the eastern side of the river. Turn right onto the trail, paralleling the highway. The remainder of the trail is well marked.

RIDE 32 *WALDO LAKE*

This single-track trip around Waldo Lake is 22 miles long. Depending on your conditioning and technical proficiency, it is a moderately difficult to difficult loop. The trails take you past rocky coves, quiet beaches, meadows, campsites, and several smaller lakes and ponds. The view across the water is of forested ridge lines and low mountains. In general, the trails are in good condition.

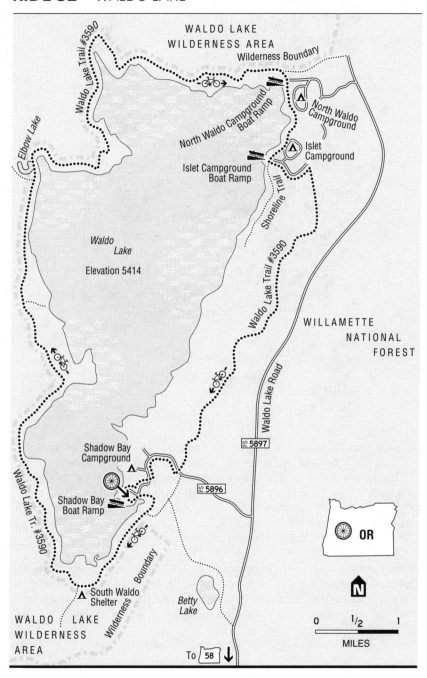

Circling Waldo Lake.

The trip starts with two easy miles along the lakeshore. Then the trail becomes more demanding, with several steep pitches and a rougher tread. Protruding tree roots, boulders, loose gravel, and sandy conditions are intermixed with smooth stretches. This more difficult terrain continues for about five miles. After passing Elbow Lake, the cycling becomes very agreeable, with an improved trail surface and rolling hills. Gentle climbing and good descents characterize the pedaling on the eastern shore.

General location: Waldo Lake is about 75 miles southeast of Eugene, Oregon.
Elevation change: The trailhead is at 5,440′. A high point of 5,700′ occurs just a few miles from the completion of the loop. There are a lot of ups and downs along the course of the ride, adding about 700′ of climbing to the outing. Total elevation gain: 960′.
Season: The trails around Waldo Lake are generally clear of snow from June

Waldo Lake.

through October. The lake is a very popular summer destination. Plan on visiting in the fall or on a weekday for a quieter experience.

Services: Water can be obtained seasonally at the trailhead. Food, lodging, gas, and groceries are available in Oakridge.

Hazards: Obstacles in the trail can cause handling problems. Common impediments include tight squeezes through boulders; slick roots and rocks; drop-offs; windfalls; and sand. There is about 1 mile of paved road riding on the eastern shore, where you may encounter vehicular traffic.

Rescue index: Help can be found in Oakridge. In an emergency, help may be available at the campgrounds on the eastern side of the lake.

Land status: Willamette National Forest.

Maps: The district map of the Oakridge Ranger District is a good guide to this ride. USGS 7.5 minute quads: Waldo Lake and Waldo Mountain.

Finding the trail: From Oakridge, follow OR 58 southeast for 27 miles, to

Waldo Lake Road/Forest Service Road 5897 (on the left). Turn north onto FS 5897 and drive 6.9 miles to FS 5896. Turn left onto FS 5896 toward Shadow Bay. Stay left toward the boat ramp. Park your vehicle in the large gravel parking area above the boat ramp.

Sources of additional information:

Oakridge Ranger District
46375 Highway 58
Westfir, OR 97492
(503) 782-2291

Notes on the trail: Waldo Lake Trail #3590 heads south from the parking area. Follow the well-marked trail around the lake. There is a tricky intersection near Elbow Lake (about 8 miles into the ride). Do not go left to follow the sign for Waldo Meadows; stay to the right, continuing on Waldo Lake Trail. You will pass through Dam Camp in another 3.3 miles; follow the signs for North Waldo Campground. The trail divides at a trail sign-in box near North Waldo Campground; bear right, following Shoreline Trail. Continue south past the North Waldo Campground boat ramp and stay on Shoreline Trail as it goes through the campground amphitheater. Then walk your bike across a sandy beach and continue on Shoreline Trail past Islet Point. Turn left onto the paved road at the Islet Campground boat ramp. After .5 miles on pavement, turn right onto signed Waldo Lake Trail. Follow the path through the woods for 4.6 miles to unsigned FS 5896 (the first paved road you come to on this section of Waldo Lake Trail). Turn right and follow FS 5896 back to your vehicle.

At the time of our research, Shoreline Trail was being extended from the boat ramp at Islet Campground to the boat ramp at Shadow Bay.

RIDE 33 *LARISON ROCK TRAIL*

If you're inclined toward inclines, you may fancy this eight-mile out-and-back trip. Leave your skinny-legged friends at home, though; this single-track rises very steeply from the get-go. Most of it is rideable, but there are several stretches that will require pushing your bike. Larison Rock Trail #3607 ascends through a dense old-growth forest of Douglas fir, cedar, and hemlock. The path is in good condition, with some narrow sections and steep drop-offs. There is a panoramic view from Larison Rock that takes in much of the Rigdon and Oakridge ranger districts. Three Sisters and Diamond Peak are visible on clear days. The return descent is extreme and requires good bike handling skills.

RIDE 33 *LARISON ROCK TRAIL*

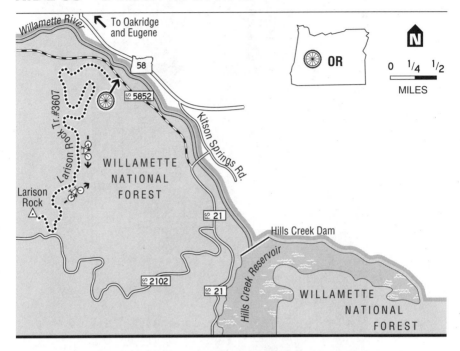

General location: This ride starts near Oakridge, approximately 40 miles east of Eugene, Oregon.

Elevation change: The trailhead is at 1,200′. The high point is 3,600′ at Larison Rock. Total elevation gain: 2,400′.

Season: This trail is open year-round but should be avoided during wet periods. The path is often muddy during the winter and spring.

Services: There is no water on this ride. All services are available in Oakridge.

Hazards: Control your speed on the descent, watch for obstacles, and anticipate others approaching from around blind corners. Equestrians and hikers also enjoy this narrow trail.

Rescue index: Help can be found in Oakridge.

Land status: Willamette National Forest.

Maps: The district map of the Rigdon Ranger District is a good guide to this ride. USGS 7.5 minute quad: Oakridge.

Finding the trail: From Interstate 5 in Eugene, drive east on OR 58 for about 40 miles to Oakridge. Continue through Oakridge to the eastern end of town and Kitson Springs Road. Turn right onto Kitson Springs Road, toward the Hills Creek Dam. Proceed for .5 miles to Forest Service Road 21 (Rigdon Road). Turn right onto FS 21, cross the bridge over the river, and turn right

Steeply inclined Larison Rock Trail.

onto FS 5852 (South Bank Road). Follow FS 5852 for 1.8 miles to the trailhead, on the left. Park on the right side of the road or continue farther along FS 5852 to locate alternative parking.

Sources of additional information:

Rigdon Ranger District
49098 Salmon Creek Road
Oakridge, OR 97463
(503) 782-2266

Notes on the trail: Cycle up Larison Rock Trail #3607. Turn right at the sign-in box for Larison Rock Trail (near FS 2102). The trail becomes impassable to bicycles as it nears the outcrop. Walk the last few yards to the top. Return the way you came.

For another option, use paved FS 2102 to create a loop.

RIDE 34 *LARISON CREEK TRAIL*

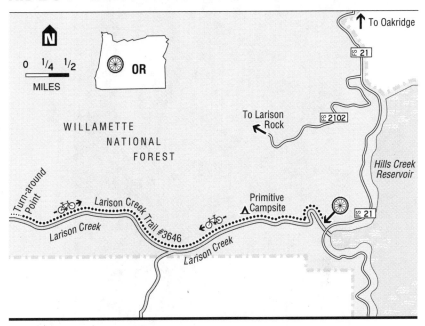

RIDE 34 *LARISON CREEK TRAIL*

Larison Creek Trail is an easy to moderate seven-mile out-and-back ride. The first 1.5 miles of single-track are in good condition. The next two miles climb higher and deeper into the woods. The trail narrows and becomes challenging, with slippery roots and short, steep climbs. Eventually the trail reaches unrideable switchbacks.

This is fun, technical single-track riding. Hanging moss, stands of old-growth timber, and the bubbling of Larison Creek combine to give this place an "enchanted" feeling. The turnaround point is signaled by an illusion-crushing clear-cut.

General location: This ride begins near the Hills Creek Reservoir, approximately 6 miles south of Oakridge, Oregon.

Elevation change: The ride begins at 1,600′ and reaches a high point of 1,900′. Ups and downs contribute about 100′ of climbing to the trip. Total

Larison Creek Trail.

elevation gain: 400′.

Season: The trail is open year-round, but it is usually too wet for mountain biking in the winter and spring.

Services: There is no water on this ride. Water can be obtained at Packard Creek Campground. Food, lodging, groceries, and gas are available in Oakridge.

Hazards: Take care when riding over slippery roots and rocks.

Rescue index: Help can be found in Oakridge.

Land status: Willamette National Forest.

Maps: The district map of the Rigdon Ranger District is a good guide to this route. USGS 7.5 minute quads: Oakridge and Holland Point.

Finding the trail: From Interstate 5 in Eugene, drive east on OR 58 for about 40 miles to Oakridge. Continue through Oakridge to the eastern end of town and Kitson Springs Road. Turn right onto Kitson Springs Road, toward the

Hills Creek Dam. Proceed for .5 miles to Forest Service Road 21 (Rigdon Road). Turn right onto FS 21. Follow FS 21 for 3.3 miles to the trailhead parking area on the right.

Sources of additional information:

Rigdon Ranger District
49098 Salmon Creek Road
Oakridge, OR 97463
(503) 782-2266

Notes on the trail: From the parking area, follow Larison Creek Trail #3646 upstream. Pass a primitive campsite and pit toilets at 1.5 miles (a good turn-around point for beginners). The trail becomes more challenging after you pass the campsite. Turn around when you have had enough hiking with your bike.

RIDE 35 ROUND MOUNTAIN

This 12.5-mile loop is physically demanding. The ride begins with one mile of pavement and then moves to dirt and gravel forest roads. These climb steeply at times, especially as you get closer to the top of the mountain. The roads are in fair shape. Rocks and ruts make the steeper parts more difficult. The descent from the mountain is on Round Mountain National Recreation Trail #805, a dirt single-track in good condition. The most technically demanding portion of the trip is a one-mile stretch of rough rock on Trail #805.

You obtain a nice view of the Ochoco Mountains and the surrounding countryside from the summit of Round Mountain. To the east is Big Summit Prairie. This huge grassy area is a privately owned cattle ranch. Numerous creeks drain this high prairie. Cottonwoods line the waterways and add splashes of color to the fall landscape.

General location: The loop begins near Walton Lake Campground, approximately 30 miles east of Prineville, Oregon.
Elevation change: The ride starts at 5,360′ and reaches 6,753′ at the top of Round Mountain. There are some downhills on the way to the summit and some uphills on Trail #805. These undulations add about 500′ of climbing to the ride. Total elevation gain: 1,893′.
Season: Warm sunny days and cool nights are typical of this region in the summer. The early fall (before hunting season) is also an excellent time for a visit. Snow and mud often create impassable conditions during the winter and

RIDE 35 *ROUND MOUNTAIN*

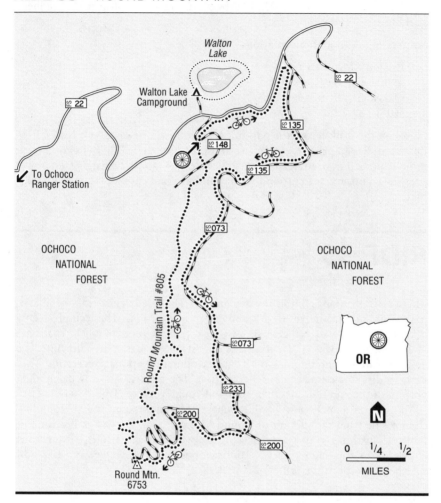

spring. The soils that make up the Round Mountain Trail are vulnerable to erosion, and when they are wet they stick like glue to mountain bike tires . If the single-track is damp, return the way you came.

Services: Water is available seasonally at Walton Lake Campground. Food, lodging, gas, and groceries can be obtained in Prineville.

Hazards: The beginning of the trip is on paved Forest Service Road 22. This road sees a moderate amount of vehicular traffic from loggers and other forest users. Round Mountain Trail drops steeply at first; walk your bike down

Round Mountain bike toss.

the switchbacks in the trail. You will come to a dilapidated footbridge after the switchbacks. It is tilted and slippery; walk your bike across it. A 1-mile stretch of rocky trail occurs near the end of the ride; again, walking may be necessary. Control your speed while descending on Round Mountain Trail— it is popular with hikers and equestrians.

Rescue index: Help may be available at the Ochoco Ranger Station during regular business hours. If the ranger station is closed, you may be able to obtain assistance at the nearby Forest Service housing area, located behind the ranger station. Aid can be found in Prineville.

Land status: Ochoco National Forest.

Maps: The district map for the Prineville Ranger District shows the roads followed on this route, but not Round Mountain Trail. The forest map for the Ochoco National Forest includes the trail, but not all of the roads. Carry both maps. USGS 7.5 minute quad: Ochoco Butte.

Finding the trail: From Prineville, travel east on US 26 for about 15 miles, to County Road 23. Turn right onto CR 23, toward the Ochoco Ranger Station and the Ochoco Campground. After 9 miles, you will come to the intersection of CR 23, FS 22, and FS 42 (.3 miles past the ranger station). Turn left onto FS 22, toward Walton Lake, where FS 42 goes right, toward Lookout Mountain. Stay on FS 22 for 7 miles to Walton Lake Campground (on the left). Pass the campground and continue straight on FS 22 for .1 miles to FS 148. This gravel road is marked by a hiking sign for Trail #805. Turn right and proceed up FS 148 for .4 miles to a parking area on the right for Trail #805.

Sources of additional information:

> Prineville Ranger District
> 155 N. Court
> Prineville, OR 97754
> (503) 447-9641

Notes on the trail: From the parking area, return the way you came on FS 148 (downhill) to FS 22. Turn right onto FS 22 and climb on pavement to signed FS 135. Turn right onto FS 135. Take note of the orange diamond-shaped symbols on trees that line the road. The next 4.5 miles of the ride are marked with these orange diamonds. The route stays on FS 135 for 2.2 miles and then follows FS 073 and FS 233. These roads are unsigned; at intersections, choose the road marked by the orange diamonds. After 4.5 miles of dirt and gravel roads, you will reach unsigned FS 200. This gravel road is marked with a sign to your right that reads "Road Closed 1 Mile Ahead—Local Traffic Only." Turn right and climb on FS 200. Stay on this switchbacking road to the top of the mountain. Just before the top, at the last switchback on FS 200, you will pass Round Mountain Trail #805 on the right (north). Visit the summit and return down FS 200, then turn left onto Round Mountain Trail #805. Continue on this trail back to your vehicle.

The Walton Lake Campground is a great base of operations for exploring miles of nearby roads and trails. There is a path around the small lake; children enjoy riding on this loop.

Oregon Coast / Coastal Range Area Rides

The Oregon Coast is 360 miles of beaches, rocky headlands, rainforests, and wildflower-stippled meadows. Sections of the coast offer promontories for watching birds, whales, and other marine life. Nestled along the shore are towns and fishing villages, and each of these communities acts as a gateway to more wilderness beauty.

Following US 101 north out of California brings you into an area known as Oregon's Banana Belt. A sheltering headland protects the area around Brookings (the first town north of the border) from prevailing northwest winds. The climate is so mild that citrus trees and palms are grown here.

Twenty-seven miles north of Brookings is the community of Gold Beach. The 40-minute drive between these two towns can easily turn into a day-long outing. Scenic overlooks from rocky capes and hikes to secluded beaches are strung out along the course of the highway. The scenes you gaze upon are little changed from those seen by early western explorers.

Searching for golden cities to conquer, the Spanish pilot Bartolome Ferrelo sailed as far north as the southern coast of Oregon in 1542. In 1579, the Englishman Sir Francis Drake challenged Spain's claim to the coast by sailing north to the Rogue River (near present-day Gold Beach). "Thicke and stinking fogges" caused him to give up his search for a passage back to the Atlantic.

The hope of a northwest passage lingered and fueled more explorations. James Cook searched the northern waters of the Pacific in the late eighteenth century. Stopping in the Orient on the way home to England, his men made a monumental discovery: they could sell their makeshift bedding of sea otter pelts to the Chinese—for a small fortune! To Europeans, the value of the Pacific Coast was forever changed; the great tide from the West had begun.

Today the coastal strip is thinly populated; only a few of its towns approach 10,000 residents. Timber, fishing, and the millions of dollars generated by tourism stoke the region's economy. US 101 is the conduit for tourists and their credit cards.

For most of its length, US 101 hugs the coast. This road is a favored destination for touring bicyclists. Thousands enjoy all or part of the Oregon Coast Bike Route annually. What draws these riders is the natural beauty of the Pacific, the excellent camping, and the state's welcoming approach to cycling. These same qualities make the area attractive to mountain bikers.

State parks and excursions on private property (with permission) provide some opportunities for mountain bike riding along the coastline. Inland from the coast are miles of river-level trails and forest roads. State and national forests offer the greatest selection of all-terrain rides.

The Siskiyou National Forest surrounds the Klamath Mountains along the southern coast of Oregon. The Klamath Mountains are the most severe subgroup of mountains within the Coastal Range. Good access into these steep and heavily upholstered peaks can be found in Brookings and Gold Beach.

Farther north, the Siuslaw National Forest covers over one-half million acres between Coos Bay and Tillamook. This large holding within the Coastal Range contains miles of gravel roads that have seldom, if ever, been explored by bicycle.

The ocean has a moderating effect on the weather along the coast. Clear, cool summers are the rule. Rain and fog are common from November until May, but pleasant, sunny winter days are not unheard of.

RIDE 36 *LOWER ROGUE RIVER TRAIL #1168*

In the late 1800s, the Rogue River Trail was an important transportation link between the coast at Gold Beach and inland settlements. After the construction of other roads, this route was all but abandoned. Today it is a well-maintained recreational trail that rambles through a dense, temperate rainforest. Sightings of the Rogue from the trail are few. The view of the river from the cliffs in Copper Canyon is a memorable exception.

Cycling this 12-mile Lower Rogue River Trail is a demanding experience. Much of the single-track is rideable, though some parts can be a real struggle. The path is a technical challenge, with roots, rocks, scree slopes, steep climbs and descents, narrow cliff experiences, lots of small creek crossings, and scratchy, encroaching vegetation. There are also plenty of hike-a-bike stretches. This route is just the ticket for strong, experienced, and slightly demented cyclists.

After pedaling and pushing your bike for 12 miles, you must decide whether to return on the trail or loop back on paved and gravel roads. Beaten up by the single-track, we chose the roads. It made for a long day (42 miles), but making a loop was probably less taxing than riding back on the trail. Any way you approach it, this is a tough ride.

General location: The trailhead is on the north side of the Rogue River, 16 miles east of Gold Beach, Oregon.

Elevation change: The ride starts at 540′ and drops to 160′ in 3.7 miles. The high point of the trail, 780′, occurs shortly after Schoolhouse Creek (about 6 miles into the trip). The small town of Agness (elevation 200′) marks the end

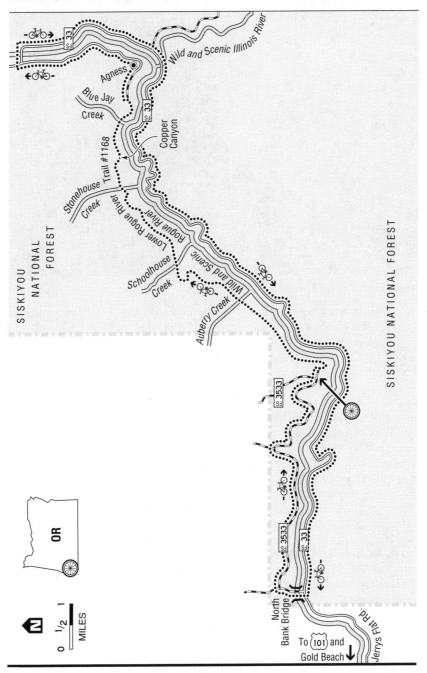

Ancient cedar on the Lower Rogue River Trail.

of the single-track portion of the circuit. Lower Rogue River Trail contains innumerable climbs and descents that are shorter than those described above. We estimate that the trail rises and falls enough to add over 1,000′ of climbing to the ride. The return to the trailhead on the roads is all up and down. From Agness, rolling terrain takes you to a bridge that crosses the Illinois River at 160′. Shortly after crossing the river, you will commence a long climb to 840′. This climb is followed by a 4-mile descent and many lesser hills. The loop closes with another longer climb—300′ in 1 mile. Undulations add about 1,000′ of climbing to the road riding. Total elevation gain: 3,600′.

Season: This tour can be fun year-round if the trail is dry. Much of the single-track is covered with leaves and other forest litter. When wet, the surface is fragile and extremely slick and should be avoided. Wood ticks are a problem in the spring and summer.

Services: There is no water on this ride. There is a small store in Agness that maintains a limited inventory of groceries. All services are available in Gold Beach.

Hazards: You should consider tackling the Lower Rogue River Trail only if you are fit and possess advanced bike handling skills; this is a long and demanding ride with no bail-out options. Turn around before passing Schoolhouse Creek if you are getting tired. The narrow trail drops off steeply in places and contains many obstacles to a safe passage. Wood ticks, rattlesnakes, and poison oak are additional concerns. In Agness, the trail deposits you onto a street. The first house on the right had a couple of mean,

Passing through Copper Canyon.

unchained dogs protecting it.

Rescue index: Help can be found in Gold Beach.

Land status: Siskiyou National Forest lands and public right-of-way through private property.

Maps: The district map of the Gold Beach Ranger District is a good guide to this ride. USGS 7.5 minute quads: Quosatana Butte, Signal Buttes, Agness, Soldier Camp Mountain, and Brushy Bald Mountain.

Finding the trail: From Gold Beach and US 101, turn east onto Jerrys Flat Road. (Jerrys Flat Road meets the highway just south of the bridge over the Rogue River.) Drive east for 9.6 miles, then turn left to cross the North Bank Bridge at Lobster Bar. Immediately after the bridge, turn right onto Forest Service Road 3533/North Bank Road. Stay on the main road and follow the signs to the Lower Rogue River Trail. After 5.8 miles on FS 3533 you will come to a Y intersection at a clearing. There is a sign here that points the way toward the Lower Rogue River Trail. Park on the right at this intersection, next to the big log.

Sources of additional information:

Gold Beach Ranger District
1225 S. Ellensburg Street, Box 7
Gold Beach, OR 97444
(503) 247-6651

Notes on the trail: Turn right to follow the sign for the Lower Rogue River Trail. When you reach the next Y intersection, turn left and ride for .1 miles to the trailhead. Turn right onto the trail. Stay left where side trails descend to summer homes along the river. After about 10 miles, the trail crosses a fence (by means of some wooden steps) and comes to a gravel road. Turn left, cross Blue Jay Creek, and follow the road a very short distance to the trail (signed on the right). Turn right, back onto the trail. Stay left at all side trails for another 1.3 miles, until you reach the streets of Agness. Stay right at the first Y intersection. Soon you will reach pavement and then the Agness Store on the left. Turn left at the Agness Store and follow the road upriver. Follow this road for 3 miles to FS 33. Turn right to cross the bridge over the Rogue River; follow FS 33 toward Gold Beach. Remain on FS 33 for 21 miles to the North Bank Bridge. Turn right to cross the bridge, then immediately turn right onto FS 3533/North Bank Road. Follow the signs to the Lower Rogue River Trail.

RIDE 37 *SILTCOOS LAKE TRAIL*

This moderately difficult four-mile circuit combines a loop with an out-and-back trip. Energetic intermediate cyclists will thrill at the challenges this trail throws at them. Seasoned cyclists may be surprised by the amount of fun that is packed into this short ride, which is a mix of twists, turns, bumps, and short, steep, rideable climbs. The compacted dirt and rock trail was in great shape at the time of our initial research in 1993. Evergreen needles carpeted the path and hushed our rolling tires. Seeing fresh skid marks on this beautiful trail certainly dampened our mood.

Early accounts of this area speak of trees that were "100 feet to the bottom limbs." The forest was said to be "so open you could ride a saddle horse anywhere." Today the trails to Siltcoos Lake lead through a 50-year-old stand of Sitka spruce, Douglas fir, cedar, and hemlock. Scattered throughout the area are huge stumps where giants once stood. Some of the stumps still contain

RIDE 37 *SILTCOOS LAKE TRAIL*

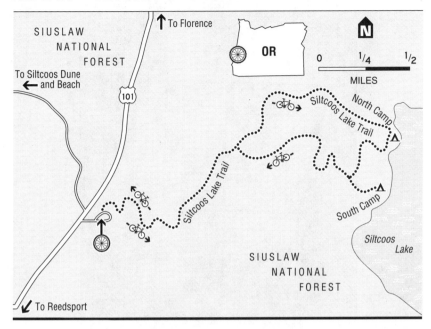

springboard holes. Fallers inserted planks into these holes and wielded their saws from these precarious perches.

General location: The trailhead is on the east side of US 101, approximately 7 miles south of Florence, Oregon.

Elevation change: The ride starts at 280′ and climbs to a high point of 540′ in the first half mile. The low point of the ride is Siltcoos Lake at 160′. You will ride from the lake to an intersection at 260′, then descend back to the lake. The trip ascends once more to 540′ before returning to the trailhead. Additional hills along the trail add about 200′ of climbing to the ride. Total elevation gain: 940′.

Season: The trail is open year-round. Avoid visiting this trail during wet times of the year. The trail can be soggy, and mosquitoes are thick in the spring and early summer.

Services: There is no water on this ride. Water can be obtained at several of the Forest Service campgrounds along US 101. Food, lodging, groceries, and gas are available in Florence.

Hazards: The trail is extremely slick when wet. Although the tread holds relatively few obstacles, common trail hindrances (like slippery roots) still occur.

Siltcoos Lake Trail.

Rescue index: Help can be found in Florence.
Land status: Siuslaw National Forest.
Maps: This trail is not depicted on forest maps. A crude map titled "Siltcoos Lake Trail" may be obtained from the offices of the Oregon Dunes National Recreation Area in Reedsport. USGS 7.5 minute quad: Florence.
Finding the trail: From Florence, drive south on US 101 for approximately 7 miles to the parking area for the Siltcoos Lake Trailhead (on the east side of the highway). From Reedsport, travel north for about 13 miles to the Siltcoos Lake Trailhead. The trailhead parking is opposite the Siltcoos Dune and Beach Access Road.

Sources of additional information:

Oregon Dunes National Recreation Area
855 Highway Avenue
Reedsport, OR 97467
(503) 271-3611

Notes on the trail: Follow the trail for .8 miles to a **Y** intersection at a huge stump. The intersection is marked with a sign that directs you left for the northern route or right to the southern route. This description covers the northern route. In another mile, you will arrive at some campsites near the lakeshore. After walking down to the water, return to the trail and stay to the left (follow the signs for US 101). The trail crosses a boardwalk over a marsh, then goes up some steep steps before depositing you at a **T** intersection. Turn left at the **T** to visit South Camp. Turn around at South Camp and retrace your path to the last intersection. Continue straight, following the sign for US 101. This route will take you back to the intersection at the big stump. Turn left to return to the parking lot.

RIDE 38 *NORTH FORK SIUSLAW RIVER LOOP*

This rigorous 15-mile loop begins and ends with easygoing paved cycling along the North Fork of the Siuslaw River. An opportunity for an easy hike through an old-growth forest comes early in the route. This interpretive hike is called the PAWN Trail. PAWN is an acronym for Poole, Akerley, Worthington, and Noland, four families that settled here in the early 1900s. The path is less than a mile in length and takes you past trees that are over 500 years old.

Back on your bike, you take on an uncommonly steep 2.5-mile quadricep tweaker. The pavement changes to a gravel surface just before you reach the top of the ridge. Following the ridge line involves some exciting descents and a lot more steep climbing. The forest roads are quiet and well maintained. Paved North Fork Road sees light traffic as it rolls by pastures, farms, and homes.

General location: This ride begins at the North Fork Siuslaw Campground, about 15 miles east of Florence, Oregon.
Elevation change: The trip starts at 260' and reaches a high point of 1,280' in 5 miles. This is followed by ridge riding that adds about 700' of climbing to the loop. When you finally descend from the crest, you lose 800' in about 2 miles. Several miles of easy climbing along the river bring you back to the starting point. Total elevation gain: about 2,000'.
Season: These roads can be ridden year-round. The summer is a nice time for a visit, because much of the route is shaded and the river lends a cool atmosphere to the tour. Native rhododendrons do well on the ridge; they are usually in bloom from mid- to late spring.
Services: There is no water on this ride. Water, food, lodging, groceries, and

RIDE 38 *NORTH FORK SIUSLAW RIVER LOOP*

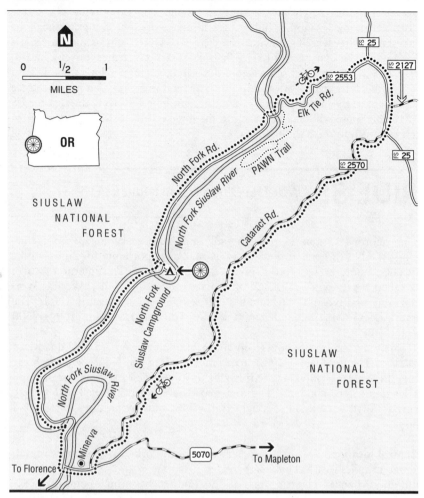

gas can be obtained in Florence.

Hazards: Much of the paved pedaling is on one-lane roads with pullouts. Remain alert for motorists, who may not expect to encounter cyclists on these roads. Control your speed and watch for patches of loose gravel on the descents.

Rescue index: Help is available in Florence.

Land status: Siuslaw National Forest lands and public right-of-way through private land.

Maps: The district map of the Mapleton Ranger District is a good guide to

North Fork Siuslaw River.

this ride. USGS 7.5 minute quads: Cummins Peak and Tiernan.

Finding the trail: From US 101 in Florence, drive east on OR 126 for 1 mile to North Fork Road/County Road 5070 (on the left). Follow North Fork Road for 11 miles to an intersection where CR 5070 goes right, toward Minerva and Mapleton. Continue straight, following the sign for the Upper North Fork. In another 3.2 miles, turn right into the North Fork Siuslaw Campground. The road into the campground is Forest Service Road 715. There is no designated day-use parking, but there is room to park in the campground.

Sources of additional information:

Mapleton Ranger District
P.O. Box 67
Mapleton, OR 97453
(503) 268-4473

Notes on the trail: Exit the campground and turn right onto the pavement. After 2.5 miles, turn right onto signed FS 2553/Elk Tie Road. For some reason, the Visitor Map of the Siuslaw National Forest shows this road's designation as FS 2500 and as FS 653. Immediately after you turn right, you will pass the trailhead for the PAWN Trail on the right. Continue cycling on FS 2553 to a Y intersection. Turn right onto FS 25 and stay on it for .8 miles to FS 2570/Cataract Road. Turn right onto FS 2570. Stay on the main road where side roads branch off. Turn right when you reach pavement; cross a bridge over the river; then turn right again to follow the sign for the Upper North Fork. Follow this road back to the campground and your vehicle.

RIDE 39 *BURNT TIMBER MOUNTAIN*

This 10.4-mile loop is moderately difficult. It begins with a three-mile ascent on a gravel road. This climb is evenly divided between easy, moderately difficult, and strenuous pedaling. (There are several short downhill stretches as well.) This leg is followed by 2.3 miles of pavement along a rolling ridge. Back on gravel, you descend for a mile, climb moderately for .2 miles, and then enjoy a three-mile grin-inducing drop along Bear Creek. The last mile back to your car is paved and easy. The scenery on this ride varies from beautiful green forests and lovely creeks to scarred mountains with massive clear-cuts.

General location: This ride begins approximately 12 miles east of the coastal community of Waldport, Oregon.

Elevation change: The circuit starts at 100′ and reaches a high point of 1,380′ on Burnt Timber Mountain. Ups and downs along the ride add about 300′ of climbing to the trip. Total elevation gain: 1,580′.

Season: This road ride is suitable for year-round use. The winter and spring are typically the wettest seasons of the year.

Services: Water is available near the start of the loop at Canal Creek Campground. Food, lodging, gas, and groceries can be obtained in Waldport.

Hazards: Control your speed while descending—some corners contain loose gravel. Watch for logging trucks and other motorists.

Rescue index: Help can be found in Waldport.

Land status: Siuslaw National Forest.

Maps: The district map of the Waldport Ranger District is a good guide to this ride. USGS 7.5 minute quads: Cannibal Mountain and Tidewater.

Finding the trail: From the intersection of US 101 and OR 34 in Waldport, follow OR 34 east toward Corvallis. After 7 miles, turn right onto Canal

RIDE 39 *BURNT TIMBER MOUNTAIN*

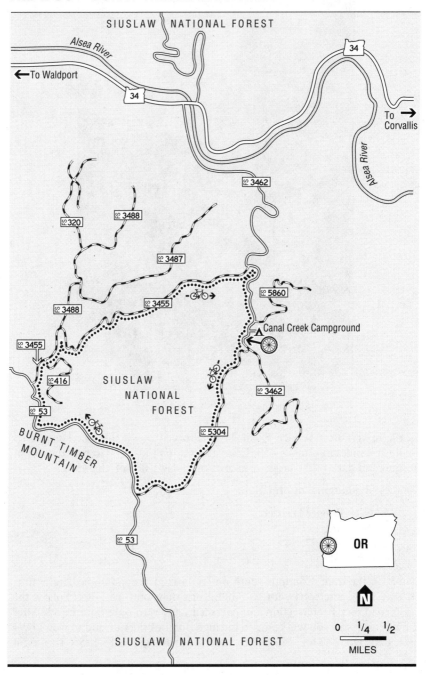

SIUSLAW NATIONAL FOREST

Alsea River

34

←To Waldport

34

To →
Corvallis

Alsea River

3462

320

3488

3487

3488

3455

-⊙🚲→

5860

Canal Creek Campground

3455

416

3462

SIUSLAW
NATIONAL
FOREST

🚲

53

🚲

5304

BURNT TIMBER
MOUNTAIN

OR

N

53

0   ¼   ½
MILES

SIUSLAW NATIONAL FOREST

Back road in the Siuslaw National Forest.

Creek Road/Forest Service Road 3462. Proceed down this one-lane paved road for 4 miles to Canal Creek Campground (on the left). Go past the campground and park in the large open area on the left side of FS 3462.

Sources of additional information:

Waldport Ranger District
P.O. Box 400
Waldport, OR 97394
(503) 563-3211

Notes on the trail: Continue south on FS 3462. The road immediately turns to gravel and intersects with FS 5304. Turn right onto FS 5304. Follow the main road to a T intersection and pavement, and turn right onto FS 53. After 2 miles on FS 53 you will come to the high point of the ride and to views over clear-cuts. Descend for .25 miles to a low point and gravel FS 3455. Turn right onto FS 3455 (an easy turn to miss). Stay on this main road as spur roads branch off. Turn right when you reach pavement, and ride back to your car.

Explorations on side roads can add many miles to this outing. Two noteworthy side roads are FS 3488 and FS 320 (see map). These head down to some stands of old-growth Douglas fir. The trees are not giants, but it is a pleasure to view larger, mature evergreens.

RIDE 40 *MARYS PEAK*

This 13-mile out-and-back ride (with a short loop) will challenge advanced cyclists with 6 miles of varied single-track riding. A sign at the summit of Marys Peak reads "The Top of the World." At 4,097 feet, Marys Peak is the highest point in the Coastal Range. On clear days (which are rare) you can look west to the Pacific Ocean or east for a view of the Cascade Range.

The initial miles on Forest Service Road 2005 are a moderately difficult warm-up. Then you get on East Ridge Trail and climb 1,500 feet in 2.7 miles, to Marys Peak. This ascent is moderately difficult to strenuous, with some very steep pitches and some easy "breathers." The trail gets rocky in places but is in good condition overall. North Ridge Trail and Tie Trail descend from the mountain and reconnect you with East Ridge Trail. Tie Trail is especially rough and includes some very technical climbing and some unrideable sections.

General location: The start of the ride is about 22 miles west of Corvallis, Oregon.

Elevation change: The ride begins at 1,700′ and reaches 4,097′ atop Marys Peak. Undulations add about 300′ of climbing to the trip. Total elevation gain: 2,697′.

Season: It is possible to ride here from spring through autumn. Temperatures can be surprisingly cold at the peak; bring extra clothing.

Services: Water can be obtained seasonally at the observation point on Marys Peak. Food, lodging, gas, and pay phones can be found in Philomath. All services are available in Corvallis.

Hazards: Tie Trail includes cliff experiences and some very rocky stretches. Control your speed on the return—watch for other trail users.

Rescue index: Help can be found in Philomath.

Land status: Siuslaw National Forest.

Maps: A pamphlet titled "Marys Peak—A Place to Discover" can be obtained from the Alsea Ranger District. It is the best map available. The USGS 7.5 minute quad, Marys Peak, does not show the trails.

RIDE 40 *MARYS PEAK*

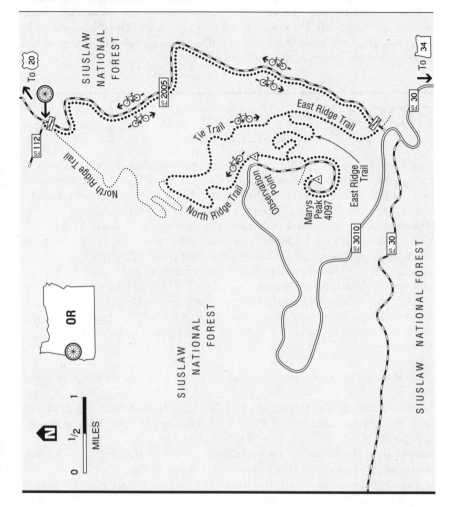

Finding the trail: From Corvallis, follow US 20/OR 34 west to Philomath. Proceed through town and remain on US 20 toward Toledo/Newport, where OR 34 goes left toward Alsea/Waldport. Turn left onto Woods Creek Road/FS 2005 near milepost marker 48 (about a mile after crossing Marys River). Follow FS 2005 for 7.4 miles to FS 112 (on the right) and a gate across FS 2005. Park in the pullout on the left.

Negotiating East Ridge Trail.

Sources of additional information:

Alsea Ranger District
18591 Alsea Highway
Alsea, OR 97324-9612
(503) 487-5811

Notes on the trail: Pedal around the gate and ride up FS 2005. Stay on the main road where trails and side roads branch off. After 3.4 miles on FS 2005, near paved FS 3010, you will arrive at a gate across the road. Go around the gate and immediately turn right onto East Ridge Trail. After 1 mile you will come to an unmarked intersection where unsigned Tie Trail goes right. Stay to the left and switchback uphill, remaining on East Ridge Trail. Carry your bike up some steps after another .7 miles. It is .4 miles from this landmark to another intersection, with five railroad tie steps on the left. Carry your bike up the steps. Soon you will emerge from the woods onto a grassy hillside. Proceed across the hillside to a gravel road. Turn left onto the gravel road and ride to Marys Peak. Turn around at the summit and backtrack to the five railroad tie steps; turn left and pedal to restrooms and a parking lot for the observation point. Ride by the restrooms and across the pavement (stay to the right) to a sign for North Ridge Trail. Bear right onto the trail and reenter the woods. Follow this trail for .6 miles to a log bench on the left. Turn right onto unsigned Tie Trail at this faint intersection (easy to miss). Take Tie Trail to East Ridge Trail. Bear left onto East Ridge Trail and return the way you came.

RIDE 41 *MCDONALD FOREST*

The 7,000-acre McDonald Forest is managed by Oregon State University's School of Forestry. The school encourages recreational use of the forest, which is very popular with local hikers, joggers, mountain bikers, and equestrians. Over 60 miles of well-maintained forest roads and multi-use trails crisscross the area. The route we describe travels on forest roads; at the time of our visit, the trails were too muddy for two-wheeled travel.

This 11.9-mile loop (with out-and-back spurs) can be labeled as an intermediate to advanced workout. The first 1.5 miles are a pleasant warm-up—the roads climb easy to moderately difficult terrain. Then the ascent gets steeper but is still mostly moderate. This initial climbing is followed by a furious 500-foot drop. Then the real exertion begins. Monster climbs find you working feverishly to keep your front wheel on the ground. Wipe the sweat from your eyes upon reaching McCulloch Peak and look out over Corvallis and the surrounding rural flatlands. Marys Peak is off to the southwest. The remainder of the circuit is nearly all downhill.

General location: This ride begins approximately 6 miles northwest of Corvallis, Oregon.
Elevation change: The ride begins at 500′ and climbs to 1,460′. Then you drop to 950′ before continuing with the climbing. The high point of the trip is 2,178′, at McCulloch Peak. A few short ups and downs add another 100′ of climbing to the loop. Total elevation gain: 2,288′.
Season: Most of the trails and roads in the forest are open year-round. Some closures occur due to management activities, special events, and wet conditions.
Services: There is no water available on this ride. All services can be found in Corvallis.
Hazards: The roads on this ride are technically easy but are often busy with

RIDE 41 McDONALD FOREST

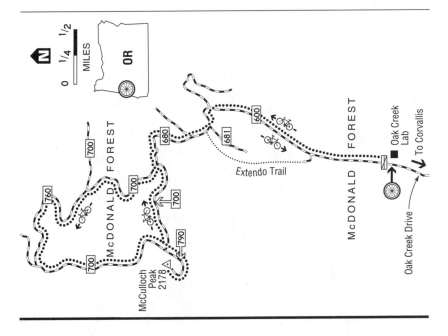

other recreationists. Extend common courtesy; control your speed and announce your presence well in advance of overtaking others.

Rescue index: Help is available in Corvallis.

Land status: OSU Research Forest and private property. The described route passes through a parcel of property owned by Starker Forests; a special land-use permit is required for access to this land. To obtain a permit, please visit the Starker Forests offices at 7240 S.W. Philomath Boulevard in Corvallis, or call (503) 929-2477.

Maps: A brochure box at the trailhead is stocked with a McDonald Forest Recreation Map and Guide. A detailed topo map of the McDonald and Paul M. Dunn forests may be purchased at local bike and sports shops. It contains directions for other rides in the forests. USGS 7.5 minute quads: Corvallis and Airlie South.

Finding the trail: In Corvallis, go west on Harrison Boulevard. Continue straight at the stop sign at S.W. 53rd Street/N.W. Walnut Boulevard. Stay on this road (now Oak Creek Drive) for 1.8 miles to an intersection where Oak Creek Drive goes right and Cardwell Hill Drive goes straight. Turn right to remain on Oak Creek Drive (Cardwell Hill Drive is marked with a "Dead End" sign at this intersection). Stay on Oak Creek Drive to the end of the

Mark Price reaching the summit of McCullough Peak.

road, at the Oak Creek Laboratory of Biology. Park in the small lot on the left.

Sources of additional information:

Oregon State University Research Forest
Peavy Hall, Room 218
Corvallis, OR 97731-5711
(503) 737-4452
For trail and road conditions: (503) 737-4434

Notes on the trail: Go around the gate and climb up Road 600 for 1.7 miles to a Y intersection at a brown information board. Turn left onto Road 680. Stay on the main road as Road 681 goes left. Stay on the main road where Extendo Trail goes left (signaled by a brown fiberglass marker). After passing Extendo Trail, you will come to an intersection with an island of vegetation in the middle of it. This junction is also marked by an evergreen tree marked with pale blue spray paint. Continue straight (left) on the main road. In another .5 miles you will come upon another intersection with an island of vegetation in the middle. Turn right onto Road 700 and descend sharply for about 1.3 miles. Control your speed and watch for Road 760 on the left. Turn left and climb briskly on Road 760. Stay on Road 760 as side roads branch off. (Road 760 becomes Road 700 after about 2 miles.) After the road levels out some, you will arrive at a major intersection and Road 790 on the right. Turn right and follow Road 790 to McCulloch Peak. Turn around at the summit and return to the last intersection. Turn right onto Road 700. Descend on the main road for .8 miles to the intersection of Road 700 and Road 680. Stay to the right, bearing onto Road 680. Backtrack to your vehicle.

RIDE 42 *MT. HEBO*

About half of this moderately difficult six-mile loop is on an old Indian trail. In the early 1850s, this trail was the Tillamook settlers' major transportation link to the Willamette Valley. The pioneers abandoned the route in 1882 when a wagon road was completed. Grande Ronde Indians continued to use it for a couple more decades. Remnants of the old trail were discovered by a Forest Service employee about 20 years ago. Reconstruction of a portion of it was completed in 1984. Today, Pioneer Trail's primary users are Mt. Hebo's deer and elk herds (with equestrians coming in a distant second).

The upper portion of the trail drops moderately and is a delightful mix of straightaways and turns. The tread is a smooth, hard-packed surface of dirt and rock. After 1.5 miles you will enter wetter environs. Hoof damage, large exposed roots, and moist conditions predominate for the remainder of the single-track riding. The trail ends at Hebo Lake Campground. The lake is bordered by a hiking trail and is a popular fishing hole. The circuit ends with 2.5 miles of steep, paved climbing.

General location: Mt. Hebo is about 20 miles south of Tillamook, Oregon.
Elevation change: The single-track drops from 2,820′ at the parking area to 1,720′ at Hebo Lake. Total elevation gain for the loop: 1,100′. You can extend your explorations by pedaling to the summits of Mt. Hebo. This side trip would add about 1,000′ of climbing to your ride.
Season: Typically, the driest period on Mt. Hebo is mid-summer through early fall.
Services: Water is available at Hebo Lake Campground. Food, lodging, groceries, gas, and pay phones can be found in Hebo.

RIDE 42 *MOUNT HEBO*

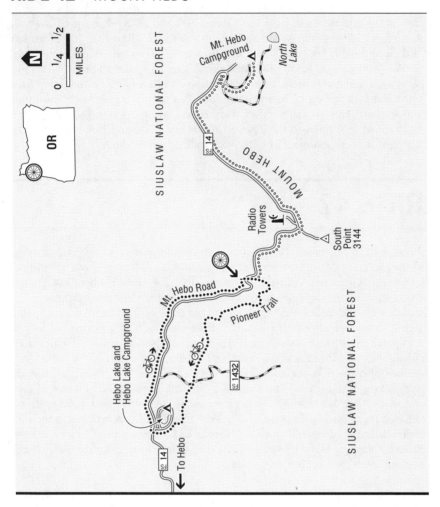

Hazards: The lower part of Pioneer Trail contains numerous exposed roots. When wet, these obstacles become cyclist launchers.

Rescue index: Help can be found in Hebo.

Land status: Siuslaw National Forest.

Maps: The district map of the Hebo Ranger District is a suitable guide to the trails and roads on Mt. Hebo. USGS 7.5 minute quads: Niagara Creek and Hebo.

Finding the trail: In Hebo, take OR 22 east from US 101. After just .1 miles,

Angler at Hebo Lake.

turn left onto Forest Service Road 14/Mt. Hebo Road (just before the Hebo Ranger Station). Drive up the mountain for 4.6 miles; you will pass Hebo Lake Campground on the right. Continue past the campground on FS 14 for another 2.6 miles. At this point, just as you are about to enter a right-hand curve, you will see two barricades on the left. Park on the left side of FS 14 in the dirt pullout.

Sources of additional information:

Hebo Ranger District
Hebo, OR 97122
(503) 392-3161

Notes on the trail: The Pioneer Trail begins across the road from the parking turnout. It is marked with a "No Motor Vehicles" sign. Follow the trail down to Hebo Lake Campground. Stay left through the campground, then turn right onto FS 14. Follow FS 14 back to your car.

If you want a longer ride, continue on up the road to the top of Mt. Hebo. Bypass the first summit and its radio towers; by pedaling northeast you will find beautiful alpine meadows and plump views of the Tillamook Valley, Cape Lookout, Sand Lake, Kiwanda Beach, and Haystack Rock. You can continue past the meadows on FS 14 to gravel FS 115 and Mt. Hebo Campground (a fire ring). A trail leads from the campground back to the radio towers. We found the trail to be wet and extremely rough, with coarse rocks.

RIDE 43 *FORT STEVENS STATE PARK*

Fort Stevens State Park contains an eight-mile network of paved, mostly level bike paths. Prominent in the park is a 600-site campground. Everywhere you look, children are absorbed in lively games and resolutely pumping their bikes around (and around and around) the many campground loops. Exploring this historic park on two wheels is a great family activity. More fun with the clan can be had by enjoying the sandy beaches and good fishing at Coffenbury Lake, hiking a nature trail, or attending an evening program at the campground amphitheater.

Fort Stevens Military Reservation guarded the mouth of the Columbia River from the Civil War through World War II. The fort is a couple of miles north of the campground and features a museum and self-guided walking tour. The abandoned gun batteries and the commander's station offer good views of the Columbia River and South Jetty. Another historic point of interest is the wreck of the Peter Iredale, an English vessel that ran aground in 1906. Its rusting skeleton is embedded in the beach about a mile west of the campground.

General location: Fort Stevens State Park is located approximately 8 miles west of Astoria, Oregon.

Elevation change: The park is quite flat. The trail dips and rises in places to surmount lesser landforms and cross bridges.

Season: The park is open year-round. For full-tilt campmania, visit on a summer holiday weekend. Other seasons of the year are less frenzied. The early fall is a good time for a ride in the park.

Services: Water is available at the campground and at various day-use areas within the park. All services are available in Astoria.

Hazards: The roads in the park can get busy, and motorists often drive too fast. Children should be supervised and given instruction on safe cycling. The park's bike safety rules are printed on the trail map available at the camp-

RIDE 43 *FORT STEVENS BICYCLE TRAILS*

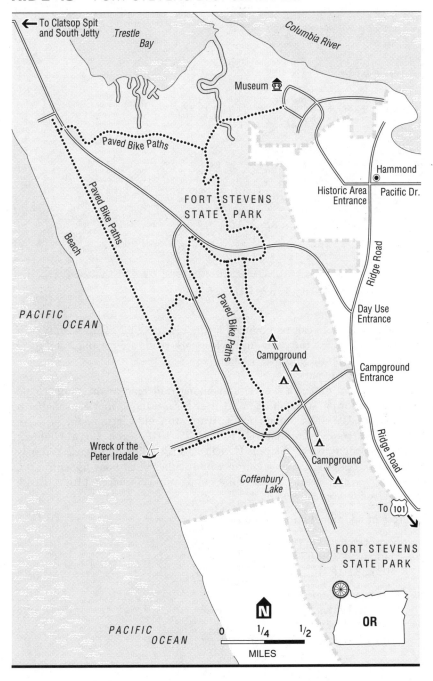

Beachfront parking at Fort Stevens State Park.

ground entrance station.

Rescue index: Help can be obtained at the campground entrance station or by contacting one of the camp hosts. The park roads are patrolled and there are pay phones at the entrance station.

Land status: State park.

Maps: You can obtain a bicycle and hiking trail map at the campground entrance station or at the museum. A flyer for a walking tour is available at the museum. USGS 7.5 minute quads: Warrenton and Clatsop Spit.

Finding the trail: From Astoria, follow US 101/Oregon Coast Highway south. The route to Fort Stevens is well marked; follow the signs. You may enter the park at the camping entrance or at either of two day-use entrances. The day-use entrances are north of the campground entrance on Ridge Road. There is a day-use fee.

Sources of additional information:

Fort Stevens State Park
Hammond, OR 97121
(503) 861-1671

Fort Stevens State Park
Historical Area and Military Museum
Hammond, OR 97121
(503) 861-2000

Notes on the trail: For those seeking a more difficult riding experience, the woods below the Astoria Column (near Astoria) are home to an extensive network of single-track trails. It is an easy place to get lost—the trails lead in many directions and are unmapped and unsigned. Drop by one of the bike shops in Astoria and see if anyone has produced a map. Perhaps they can set you on course; if not, they can at least sell you a compass and a Power Bar.

Mt. Hood National Forest

For over a century, Mt. Hood has captured the imagination of Americans. After thousands of arduous miles on the Oregon Trail, emigrants came up against one final obstacle: the massive bulk of Mt. Hood. Today tourists travel around the mountain on highways, and sportsmen and recreation-minded people flock to its slopes. All who behold it are struck by the beauty of this isolated and majestic peak. In Portland, Mt. Hood is visible from every section of the city. The people lovingly refer to it as "our mountain."

Just a couple of hours east of Portland is the town of Hood River. It sits at the foot of Mt. Hood on the banks of the mighty Columbia River. The steady, intense winds that blow up the Columbia Gorge have made Hood River the windsurfing capital of the Northwest. This young recreation-oriented community also enjoys access to some fine single-track mountain biking.

From Hood River, the Mt. Hood Highway climbs away from the Columbia Gorge. The drive up this two-lane highway is a scenic trip. On either side of you are the apple and pear orchards of the wide Hood River Valley. Before you is the shining volcanic cone of Mt. Hood. To the east, high above the roadway, is Surveyors Ridge. A trail follows the ridge for 17 miles and offers incredible views of the snowfields and glaciers on Mt. Hood. It is an outstanding place to ride a mountain bike.

Still heading south along the highway, the valley narrows rapidly and gives way to evergreen forests. The East Fork of the Hood River runs beside the highway; good camping and mountain biking can be found on its banks. Connecting the Sherwood and Robinhood campgrounds is East Fork Trail, which parallels the vigorous river and offers cyclists a short, less demanding single-track experience. A hiking trail leads from Sherwood Campground to beautiful Tamanawas Falls.

Climbing higher, the highway brings you to Bennett Pass. A gravel road leads from the pass to a quiet trail that follows Gunsight Ridge to Gumjuwac Saddle. The ridge provides breathtaking vistas of nearby Mt. Hood and distant views of many other Cascade peaks.

South of Barlow Pass, the Mt. Hood Highway meets US 12 and swings west toward Portland. Here you pass the towns of Government Camp and Zigzag. The resort hotel Timberline Lodge is accessed from Government Camp. The lodge sees many visitors in the winter for downhill skiing. In the summer, it is the trailhead for the popular southside climb of Mt. Hood and the Round-the-Mountain Trail. Good camping and gravel road riding can be found below Government Camp at lovely Trillium Lake.

Head south from Government Camp on US 12 to access rides in the Bear Springs Ranger District, or drive west toward Portland and stop in at the ranger station in Zigzag. All of the ranger districts in the Mt. Hood National Forest supply handouts on mountain bike opportunities in their section of the forest.

Due to its proximity to Portland, the Mt. Hood National Forest is a hugely popular destination. The increased use of mountain bikes has not gone unnoticed by the forest's recreation managers. We recommend that you make a visit or phone call before your trip to check on special conditions that could affect your ride. Some trails are closed periodically to reduce erosion or to lessen user conflicts.

RIDE 44 *EAST FORK TRAIL #650*

This is a moderately difficult ten-mile out-and-back trip on single-track. It begins with the ride's most demanding terrain. The pedaling gets much easier near Robinhood Campground (at the south end of the trail). Technical challenges include roots, embedded boulders, waterbars, and whoop-dee-doos. The path is in mostly good condition, with some pummy sections and wet areas.

This fun route parallels the East Fork of the Hood River and travels through some nice old-growth forest. Trail #650A to Tamanawas Falls makes for an excellent side trip (no bikes—hiking only).

General location: This ride begins near Sherwood Campground, approximately 25 miles south of Hood River, Oregon, on OR 35.
Elevation change: The trip begins at 3,000' and reaches 3,550' at Robinhood Campground. Undulations on the route add about 200' of climbing to the ride. Total elevation gain: 750'.
Season: The Hood River Ranger District recommends this trail as an early and late season ride. Dry summer conditions turn the soil to dust, which can lead to trenching by mountain bike tires. Call ahead to check on seasonal closure.
Services: Water can be obtained seasonally at Sherwood and Robinhood campgrounds. All services are available in Hood River.
Hazards: Good bike handling skills are required to safely negotiate obstacles in the trail. The route includes some wooden bridges that are slippery, especially

RIDE 44 *EAST FORK TRAIL #650*

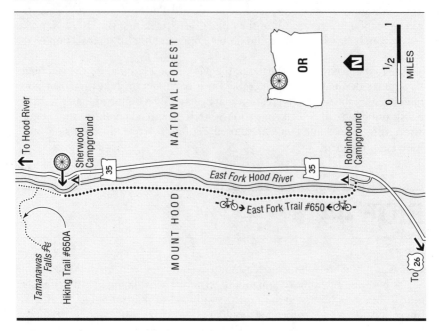

when wet. Minimize trail damage by walking your bike over the steepest and most fragile segments of the path.

Rescue index: Help can be found in Mt. Hood and Hood River.

Land status: Mt. Hood National Forest.

Maps: The district map of the Hood River Ranger District is a good guide to this route. USGS 7.5 minute quads: Badger Lake and Dog River.

Finding the trail: From the community of Hood River, follow OR 35 south for 24 miles. Turn right to park in the gravel pullout signed "East Fork Trailheads."

Sources of additional information:

Hood River Ranger District
6780 Highway 35
Mt. Hood, OR 97041
(503) 352-6002

Notes on the trail: From the parking area, walk your bike to the river and across the footbridge. Turn left onto East Fork Trail #650. Follow the single-track to Robinhood Campground. Turn around and return the way you came.

Footbridge over the East Fork of the Hood River.

Beginners can explore this trail by starting at Robinhood Campground and heading north. Turn around when the terrain gets too demanding.

RIDE 45 *SURVEYORS RIDGE TRAIL #688*

Surveyors Ridge Trail is 17 miles long and is mostly single-track. Parts of the trail require excellent bike handling skills, while others are smooth and dreamy. We describe a 20-mile loop that utilizes 12.4 miles of the trail, with a return on paved and gravel roads. Longer and shorter loops are possible. This demanding ridge ride passes through grassy meadows, through stands of

Boardwalk near Robinhood Campground.

heavy timber, and around rocky outcroppings. On clear days, views of the Hood River Valley, Mt. Hood, and Mt. Adams are spectacular. Sunshine or clouds, Surveyors Ridge will bring a smile to fans of single-track cycling.

The trail loses elevation as it heads north, but it undulates continually. Most of the uphills are easy to moderately difficult; there are about 1.5 miles of steep climbing (some sections are unrideable). The trail is in fair to good condition, with some rocky and pummy stretches. Returning on the roads involves mostly moderately difficult to easy climbing.

General location: The trailhead is approximately 30 miles south of Hood River, Oregon.

Elevation change: The southern terminus of the trail lies at 4,200′. The northern end of the trail, for this ride description, lies at 3,400′. The path nears

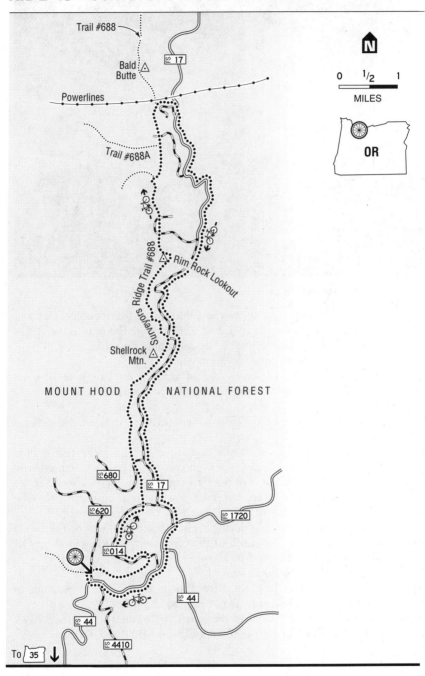

Trail #688

Bald
Butte △

FS 17

Powerlines

N

0   1/2   1
MILES

OR

Trail #688A

△ Rim Rock Lookout

Surveyors Ridge Trail #688

Shellrock △
Mtn.

MOUNT HOOD   NATIONAL FOREST

FS 680

FS 17

FS 620

FS 1720

FS 014

FS 44

FS 44

To 35

FS 4410

Mt. Hood from Surveyors Ridge Trail.

4,300′ several times and stays above the 4,000′ mark for 10 miles. Ups and downs on the trail add up to about 1,200′ of climbing. The road return takes you to the trip's low point—3,300′. Hills contribute an estimated 1,500′ of climbing to the road miles. Total elevation gain: 2,700′.

Season: Surveyors Ridge is usually free of snow from late June through October. Wildflowers are abundant in June and July, especially at the northern end of the trail.

Services: There is no water on the ride. Water and all services are available in Hood River.

Hazards: Watch for pummy segments of trail, especially while descending. Expect rocky terrain and obstacles like exposed roots. There is a barbed-wire gate across the trail, 1 mile north of the trail's intersection with Forest Service Road 17. The gate is on a steep descent if you are heading north. Warning signs were in place in the fall of 1993. Watch for traffic on the roads.

Rescue index: Help is available during regular business hours at the Hood River Ranger Station, .3 miles south of the community of Mt. Hood on OR 35. Pay phones can be found in Mt. Hood.

Land status: Mt. Hood National Forest.

Maps: The district map of the Hood River Ranger District is a good guide to this ride. USGS 7.5 minute quads: Dog River and Parkdale.

Finding the trail: From locations to the north, drive south from Hood River on OR 35 for 25 miles. Turn left onto FS 44/Dufur Mill Road. From locations to the south, FS 44/Dufur Mill Road will be on your right, 6.8 miles north of Bennett Pass. Follow FS 44 for 3.6 miles to a sign on the right that points left toward Surveyors Ridge Trail #688. Turn left here onto FS 620; you will immediately arrive at the trailhead for Surveyors Ridge Trail, on the right. Park on the side of the road.

Sources of additional information:

Hood River Ranger District
6780 Highway 35
Mt. Hood–Parkdale, OR 97041
(503) 352-6002

Notes on the trail: The path goes east from the large trailhead sign at FS 620. The trail passes through Cooks Meadow (signed) and then arrives at unsigned FS 014. Turn left to follow the sign for Trail #688. Stay on the road for about 3 miles as it travels through clear-cuts and parallels the buried Dog River Aqueduct. Turn left onto signed Trail #688 just before FS 014 commences a steep climb up to FS 17. At intersections, follow the signs for Surveyors Ridge Trail #688. After 9.2 miles of pedaling, you will pass Rim Rock Lookout (signed) on your left. You will cross two gravel spur roads in the next .6 miles, then you will arrive at a poorly marked Y intersection in a grove of old-growth Douglas fir (.7 miles north of the second spur road crossing). Stay to the right to follow Trail #688. You will come to the next intersection of trails in 1 mile; continue straight where Oak Ridge Trail #688A goes left. Surveyors Ridge Trail quickly arrives at another unsigned spur road. Cross the road to continue north on Surveyors Ridge Trail. (The trail is marked by a sign that directs you toward Bald Butte.) Next you will approach four huge electric towers and a trailhead sign on your right. Bear right toward the trailhead sign and onto a faint trail that leads out to a dirt road. Turn right onto the road and descend a short distance to a T intersection at unsigned FS 630. Turn left and drop down to paved FS 17 (unsigned). Turn right onto the pavement. FS 17 becomes a gravel road in 2.8 miles. It changes back to pavement in 5.5 miles. After following FS 17 for 9 miles, you will come to a T intersection where FS 1720 goes left toward Knebal Springs Campground. Turn right here to stay on FS 17 (a sign directs you right toward FS 44). In .4 miles, FS 17 intersects with FS 44. Continue straight onto FS 44 toward Highway 35. You will remain on FS 44 for 1.6 miles. Pass FS 4410 (which goes left to High Prairie) and take the next right onto FS 620 to reach your vehicle.

RIDE 46 *GUNSIGHT TRAIL*

Gunsight Trail is a fun and challenging single-track that takes you to some spectacular sights. There is a great view of Mt. Hood near the halfway point. Another overlook is reached farther down the path. This vista includes the Upper Hood River Valley and Mt. Adams. The return on Forest Service Road 3550 sports some outstanding scenery as well. The ridge you are riding along suddenly drops away to the east. Far below are Jean and Badger lakes, and in the distance is Mt. Jefferson.

This demanding 19-mile circuit is well suited to strong intermediate cyclists and advanced cyclists. It is a combination of an out-and-back trip and a loop. The route follows gravel FS 3550 for 14 miles and Gunsight Trail for 5 miles. There are some sustained grades and plenty of short ups and downs. Most of the climbing is easy to moderately difficult. You will encounter a lot of rough surfaces, so wear your most heavily padded bike shorts.

Gunsight Trail packs in a real mixture of riding surfaces and terrain. This fine path goes from stretches of smooth compacted dirt to areas littered with obstacles. Negotiating the trail requires good bike handling skills. There are several places where you will need to push your bike.

General location: This ride begins at Bennett Pass on OR 35, approximately 35 miles south of Hood River, Oregon.
Elevation change: The trailhead elevation at Bennett Pass is 4,674′. The route climbs to 5,340′ at the intersection of FS 3550 and Gunsight Trail. A high point of 5,900′ occurs on Gunsight Trail. Then you pedal to Gumjuwac Saddle, at 5,260′. Back on FS 3550, you reach 5,820′ before the return to Bennett Pass. Rolling topography adds about 1,000′ of climbing to the tour. Total elevation gain: 2,786′.
Season: The best opportunities for finding dry conditions are in the summer and fall.
Services: There is no water on the ride. Water, food, lodging, limited groceries, gas, and pay phones can be found in Government Camp. All services are available in Hood River.
Hazards: Much of FS 3550 is degraded, with ruts, washboarding, rocks, and coarse gravel. Use extra caution when descending on this road. You may encounter motorists on the roads. Gunsight Trail presents obstacles including rocks, scree, sand, windfalls, narrow openings between boulders, drop-offs, and steep, switchbacking descents.
Rescue index: Help is available in Government Camp.
Land status: Mt. Hood National Forest.
Maps: The district map of the Hood River Ranger District is a good guide to

RIDE 46 *GUNSIGHT TRAIL*

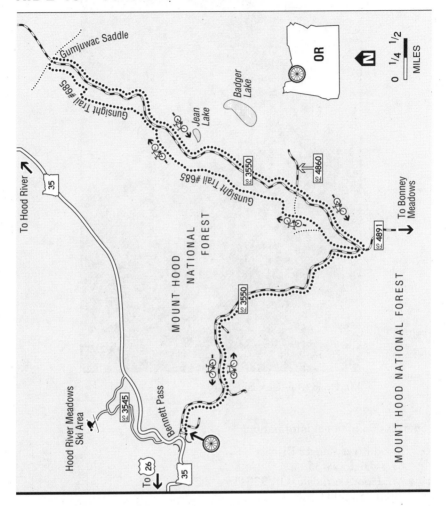

this ride. USGS 7.5 minute quads: Badger Lake and Mount Hood South.
Finding the trail: From Hood River, drive south on OR 35 for 34 miles to Bennett Pass (about 1 mile south of the turnoff for the Hood River Meadows Ski Area). From locations to the south, drive to the intersection of US 26 and OR 35, then follow OR 35 northeast (toward Hood River) for 6 miles to Bennett Pass. Park in the paved pullout on the east side of the highway or turn east onto FS 3550/Bennett Pass Road and park in the gravel parking area on the right.

Mt. Hood from Gunsight Trail.

Sources of additional information:

Hood River Ranger District
6780 Highway 35
Mt. Hood–Parkdale, OR 97041
(503) 352-6002

Notes on the trail: Follow FS 3550 east. Stay on the main road as several side roads branch off. After 4.2 miles, you will reach an intersection where FS 3550, FS 4891, and Gunsight Trail #685 meet. Turn left onto Gunsight Trail. After .6 miles on Gunsight Trail stay right and uphill where an unsigned single-track goes left and descends. In another .5 miles, continue straight where a trail branches off to the right toward Windy Camp. From this intersection it is 1.3 miles to a large rock outcropping on the left. Climb up onto the outcropping for a view of Mt. Hood. Back on Gunsight Trail, you will descend rapidly and come to another observation point on the left (look to the left for a clearing in the trees near a pile of large, angular boulders). It is .7 miles from this second overlook to FS 3550. Turn left onto FS 3550 and follow it for .2 miles to rejoin Gunsight Trail on the left. This stretch of Gunsight Trail lasts for 1.8 miles and deposits you at Gumjuwac Saddle and FS 3550. Turn right onto FS 3550 and follow it back to your car.

You can shorten this loop without missing the nicest views. To do this, ride to the intersection of Gunsight Trail and FS 3550 (.7 miles beyond the second overlook). Instead of turning left onto FS 3550, turn right and shorten the circuit by 4 miles. You will miss some exciting downhill single-track, but you will also avoid some bumpy climbing on FS 3550.

For an easy out-and-back trip, start at the described trailhead and follow FS 3550 for 1.8 miles. This stretch of FS 3550 is in excellent condition and takes you to a good view of Mt. Hood.

RIDE 47 *FROG LAKE BUTTES*

This ride is a 14-mile loop with a short out-and-back spur. One mile is paved cycling, and .3 miles use a snowmobile trail; the remainder of the circuit is on gravel roads. The first 3.5 miles of the loop are the most demanding. A short warm-up is followed by two miles of moderately difficult climbing and then by a steep mile over a rough road. This ascent brings you to the top of Frog Lake Buttes and a big view of Mt. Hood. You make a technical descent from this high point, then do some route finding to locate an overgrown trail. Then you enjoy a fun three-mile descent. The remainder of the ride is an easy cruise over mostly level and downhill terrain.

General location: This ride starts at Frog Lake Sno-Park, 7 miles south of Government Camp (approximately 60 miles east of Portland, Oregon).
Elevation change: The ride begins at 3,920′ and reaches 5,294′ atop Frog Lake Buttes. Undulating topography adds about 600′ of climbing to the loop. Total elevation gain: 1,974′.
Season: The roads followed on this ride are generally clear of snow from July through September. A great time for a visit is the period after Labor Day and before the beginning of hunting season.
Services: Water is available seasonally at Frog Lake Campground. The community of Government Camp has lodging, gas, pay phones, and limited groceries. All services are available in Hood River.
Hazards: There are loose rocks and ruts on the descent from Frog Lake

RIDE 47 *FROG LAKE BUTTES*

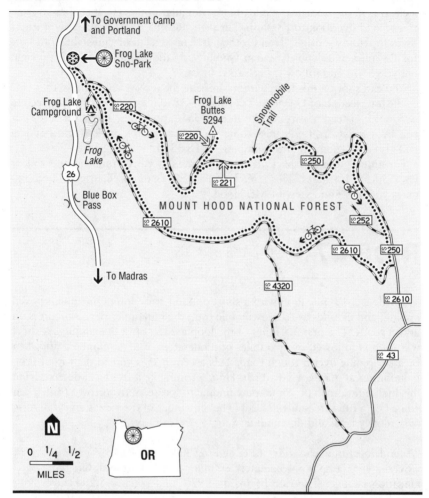

To Government Camp and Portland

Frog Lake Sno-Park

Frog Lake Campground

FS 220

Frog Lake Buttes 5294

Snowmobile Trail

FS 220

Frog Lake

26

FS 250

FS 221

Blue Box Pass

MOUNT HOOD NATIONAL FOREST

FS 2610

FS 252

To Madras

FS 2610

FS 250

FS 4320

FS 2610

FS 43

N

0   ¼   ½

MILES

OR

Buttes. Walk your bike down the steep, degraded snowmobile trail that connects Forest Service Road 221 and FS 250. Watch your speed while descending on FS 250. This road contains some washboarding, and there is loose gravel in its corners. You may encounter some vehicular traffic on this ride.

Rescue index: Help can be found in Government Camp. The nearest pay phone is at a gas station 2 miles north of the trailhead on US 26.

Land status: Mt. Hood National Forest.

Maps: The district map of the Bear Springs Ranger District is a good guide

Vista from Frog Lake Buttes.

to this route. USGS 7.5 minute quads: Post Point and Wapinitia Pass.

Finding the trail: The intersection of US 26 and OR 35 is about 50 miles east of Portland and approximately 40 miles south of Hood River. From this interchange, follow US 26 south for 4.7 miles to the Frog Lake Sno-Park (on the left). From locations to the south, follow US 26 north from Madras for about 60 miles to the Frog Lake Sno-Park (on the right). Park in the large paved lot.

Sources of additional information:

Bear Springs Ranger District
Route 1, Box 222
Maupin, OR 97037
(503) 328-6211

Notes on the trail: From the parking lot, head south on FS 2610 toward Frog Lake. Turn left onto FS 220. Climb on FS 220 for 2 miles, then turn left to continue on FS 220 where FS 221 goes right. FS 220 ends at a clearing. Backtrack to the intersection of FS 220 and FS 221. Turn left onto FS 221. Follow FS 221 to its terminus at a clear-cut. Walk your bike straight across the clear-cut; do not lose or gain elevation. After about 150′, you will come to the edge of the woods. Look for a faint snowmobile trail that enters the forest. Follow this rough track downhill. After a few hundred yards, the trail becomes more obvious, and you will notice some orange and yellow diamond-shaped markers on the trees that border the path. The trail deposits you into another clear-cut at the bottom of the slope. Walk your bike out of the woods and bear to the right. Shortly you will come to a gravel road—the beginning of FS 250. Follow FS 250 downhill. Stay on this main road as it continues to descend. The road surface eventually changes to pavement. Coast down the pavement for just .4 miles to FS 2610 on the right (easy to miss). Turn right onto gravel FS 2610. Stay on this road to complete the loop.

WASHINGTON

Washington is a uniquely beautiful state with incredibly diverse environments. Ocean beaches, tidelands, temperate rainforests, large freshwater lakes, all set amid snow-capped peaks. How's that for variety? And that's just the Olympic Peninsula. The state is covered with mountains. The Cascade Divide stretches northward and is punctuated by huge volcanoes. Mt. Rainier is the largest and most dramatic of these sentinels. At over 14,000 feet, it dominates the skyline throughout the Puget Sound region. The Cascades culminate in North Cascades National Park. Just east of the park is the Methow Valley—a mountain biker's haven. Welcoming communities, breathtaking scenery, endless trails and roads, and an abundance of espresso bars all contribute to make Washington a magical place.

Mt. Adams Area Rides

The jump-off point for exploring the area around Mt. Adams is Trout Lake, Washington. This town is about 23 miles north of Hood River, Oregon. From Portland, Trout Lake is a few hours' drive away.

At 12,307 feet, Mt. Adams is a massive bulk of a mountain, the third largest peak in the Cascade Range. To the east of Mt. Adams is the Yakima Indian Reservation. To the west is the Gifford Pinchot National Forest, named for the first chief of the U.S. Forest Service. Pinchot was an active conservationist. He played a key role in establishing environmental awareness as a cornerstone of forest management.

The forests blanketing the lower slopes of Mt. Adams contain several varieties of trees of high commercial value. While the economy of the region has long centered around timber, logging of the great forests has slowed. You still encounter logging trucks and hear chainsaws, but the woods seem quieter than they were a few years ago. Ranger districts throughout the Pacific Northwest are welcoming people to come and take part in their favorite recreational pursuits.

One very popular activity in this part of the forest is berry picking. The hillsides leading up to Mt. Adams contain vast open areas thick with huckleberry bushes. Large numbers of people come to gather the berries when they ripen (usually around Labor Day). Many of the pickers are Native Americans. In the old days, berries of all kinds were an important part of the Indian diet. The Indians would arrive on horseback and foot, then set up camps on the slopes of the mountain. Huge quantities of huckleberries were gathered and then dried. These berries were formed into cakes that sustained the Indians through the long months of winter.

Today a couple of bed-and-breakfasts, a café, and a general store meet the needs of travelers to this part of the world. Camping facilities are plentiful, and the fishing in the area's many mountain lakes and streams is good. Thanks to the timber industry, miles of gravel roads await two-wheeled adventures. Trails wander for miles through the woods and make for some good mountain biking.

RIDE 48 *GOTCHEN CREEK TRAIL*

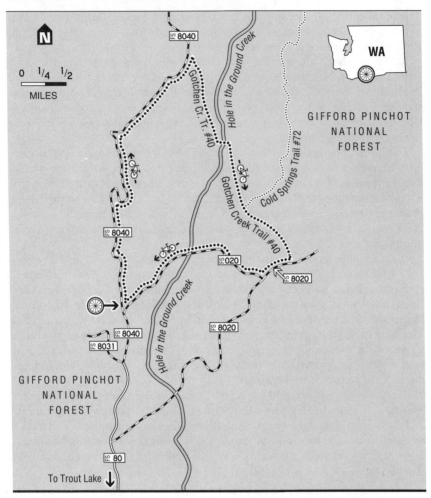

RIDE 48 *GOTCHEN CREEK TRAIL*

Combining Gotchen Creek Trail with fire roads makes for a moderately difficult 9.6-mile loop. Well-maintained gravel and dirt roads account for 6.6 miles of the trip. Gotchen Creek Trail descends overall and is in fair shape. The path is bumpy and hoof-worn in places.

Creek crossing on Gotchen Creek Trail.

The trip begins with a four-mile climb to the upper trailhead. This grade begins easily with a nice warm-up; the remaining three miles are moderately difficult. There are some views of Mt. Adams through the trees as you near the top of the climb. For a trail that drops over 1,000 feet in three miles, Gotchen Creek Trail contains a surprising number of short ascents, some steep. The ride from the lower trailhead back to your vehicle is an enjoyable descent along winding dirt roads.

General location: The ride begins approximately 7 miles north of Trout Lake, Washington. Trout Lake is located about 23 miles north of Hood River, Oregon.
Elevation change: The ride starts at 3,160′ and reaches a high point of 4,660′ just past the start of Gotchen Creek Trail. Ups and downs add approximately 300′ of climbing to the loop. Total elevation gain: 1,800′.
Season: This trail is open to recreational use by equestrians, hikers, and cyclists from June 1 to November 1.
Services: Food, lodging, limited groceries, gas, showers, and pay phones can be found in Trout Lake.
Hazards: Sections of the trail descend sharply and are rough; control your speed. Expect technical riding on the trail, which contains embedded, loose, and moss-covered rocks; soft conditions; creek crossings; and forest litter, including windfall. You may encounter vehicles on the roads.
Rescue index: Help is available in Trout Lake.

Southern trailhead of Gotchen Creek Trail.

Land status: Gifford Pinchot National Forest.

Maps: The district map for the Mt. Adams Ranger District is a good guide to this route. USGS 7.5 minute quads: King Mountain and Trout Lake.

Finding the trail: From the ranger station in Trout Lake, turn right onto WA 141. In .9 miles, turn left at the gas station and head north on Forest Service Road 17. You will arrive at the intersection of FS 17 and FS 23 in another 1.3 miles. Bear right, taking FS 17 toward the Mt. Adams Recreation Area. Turn left in .6 miles onto FS 80. Follow FS 80 for 3.7 miles to the end of pavement; here you will see FS 8040. Turn right onto FS 8040 and drive .6 miles to FS 020 (on the right). Park on the left at this intersection.

Sources of additional information:

Mt. Adams Ranger District
2455 Highway 141
Trout Lake, WA 98650
(509) 395-2501

Notes on the trail: Follow FS 8040 uphill for 4.1 miles to the upper trailhead for Gotchen Creek Trail #40 (on the right). There is a weathered wooden signpost next to the road. Push your bike up the dirt slope to find a larger trailhead sign. After 2 miles on the path, continue straight on Gotchen Creek Trail #40 as Cold Springs Trail #72 goes left. In another mile you will reach the lower trailhead. Ride past the corrals and up to the road. Turn right onto FS 8020 and descend. In .5 miles turn right onto FS 020 and follow it back to its intersection with FS 8040.

RIDE 49 *BUTTES LOOP*

This 15-mile loop begins with 5 miles on Squaw Butte Trail, which is a single-track in some places and an old double-track in others. It starts with a moderately difficult mile-long climb around the southern flank of Squaw Butte. This rise contains .2 miles of steep climbing. The trail levels out and begins a long descent that is both thrilling and technical. Erosion has created ditchlike conditions—there are steep drop-offs, rocks, and menacing roots. The last part of the trail involves easy to moderately difficult climbs as well as level riding. There are some pummy sections of trail in the last quarter mile.

The remainder of the circuit is on gravel and paved roads that are evenly split between ups and downs. There are a couple of demanding, sustained climbs. The second is steeper and leads to the summit of West Twin Butte. A short hike through thick brush takes you to the remains of an old lookout. The view is panoramic; Mt. Adams, Mt. St. Helens, Mt. Rainier, Goat Rocks, and Sawtooth Mountain are prominent. The loop ends with a 2.3-mile descent back to your vehicle.

General location: The trailhead for Squaw Butte Trail is approximately 20 miles north of Trout Lake, Washington.

Elevation change: The ride begins at 3,760′ and climbs to 4,360′ in 1 mile. The trail drops for about 3 miles to a low point of 3,260′ at Big Creek. The route follows roads to 4,120′, then descends to 4,040′ before the ascent to the top of West Twin Butte (4,716′). Ups and downs add about 100′ of climbing to the loop. Total elevation gain: 2,236′.

Season: The roads and trails are usually free of snow from July through October. The area is popular with mushroom hunters in the spring and huckleberry pickers in the late summer.

Services: Water is available seasonally at Tillicum Campground. Food, lodging, gas, showers, and limited groceries can be obtained in Trout Lake. All services are available in Hood River.

RIDE 49   *BUTTES LOOP*

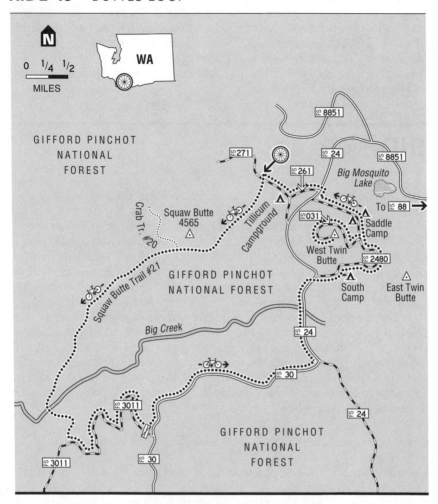

Hazards: The descent on Squaw Butte Trail is treacherous—ideal conditions for being thrown over your handlebars. There is no bridge where Squaw Butte Trail crosses Big Creek; you must either wade through deep water or cross one of the logs that span the creek. Some of the roads contain large amounts of loose gravel. Watch for traffic on the roads.

Rescue index: Help can be found in Trout Lake.

Land status: Gifford Pinchot National Forest.

Mt. Adams from West Twin Butte.

Maps: The district map of the Mt. Adams Ranger District is a good guide to this ride. USGS 7.5 minute quad: Lone Butte.

Finding the trail: Turn left out of the Mt. Adams Ranger Station in Trout Lake and head west on WA 141. In .8 miles, turn right onto Trout Lake Creek Road/Forest Service Road 88. Follow FS 88 for 12.4 miles to Big Tire Junction—you will see FS 8851 on the left. Turn left onto FS 8851. You will pass Mosquito Lake after 3 miles on FS 8851. Then you will arrive at a Y intersection where FS 8851 goes right and FS 24 goes left. Turn left and proceed on FS 24 for 1 mile to a sign on the right that directs you toward Tillicum Campground and Squaw Butte Trail #21. Turn right onto this road, which is FS 261. Follow FS 261 for a short distance to an intersection where FS 261 meets FS 271. Turn right onto FS 271 and drive through Tillicum Campground for .2 miles to the trailhead for Squaw Butte Trail #21 (on the left). Park in the campsite on the right. Additional parking can be found off FS 271.

Sources of additional information:

Mt. Adams Ranger District
2455 Highway 141
Trout Lake, WA 98650
(509) 395-2501

Notes on the trail: Follow the trail and stay to the left at the first two intersections. After 1.6 miles you will come to Crab Trail #20 on the right; continue straight on Squaw Butte Trail #21. You will cross Big Creek in another 2.6 miles. In .3 miles from Big Creek, cross a small wooden bridge over a lesser creek. The trail becomes faint after the bridge, but well-placed trail markers make it is easy to follow. Follow the markers out to a trailhead sign at unsigned FS 3011. Turn left onto the road and climb. The road contains a lot of loose gravel for the first 1.5 miles, then becomes a degraded double-track, then changes to a cinder road. You will reach paved, unsigned FS 30 after 2.4 miles of pedaling on FS 3011. Turn left onto the pavement and ride 1.7 miles to a T intersection and FS 24. Turn left onto FS 24 (paved). In 1.1 miles, turn right and climb on FS 2480 toward South Camp and Saddle Camp. After 1.1 miles, FS 2480 levels out and comes to an unsigned spur road on the left. Turn left here onto FS 031. (This turn is easy to miss; you will enter Saddle Camp if you go too far.) Take FS 031 to its terminus and look to the right for an overgrown trail. Walk up the steep path to the summit of West Twin Butte. Return the way you came down FS 031, and turn left onto FS 2480. Enter Saddle Camp and stay on the main road through it. Cross through a trench at the lower end of the camp and continue to descend, now on a closed road. Turn right when you reach pavement, then make a quick left onto FS 261 to enter Tillicum Campground and complete the loop.

RIDE 50 *FORLORN LAKES*

This is a 9.2-mile loop on gravel roads. The 1.5-mile climb to Forlorn Lakes Basin involves easy and moderately difficult climbing. The remainder of the ride is easy. The roads are in good condition, with some ruts, rocks, and loose gravel. Level pedaling through the basin takes you past several small lakes with good fishing and campsites. The descent from Forlorn Lakes affords some nice views of Lemei Rock and Mt. Adams.

RIDE 50 *FORLORN LAKES*

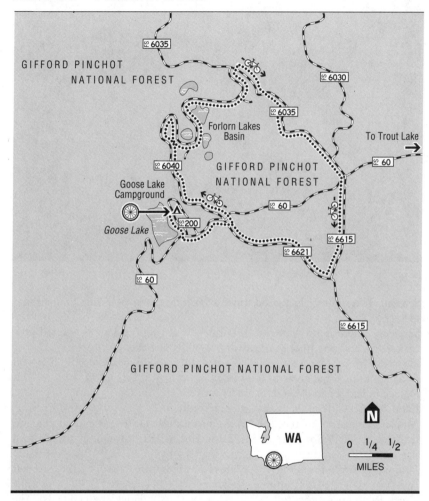

General location: This ride begins at Goose Lake, approximately 13 miles southwest of Trout Lake, Washington.

Elevation change: This loop begins at 3,130′. You reach Forlorn Lakes basin at 3,700′, then descend to 3,040′ at the intersection of Forest Service roads 6615 and 6621. Ups and downs add about 60′ of climbing to the ride. Total elevation gain: 720′.

Lovers Stump, Forlorn Lakes.

Season: The summer is a good time for visiting the area—bring your fishing tackle.

Services: There is no water on this ride. Water, food, lodging, limited groceries, gas, and pay phones are available in Trout Lake.

Hazards: Watch for motorists. Control your speed while descending—FS 6035 contains some areas of loose rock.

Rescue index: Help is available in Trout Lake.

Land status: Gifford Pinchot National Forest.

Maps: The district map of the Mt. Adams Ranger District is a good guide to this ride. USGS 7.5 minute quads: Little Huckleberry Mountain and Gifford Peak.

Finding the trail: From the Mt. Adams Ranger Station in Trout Lake, turn left (west) onto WA 141. Continue straight on WA 141 where FS 88/Trout Lake Creek Road goes right (follow the signs for Carson/Huckleberry Fields). The road's designation changes from WA 141 to FS 24 where it enters the Gifford Pinchot National Forest. You will arrive at an intersection after passing Peterson Prairie Campground. At this junction, continue straight onto FS 60 toward Goose Lake (FS 24 goes right). The remaining intersections are well marked—simply follow the signs to take FS 60 toward Goose Lake. Turn right into Goose Lake Campground and park on the left across from the vault toilets. Do not block the boat ramp.

Sources of additional information:

Mount Adams Ranger District
2455 Highway 141
Trout Lake, WA 98650
(509) 395-2501

Notes on the trail: Pedal out of the campground and turn left onto FS 60. In .6 miles, turn left onto FS 6040 toward Forlorn Lakes. Pedal past the lakes to a T intersection (4 miles into the ride). Turn right and descend on FS 6035. Continue straight where FS 6035 meets FS 6030. When you arrive at FS 60, go straight across FS 60 onto FS 6615. Follow FS 6615 for 1.2 miles to FS 6621. Turn right onto FS 6621 and follow the signs back to Goose Lake.

RIDE 51 *VALLEY TRAIL #270*

Valley Trail is a new ORV route in the Randle District of the Gifford Pinchot National Forest. A moderately difficult 16.5-mile loop is formed by following the trail for 8.5 miles and then returning on pavement. The path contained some sandy sections but was still in good shape at the time of our research. Expect more degraded conditions as the trail becomes more popular with ORV enthusiasts.

This is a fun and challenging route for intermediate and advanced mountain bikers. The single-track goes up and down like a yo-yo. The path loses elevation overall as it heads north, but its rolling character creates about 1,000 feet of climbing. Through clear-cuts you can see Burley Mountain, Surprise Peak, and Juniper Peak.

General location: The trailhead is located approximately 25 miles southeast of Randle, Washington.
Elevation change: The trip begins at 2,700' at Cat Creek Campground. The high point along the trail is 2,900'. The single-track portion of the loop ends at 1,920'. The pedaling on Valley Trail contributes an estimated 1,000' of climbing to the loop. Ups and downs on the roads add about 100' of climbing to the ascent back to Cat Creek Campground. Total elevation gain: 1,880'.
Season: The heaviest ORV use is on summer weekends. This is a good early season ride.
Services: There is no water on the ride. Water is available seasonally at Adams Fork and Blue Lake Creek campgrounds (en route to the trailhead). Food, lodging, groceries, gas, and pay phones can be found in Randle.

RIDE 51 *VALLEY TRAIL #270*

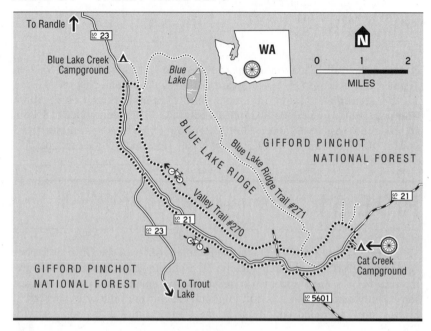

Hazards: Watch for other trail users. Control your speed while descending—there are rocky stretches and pummy areas. Expect some traffic on the paved roads.

Rescue index: Help is available in Randle.

Land status: Gifford Pinchot National Forest.

Maps: The forest map of the Gifford Pinchot National Forest is a good guide to this ride. Valley Trail #270 is not delineated on the Randle District map or USGS quads.

Finding the trail: From US 12 in Randle, head south on WA 131, following the signs for "Cispus Road/Mount St. Helens/Forest Service Road 23/FS 25." Cross the bridge over the river; here the road's designation changes to FS 23. In .8 miles, turn left, taking FS 23 toward Cispus Center/Trout Lake. Stay on FS 23 for another 17.3 miles to FS 21. Turn left onto FS 21. Follow FS 21 for 6 miles to Cat Creek Campground. Turn right into the campground and park your vehicle.

Valley Trail.

Sources of additional information:

Randle Ranger District
10024 Highway 12
Randle, WA 98377
(206) 497-7565

Notes on the trail: Turn right onto FS 21, then immediately turn left onto Valley Trail #270. A couple of trails branch off to the right near the start of the ride; stay left on the main trail. You will cross Blue Lake Ridge Trail #271 in less than a mile of riding; continue straight on Valley Trail #270. The route meets a gravel road in another .7 miles. Pick up the trail on the opposite side of the road, a little to the right and uphill. Follow the trail for nearly 7 miles to an intersection with several signs. Turn left and descend. You will immedi-

Creek crossing on Valley Trail.

ately arrive at another intersection. Stay left and downhill. Soon you will reach a trailhead and a parking area for Valley Trail. Ride out to the pavement and turn left onto FS 23. After 1.8 miles on FS 23, turn left onto FS 21 at a Y intersection. Follow FS 21 back to Cat Creek Campground.

Wenatchee National Forest

The Wenatchee National Forest is an enormous piece of public real estate. It encompasses 2.2 million acres and extends from Lake Chelan in the north to the Yakima Indian Reservation in the south—135 miles! Bordering the forest to the west is the Cascade Range, a formidable barrier to the humid air that flows inland from the Pacific Ocean. The forests on the west side of the Cascades receive great quantities of rainfall. By comparison, the Wenatchee is dry and sunny.

For millions of people, a retreat to the Wenatchee National Forest is within easy reach. The vast open areas of the Inland Empire stretch out to the east of the forest. Hubs of commerce like Wenatchee and Yakima border this expanse of agricultural, mining, and timber wealth. Several highway systems provide access from the Puget Sound region. From Seattle, Interstate 90 climbs Snoqualmie Pass and cuts right through the forest. The Wenatchee's proximity to population centers and its wealth of recreation opportunities make it the most heavily visited national forest in the United States.

Mountain bikers find the forest full of interesting gravel road treks. Some of the easier outings in the region run beside rivers and take in great scenery. Moderately difficult riding can be found on many quiet roads in the forest. The area has several memorable trips of a more demanding nature. Many rides mount high ridges or clamber up mountains for incredible views of the rugged Cascades.

RIDE 52 BETHEL RIDGE

This is an easy eight-mile out-and-back ride. The route follows a compacted dirt and gravel road for two miles to Bethel Ridge. This road is in good condition, with some exposed rocks and loose gravel. Once on the ridge, you follow a dirt double-track that is in poor condition, with large, sharp rocks and lots of ruts.

Bethel Ridge drops off to reveal a sweeping panorama. The view to the south takes in the Tieton Basin and Divide Ridge. Farther to the west lies Goose Egg Mountain, at the eastern end of Rimrock Lake. Vistas extend for many miles; Mt. Adams can be seen in the southwest on clear days.

RIDE 52 BETHEL RIDGE

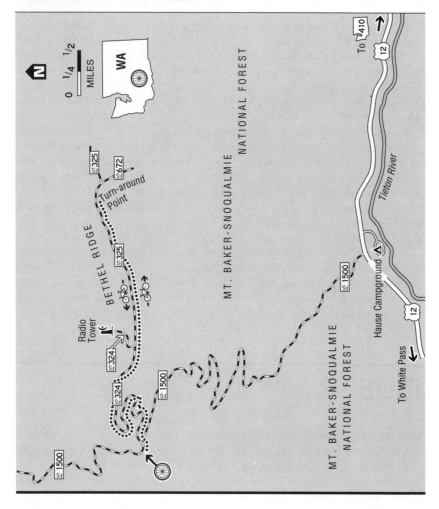

General location: The ride is about 50 miles northwest of Yakima, Washington.

Elevation change: The trailhead lies at 5,600′. The high point of the trip, 6,160′, occurs on Bethel Ridge. Total elevation gain: 560′.

Season: Cooler temperatures at its higher elevation makes the ridge an inviting destination on hot summer days. Cyclists also enjoy exploring the area in the spring and fall.

Bethel Ridge.

Services: There is no water on this ride, but it can be obtained seasonally at Hause Campground. There are two convenience stores on US 12. One is located 2.5 miles west of Hause Campground, the other 4.5 miles to the east. Food, lodging, gas, and groceries can be found in Naches. All services are available in Yakima.

Hazards: You will cross a cattle guard near the start of the trip. Expect some vehicular traffic on the roads. Control your speed and watch for loose gravel while descending.

Rescue index: The nearest pay phones are at the convenience stores on US 12. Help is available in Naches.

Land status: Mt. Baker–Snoqualmie National Forest lands administered by the Wenatchee National Forest.

Maps: The district map of the Naches Ranger District is a good guide to this ride. USGS 7.5 minute quad: Tieton Basin.

Finding the trail: From locations to the west, drive approximately 18 miles east of White Pass on US 12 to Forest Service Road 1500 (on the left). FS 1500 is .3 miles east of milepost 168. From locations to the east, travel west from Naches on US 12 for about 26 miles to FS 1500 (on the right). Turn north onto FS 1500 and follow it for 6.9 miles to FS 324 (on the right). There is room to park on the left side of FS 1500.

Sources of additional information:

Naches Ranger District
10061 Highway 12
Naches, WA 98937
(503) 653-2205

Notes on the trail: Ride up FS 324 to FS 325. Turn right onto FS 325 and ride under the power lines. Stay on the main road that borders the cliff. Ride along Bethel Ridge for about 1.5 miles to where FS 325 enters the woods and begins to descend rapidly. Turn around and return the way you came.

RIDE 53 OLD RIVER ROAD

This 12-mile out-and-back trip on Old River Road offers cyclists a pleasant outing. The terrain is level to rolling, and the gravel road is in good condition. The route includes 1.5 miles of paved road cycling.

The cycling is easy along this stretch of the popular Naches River. Old River Road rolls past developed and undeveloped campsites, fishing holes, shady picnic spots, and summer homes. This route also passes the trailhead for the Boulder Cave Recreation Trail.

General location: The trailhead is approximately 40 miles northwest of Yakima, Washington.

Elevation change: The ride begins at 2,600'. The turnaround point lies at 2,400'. Undulations in the terrain add another 200' of climbing to the ride. Total elevation gain: 400'.

Season: This circuit may be ridden year-round. Wet, cold winter weather may be a limiting factor.

Services: Water can be found at the Boulder Cave Picnic Area, located 2.8 miles into the ride. The Whistlin' Jack Lodge in Cliffdell has food, lodging, gas, limited groceries, and a pay phone. All services are available in Yakima.

Hazards: Although traffic is generally light, you can expect some motorists traveling to homes, campsites, and the trail to the cave. Approach blind corners with caution.

Rescue index: Help can be found in Cliffdell.

Land status: Mt. Baker–Snoqualmie National Forest lands administered by the Wenatchee National Forest.

Maps: The district map of the Naches Ranger District is a good guide to this ride. USGS 7.5 minute quad: Cliffdell.

Finding the trail: From Yakima, drive north on US 12 for 16 miles to the

RIDE 53 OLD RIVER ROAD

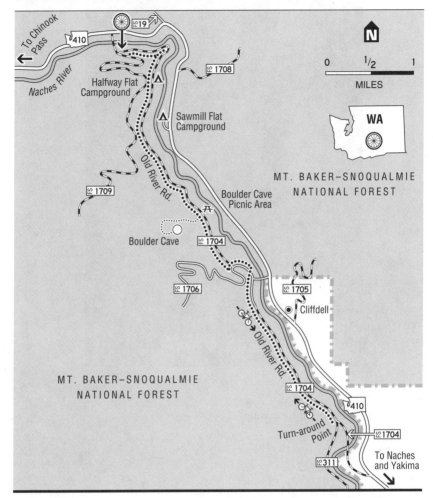

intersection of US 12 and WA 410. Continue straight on WA 410 where US 12 goes left toward White Pass. Follow WA 410 north for 25 miles to Old River Road (on the left, 2 miles north of the Sawmill Flat Campground entrance). A sign marks this turn and directs you left toward Halfway Flat Campground and Old River Road/Forest Service Road 1704. Turn left onto FS 1704 and proceed over the bridge spanning the Naches River. Bear left after crossing the bridge, and park on the left side of FS 1704.

Roving with Rover.

Sources of additional information:

Naches Ranger District
10061 Highway 12
Naches, WA 98937
(509) 653-2205

Notes on the trail: Follow the river downstream on Old River Road/FS 1704. In 2.2 miles, you will arrive at a sign that reads "Road Closed due to Flood Damage." Walk your bike over the earthen berm and then over a small creek bridged by a couple of planks. Ride another .5 miles, crossing a second berm. Soon you will arrive at the Boulder Cave Picnic Area. If you wish to explore the cave, stay to the right, toward the hiking trailhead. To remain on the route, pass through the picnic area on Old River Road. Continue straight where Swamp Creek Road/FS 1706 goes right. Go straight at the next intersection, where a spur road goes left to the highway. It is another 2 miles to the turnaround point at FS 311. Return the way you came.

Bring a flashlight and a bike lock if you plan on exploring Boulder Cave.

RIDE 54 *RAVEN ROOST*

This demanding 27-mile trip combines a loop and an out-and-back ride. Although this circuit is not technical, the long climb requires strength and stamina. The route is entirely on gravel roads in good condition. The first half of the ride is a long ascent to a viewpoint at Raven Roost. The climbing is mostly easy to moderately difficult, with some short steep stretches. The last 1.5 miles to the summit are steep. The return is an exhilarating downhill cruise.

Vistas extend in every direction from Raven Roost. On the approach, you obtain a spectacular view of Fifes Ridge and Fifes Peaks to the south. From the top, the snowfields of Mt. Rainier are prominent in the southwest. The distant horizon to the north is filled with rugged peaks.

General location: This ride begins at Crow Creek Campground, approximately 45 miles north of Yakima, Washington.

Elevation change: The ride starts at 2,720′ and climbs to 6,200′ at Raven Roost. Ups and downs encountered along the route add approximately 200′ of climbing to the ride. Total elevation gain: 3,680′.

Season: These roads are usually clear of snow from June through October.

Services: There is no water on this ride. Water may be obtained at Sawmill Flat Campground on WA 410. The Whistlin' Jack Lodge in Cliffdell has food, lodging, limited groceries, pay phones, and gas. All services are available in Yakima.

Hazards: You may encounter some vehicular traffic on these roads. Remain alert for loose gravel, particularly while descending. Be prepared for changes in the weather; it may be windy and cold at the top.

Rescue index: Help can be found in Cliffdell.

Land status: Mt. Baker–Snoqualmie National Forest lands administered by the Wenatchee National Forest.

Maps: The district map of the Naches Ranger District is a good guide to this ride. USGS 7.5 minute quads: Mt. Clifty and Raven Roost.

Finding the trail: From Yakima, drive north on US 12 for about 16 miles to the intersection of US 12 and WA 410. Continue straight on WA 410 where US 12 goes left toward White Pass. Follow WA 410 north for 24 miles to Forest Service Road 19 (on the right, 1.2 miles north of the Sawmill Flat Campground entrance). From Enumclaw, take WA 410 east toward Chinook

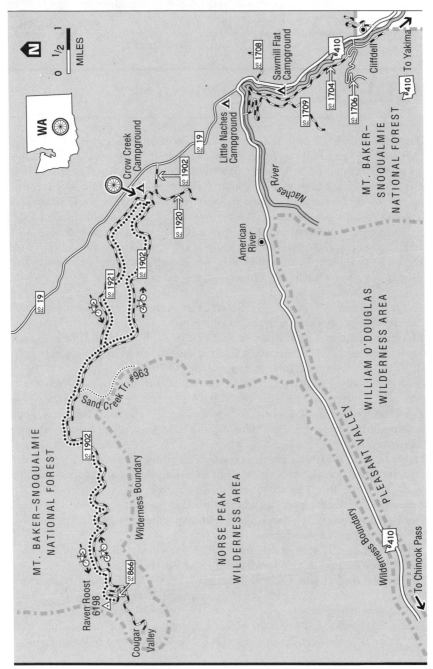

Mt. Rainier from Forest Service Road #866.

Pass. From the pass, continue east on WA 410 for approximately 24 miles to FS 19 (on the left, about 3.5 miles east of American River). Turn northwest onto unsigned FS 19, following the signs for Little Naches Campground. Drive up FS 19 for 2.7 miles to unsigned FS 1902. Turn left onto FS 1902, which is marked by a sign that points left and reads "Raven Roost—14 miles." Cross a concrete bridge spanning the Little Naches River and drive another .4 miles to an intersection where signed FS 1920 goes left toward Fifes Ridge. Turn right to stay on unmarked FS 1902; you will cross a one-lane wooden bridge over Crow Creek. Immediately after crossing this bridge, you will arrive at another intersection. The road to the left—signed "Raven Roost—13 miles"— is FS 1902. The road to the right is signed FS 1921. Turn right onto FS 1921, then turn right again into the Crow Creek Campground. Park in a site if you intend to camp; otherwise, park on the roadside.

Sources of additional information:

Naches Ranger District
10061 Highway 12
Naches, WA 98937
(509) 653-2205

Notes on the trail: Exit the campground and turn right onto FS 1921. After 5.5 miles of riding you will arrive at the intersection of FS 1921 and FS 1902. Bear right onto FS 1902 toward Raven Roost. After 1 mile of pedaling on FS

1902, you will pass Sand Creek Trail #963 at a primitive campground. Stay on FS 1902 for another 6.6 miles to FS 866. Turn right onto FS 866 toward Raven Roost. Turn around at the top and return the way you came, to the intersection of FS 1902 and FS 1921. Keep right, staying on FS 1902. In another 5.3 miles, you will come to the intersection where FS 1902 meets FS 1921 again. Turn left onto FS 1921, then immediately turn right into the Crow Creek Campground to reach your vehicle.

Adventurous cyclists may wish to check out some of the ORV trails in the area. The Sand Creek Trail #963 can be incorporated into the return from Raven Roost. It is indicated on the recommended district map, but like most ORV routes, it is inadequately signed in the field. Be prepared to do some route finding if you venture off the roads.

RIDE 55 *BOUNDARY BUTTE*

This 13-mile ride is a loop combined with two out-and-back legs. The first part of the trip is a climb to Boundary Butte. The grade of the climb changes from moment to moment—it is mostly easy and moderately difficult pedaling. There are about a dozen short, steep pitches (totaling less than one mile). Double-track Canyon Crest Trail makes up 2.4 miles of the route. The trail is eroded in places and quite challenging. Mounds of earth have been built across the road in an effort to divert runoff. The rest of the excursion is on dirt and gravel roads in good condition. One exception is the final .3 miles below the summit. This stretch is rough and extremely steep.

Views of Leavenworth, the Stuart Range, Icicle Ridge, and Icicle Valley are this ride's main attraction. Canyon Crest Trail is part of the Mountain Home Lodge trail system. This full-service lodge has a nice deck, with views of the Stuart Range to the west.

General location: This ride begins on Mountain Home Road, approximately 2 miles south of Leavenworth, Washington.
Elevation change: The ride begins at 1,600′ and climbs to 3,168′ at Boundary Butte. Undulations on the ride add an estimated 200′ of climbing to the trip. Total elevation gain: 1,768′.
Season: Portions of the route are lined with wildflowers in the spring. You can ride here from the early spring into the late fall.
Services: All services are available in Leavenworth.
Hazards: Watch for motorists, equestrians, hikers, and fellow mountain bikers. Watch for loose gravel on the descents.
Rescue index: Help can be obtained in Leavenworth.
Land status: Lands within the Wenatchee National Forest and public right-of-way through private property.

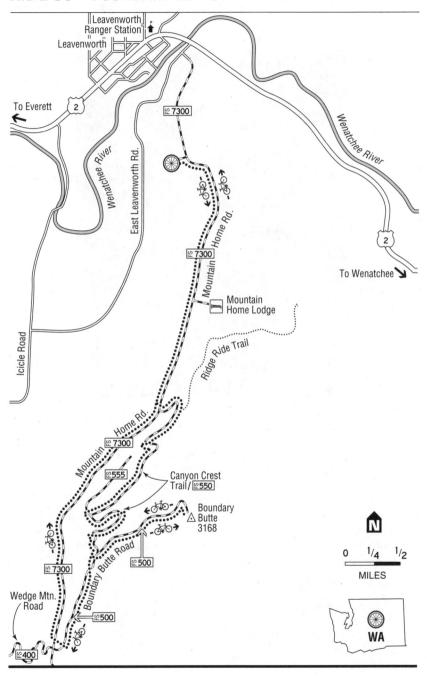

The Stuart Range from Boundary Butte.

Maps: The district map of the Leavenworth Ranger District is a good guide to this ride. USGS 7.5 minute quad: Leavenworth.

Finding the trail: From the ranger station in Leavenworth, turn left onto US 2. Cross the bridge over the Wenatchee River and immediately turn right onto East Leavenworth Road. Take the next left onto Mountain Home Road. Soon this road changes to a gravel road and climbs very steeply. Mountain Home Road narrows as it passes a couple of large boulders. Proceed beyond the second boulder for .2 miles to a closed spur road on the right. Park on the side of the spur road.

Sources of additional information:

Leavenworth Ranger District
600 Sherbourne
Leavenworth, WA 98826
(509) 782-1413

Mountain Home Lodge
P.O. Box 687
Leavenworth, WA 98826
(509) 548-7077

Notes on the trail: From your car, follow Mountain Home Road/Forest Service Road 7300 uphill past homes and Mountain Home Lodge. One mile past the lodge, turn left onto Canyon Crest Trail (a dirt spur road). This turn comes shortly after you pass a sign indicating that you have been traveling on FS 7300. Ride up Canyon Crest Trail to FS 555, at a T intersection, and turn left. At the next T intersection, turn left onto unsigned FS 500 and pedal to the summit. Turn around at the top and descend on FS 500. You will arrive at a major intersection of roads in 2 miles. Turn right onto unsigned FS 7300 and ride back to your vehicle.

RIDE 56 *WENATCHEE RIVER ROAD*

This is an easy 8.5-mile out-and-back ride. There are a couple of steep climbs and descents, which make it a tough ride for a novice. The Wenatchee River Road is a dirt and gravel road in good condition, with some areas of rough tread and patches of loose sand. The road follows the river past many good picnic and camping spots. Wildflowers grow along the roadside; lupine, Indian paintbrush, Chinese houses, and phlox are in bloom in the late spring. Maples and other deciduous trees line the route and add some color to the fall landscape.

General location: The trailhead is located approximately 11 miles north of Leavenworth, Washington.
Elevation gain: The ride begins at 1,800' and quickly descends to 1,760'. This descent is followed by a climb to the trip's high point—2,000'. Then the road drops to the river, at 1,760'. Rolling terrain adds about 200' of climbing to the outing. Total elevation gain: 720'.
Season: The relatively low elevation of the road makes it a good early and late season trip.
Services: There is no water on the ride. Water can be found seasonally at Tumwater Campground, .6 miles south of the trailhead on US 2. All services are available in Leavenworth.
Hazards: Control your speed on the descents. You may encounter limited traffic on Wenatchee River Road—residents hold keys to the locked gate.
Rescue index: Help is available in Leavenworth.

RIDE 56 *WENATCHEE RIVER ROAD*

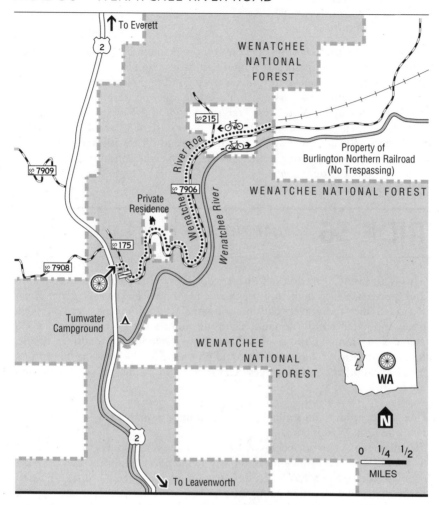

Land status: Wenatchee National Forest.

Maps: The district map of the Lake Wenatchee Ranger District is a good guide to this ride.

Finding the trail: From Leavenworth, follow US 2 north for 10.8 miles and turn right onto Forest Service Road 7906 (.6 miles north of Tumwater Campground). Immediately turn left onto FS 175 and park on the side of the road.

Wenatchee River Road.

Sources of additional information:

Leavenworth Ranger District
600 Sherbourne
Leavenworth, WA 98826
(509) 782-1413

Notes on the trail: Follow FS 7906 to the gate. Go around the locked gate and proceed on the main road. Turn around when, after pedaling 4 miles, you arrive at a Burlington Northern Railroad "No Trespassing" sign. Return the way you came.

RIDE 57 _POLE RIDGE_

This is a 12-mile loop on dirt and gravel roads. The roads are in fair condition, with some washboarding and loose gravel on the steeper hills. A good warm-up leads into a moderately difficult five-mile climb (with about one mile of steep grades). The ride ends with a four-mile descent from Pole Ridge.

Much of the timber in this section of the forest has been logged out. There is a bright side to the clear-cuts: they open up nice vistas. The view from Pole Ridge is excellent. To the north are snowfields and mountain ranges in the Glacier Peaks Wilderness.

General location: This ride begins approximately 25 miles north of Leavenworth, Washington.

Elevation change: The ride starts at 2,400′ and climbs to a high point of 3,880′. Ups and downs add an estimated 200′ of climbing to the loop. Total elevation gain: 1,680′.

Season: You can ride here from spring through fall. Avoid hunting season and summer holiday weekends.

Services: There is no water on this ride. Water can be obtained seasonally at the campgrounds on Lake Wenatchee. You will pass several convenience stores on the way to the trailhead. All services are available in Leavenworth.

Hazards: Finding your way will require some route finding—many of the roads are unsigned. Control your speed on the steep descents. Stay alert for logging trucks and other vehicles. Black bears are not uncommon in this part of the forest.

Rescue index: In the summer, help is available during regular business hours at the Lake Wenatchee Ranger Station on the north shore. You may be able to summon aid at Lake Wenatchee State Park (at the eastern end of the lake). The nearest pay phone is at the Midway Village Trailer Park, 5.5 miles south of the trailhead.

Land status: Wenatchee National Forest.

Maps: The district map of the Lake Wenatchee Ranger District is an adequate guide to this route. USGS 7.5 minute quads: Plain, Lake Wenatchee, Chikamin Creek, and Schaefer Lake.

Finding the trail: From locations to the west, take US 2 east to Stevens Pass. Continue east from the pass for 19 miles to WA 207 (on the left, at Coles Corner). From Leavenworth, follow US 2 north for 16 miles to Coles Corner and WA 207 (on the right). Turn north onto WA 207—follow the signs for Lake Wenatchee State Park. WA 209 goes right, toward Plain/Wenatchee, after 3.5 miles. Continue straight, staying on WA 207. Shortly you will cross the bridge over the Wenatchee River and arrive at a Y intersection; here, WA

RIDE 57 *POLE RIDGE*

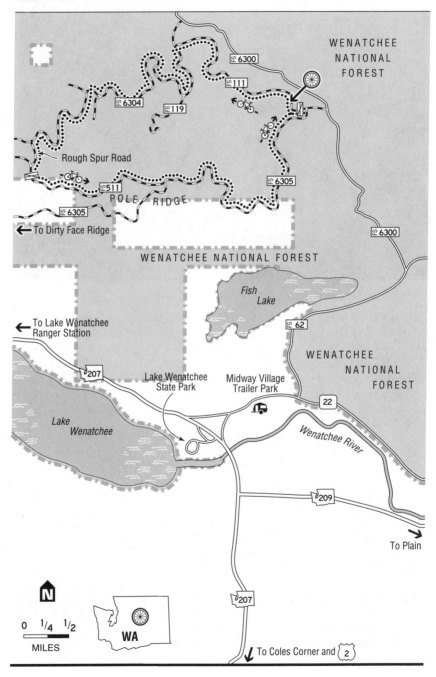

View into the Glacier Peaks Wilderness from Pole Ridge.

207 goes left toward the ranger station and state park. Turn right and follow the road as it swings to the right and feeds into another road. Drive past Midway Village Trailer Park. At the next major intersection, .5 miles beyond the trailer park, turn left onto Forest Service Road 62. Follow FS 62 for 2.3 miles to FS 6300. Turn left onto FS 6300 and drive 2.1 miles to FS 6305. Turn left onto gravel FS 6305 and proceed .3 miles to FS 111. Turn right onto FS 111 (pass through the gate) and follow the road for .2 miles to a borrow pit and a pullout on the left. Park in the pullout.

If FS 111 is blocked by the gate, park at the intersection of FS 6305 and FS 6300.

Sources of additional information:

Lake Wenatchee Ranger District
22976 Highway 207
Leavenworth, WA 98826
(509) 763-3103

Notes on the trail: Turn left out of the parking area, following FS 111. FS 111 ends at a T intersection in 2 miles. Turn left here onto unsigned FS 6304. Stay on the main road as spur roads branch off. The surface of FS 6304 changes from gravel to dirt after 3.5 miles. There is also a sign here that reads "National Forest Firewood Cutting Area." Continue on FS 6304 for .8 miles to a high point in the road. This high point occurs after the road switchbacks hard to the right and climbs steeply (there is a clear-cut to your right). Roll over the crest and immediately turn left onto an unsigned spur road. (This turn is easy to miss—do not follow the main road downhill.) Proceed on the rough spur road past "Wildlife Habitat" signs to a gravel road (unsigned FS 511). Turn left onto FS 511 and pedal past a gate. Stay on the main road as a couple of spur roads branch off. You will arrive at a T intersection after a short but fast descent. Turn left onto FS 6305, which also heads to the right toward Dirtyface Ridge. Descend on FS 6305 for 3.5 miles to FS 111. Turn left onto FS 111 and ride back to your vehicle. FS 111 is easy to miss; you will quickly come to paved FS 6300 if you go too far.

RIDE 58 *AMABILIS MOUNTAIN*

This 11.2-mile ride is a combination of two out-and-back spurs and a loop. Of the climbing, 2 miles are easy, 2.5 miles are moderately difficult, and 1 mile is demanding. The route follows good gravel roads, with some exposed rocks and a loose, coarse tread in the steepest areas. There is a short stretch of dirt double-track in good condition. The second half of the ride is a long descent that starts out roughly: the road is washed out and rutted at the top, but it quickly improves.

Freeway noise and views of clear-cut forests are predominant as you climb. Your senses are rewarded with less assaulting stimuli as you near the summit of Amabilis Mountain. At the top, the view of Kachess Lake, with its mountain backdrop, is lovely. To the north you can see the rugged Rampart and Chikamin ridges, which lie in the Alpine Lakes Wilderness Area. Mt. Rainier looms large on the horizon in the southwest.

General location: This ride begins near Cabin Creek Road, approximately 65 miles southeast of Seattle.

Elevation change: The ride starts at 2,520′ and reaches a high point of 4,500′ atop Amabilis Mountain. Ups and downs along the way add about 100′ of climbing to the ride. Total elevation gain: 2,080′.

Season: Amabilis Mountain is usually free of snow from May through October. A good time to visit is in the late summer or early fall—the weather is drier and the roads are quieter.

Services: There is no water on this ride. Water, gas, and limited groceries are available in Easton. All services can be found in Cle Elum.

Hazards: Exercise caution while crossing the freeway overpass—watch for motorists exiting the highway. Expect some traffic on the gravel roads. The descent from the mountain can get very fast. Watch for areas of loose gravel as you descend.

RIDE 58 *AMABILIS MOUNTAIN*

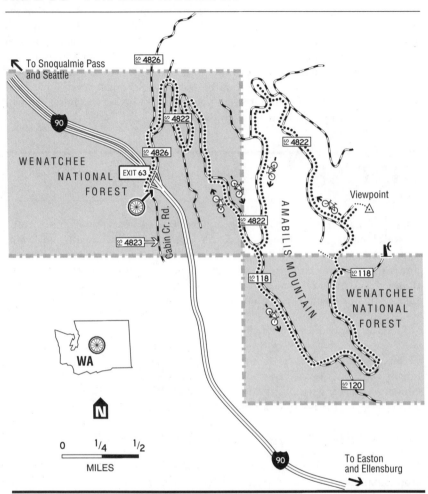

Rescue index: Help is available in Easton (Exit 71), 8 miles southeast of the trailhead on Interstate 90.

Land status: Public and private lands within the boundaries of the Wenatchee National Forest.

Maps: The district map of the Cle Elum Ranger District is a good guide to this ride. USGS 7.5 minute quad: Stampede Pass.

Finding the trail: From Seattle, drive east on I-90 for 63 miles, to Exit 63/Cabin Creek Road. From Yakima, follow I-82 north for 37 miles to I-90.

Rampart and Chikamin ridges from Amabilis Mountain.

Proceed northwest on I-90 for 56 miles to Exit 63/Cabin Creek Road. Exit the highway and follow the signs to the Sno-Park parking area. This gravel lot lies adjacent to the freeway on the southwest side.

Sources of additional information:

Cle Elum Ranger District
803 W. 2nd Street
Cle Elum, WA 98922
(509) 674-4411

Notes on the trail: Head northeast from the parking area and cross over the highway. Continue straight onto Forest Service Road 4826. Follow this road for about .25 miles, to FS 4822. Turn right onto FS 4822 and stay on the main road as side roads branch off. After 2.4 miles, turn right onto FS 118. The sign marking FS 118 is on the right, partially obscured by weeds. Turn right onto FS 118. The pedaling on FS 118 is more demanding, and the road is rougher. This more demanding section lasts for about 1 mile. At the end of this tougher stretch, you will be pedaling next to a large clear-cut on your left. Proceed to the end of the clear-cut, where FS 118 veers to the right and reenters the woods. Look to your left here and find a double-track that heads west across the clear-cut. Turn left onto the double-track and follow it as it curves around in a more northerly direction. You will come to an intersection after just .1 miles. Go right (toward the east, roughly) and climb steeply on a double-

Kachess Lake from Amabilis Mountain.

track—the woods are on your right, the clear-cut is on your left. From the last intersection it is .2 miles to a small knoll and a maintained gravel road. This unsigned road is FS 4822. Follow this road as it swings to the left and goes downhill. Turn right at the first intersection (after .1 miles on FS 4822). Pursue this spur road for about .2 miles to its terminus at a gravel turnaround. Park your bike and walk up the trail to the right to visit a viewpoint. Return on the spur road to FS 4822. Turn right onto FS 4822 and begin a long descent. Side roads branch off left and right, but you should stay on the main road. After more than 5 miles of downhill coasting, you will arrive at a "Yield" sign at the intersection of FS 4822 and FS 4826. Bear left onto FS 4826 to return to your vehicle.

Bikers can also follow a 16-mile loop around the base of Amabilis Mountain. This loop and other rides in the region are described in a mountain bike pamphlet produced by the Cle Elum Ranger District.

Greenwater and Elbe Area Rides

The town of Greenwater is on WA 410 about an hour east of Tacoma. Beyond Greenwater is the north entrance to Mt. Rainier National Park. Just before entering the park, you pass some outstanding mountain bike country. Single-track masters love the challenge of Skookum Flats Trail and White River Trail.

Forest roads and single-tracks are abundant in the area and make for some prime rides for strong cyclists. The mountain roads in this neck of the woods tend to be steep. The trails are no slouches either, but it's their obstacles that leave you gasping. The paths throw everything they have at you, all at once.

Elbe is a small town that lies about 40 miles south of Tacoma on WA 7. The road that heads east out of Elbe leads into Mt. Rainier National Park (by way of the Nisqually River Entrance). This road winds up the south flank of the mountain to Paradise Valley, a rolling parkland mottled with stately fir trees and wildflowers. The valley sits about 9,000 feet below the rounded white summit of the Big Mountain. The area is rich with fascinating day hikes.

Outside of the park, in the adjacent Mt. Baker–Snoqualmie National Forest, is a popular hike that leads to High Rock Lookout. The lookout is one of the forest's few remaining manned fire observation posts. While most people drive to the trail, we recommend mountain bikes. Once you reach the trailhead, you can stash your bike and climb the ridge to the overlook. This view of Rainier is unparalleled.

RIDE 59 SKOOKUM FLATS

Skookum Flats Trail is one of the most entertaining pieces of extreme single-track in the Pacific Northwest. This popular loop utilizes Skookum Flats Trail, Dalles River Trail, a short stretch on WA 410, and White River Trail. This is an excellent and challenging 11-mile circuit.

Difficulty rating for the loop: strenuous. Skookum Flats Trail is a lesson in humility. It is technically demanding, with innumerable roots, rocks, drop-offs, staircase climbs, and switchbacks. Remember, there is no shame in walking; besides, it is better than dying. Beginners and intermediates will enjoy out-and-back excursions from the south end of Skookum Flats Trail.

General location: This ride begins at the intersection of Buck Creek

RIDE 59 *SKOOKUM FLATS*

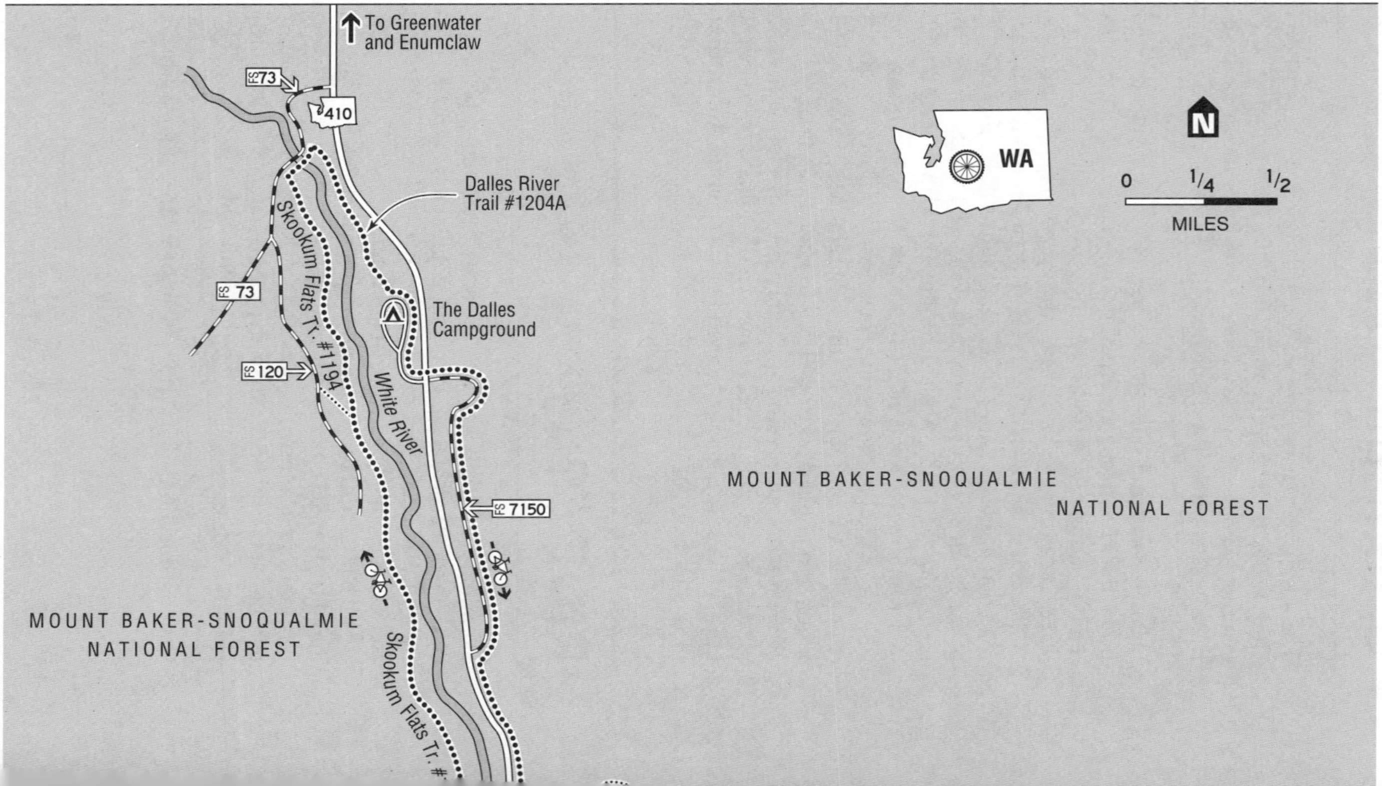

WA

N

0   1/4   1/2
MILES

To Greenwater
and Enumclaw

FR 410

FS 73

FS 73

FS 120

Dalles River
Trail #1204A

The Dalles
Campground

Skookum Flats Tr. #1194

White River

Skookum Flats Tr. #

FS 7150

MOUNT BAKER-SNOQUALMIE
NATIONAL FOREST

MOUNT BAKER-SNOQUALMIE NATIONAL FOREST

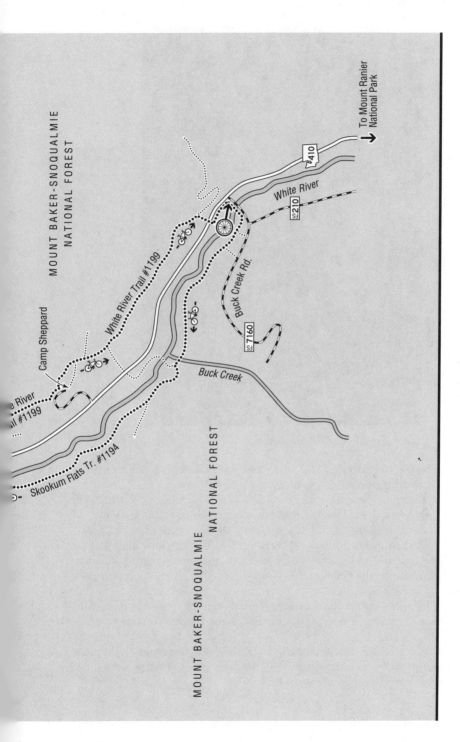

MOUNT BAKER-SNOQUALMIE NATIONAL FOREST

To Mount Ranier National Park

410

White River

FS 210

Buck Creek Rd.

FS 7160

White River Trail #1199

Camp Sheppard

e River

al #1199

Buck Creek

Skookum Flats Tr. #1194

MOUNT BAKER-SNOQUALMIE NATIONAL FOREST

217

Look at me, I can ride this part!

Road/Forest Service Road 7160 and WA 410, about 28 miles east of Enumclaw, Washington.

Elevation change: The trailhead at Buck Creek Road lies at 2,480′. The northern terminus at FS 73 is the low point of the loop, at 2,060′. Hilly terrain produces about 500′ of climbing on this trail. The route climbs to 2,280′ on FS 7150, then meets up with WA 410 at 2,220′. The ride's high point—2,580′—occurs on White River Trail. Lesser ups and downs contribute about 300′ of climbing to the pedaling on White River Trail. Total elevation gain: 1,380′.

Season: Dry spells during the summer and early fall offer good opportunities for low-impact cycling. These trails are popular and can be crowded on weekends.

Services: Water is available seasonally at the Dalles Campground. The nearby community of Greenwater offers food, lodging, gas, limited groceries, and showers. All services are available in Enumclaw.

Hazards: The single-track portions of the loop are intensely technical. The trails are perilous when wet—bridges and roots become very slick. Anticipate others approaching from around corners. Be extra cautious while riding on the highway.

Rescue index: Help can be found in Greenwater.

Land status: Mt. Baker–Snoqualmie National Forest.

Maps: The district map of the White River Ranger District is a good guide to this ride. USGS 7.5 minute quad: Sun Top.

Finding the trail: From locations to the north, follow WA 410 east from Greenwater. You will pass the Dalles Campground on the right after about 7 miles. Continue for another 3.8 miles to FS 7160/Buck Creek Road (on the right, just beyond milepost 54). From locations to the south, take WA 410 west (toward Seattle) from Cayuse Pass. It is about 11 miles from the pass to Buck Creek Road (on the left, just past milepost 55). Coming from either direction, look for the big wooden sign for Buck Creek Organization Site, opposite Buck Creek Road. Park in the small parking area on the west side of WA 410.

Sources of additional information:

White River Ranger District
Enumclaw, WA 98022
(509) 825-6585

Notes on the trail: Cross the bridge over the White River, and immediately turn right onto Skookum Flats Trail #1194. Turn right after .1 miles to stay on Trail #1194. Turn right again in another .2 miles at an unmarked intersection. One more mile brings you to a suspension bridge that leads out to WA 410. Bear to the left before the bridge to remain on Trail #1194. Pedal .4 miles to another intersection; here, turn right. The trail enters a camp area after 3 more miles; stay to the right and on the main trail until you reach unsigned FS 73. Turn right onto the gravel road and cross the bridge. Turn right onto Dalles River Trail #1204A immediately after crossing the river. Proceed along this path for .5 miles to the Dalles Campground. Turn left and follow the paved road through the campground to WA 410. Continue straight across the highway and ride up FS 7150. This road passes cottages and ends up back at WA 410. Turn left onto the highway and pedal .4 miles to a faint trail on the left. The path is hard to find—it looks like a small traffic pullout. Turn left onto the trail and climb very steeply under power lines to the White River Trail #1199. Turn left and follow the trail signs to remain on Trail #1199. After passing through a couple of clearings you arrive at a double-track and some power lines. Turn left and ride past a grassy field. Turn left at the next power pole onto a trail, then bear to the right to follow White River Trail as it passes behind Camp Sheppard. Follow the signs and stay on White River Trail #1199 for another 1.6 miles. Leave White River Trail where a sign indicates that White River Trail #1199 continues on to Ranger Creek Trail, Deep Creek Trail, and Corral Pass Road. Turn right at this sign and descend to WA 410. Turn left and ride up the highway .2 miles to your vehicle.

RIDE 60 DALLES RIDGE LOOP

This is a demanding 22.3-mile training ride. The loop begins with a real lip-chapper—10 miles of steady climbing on gravel roads (including 3.5 miles of steep climbing). Your stay on Dalles Ridge is brief—one-half mile of moderately difficult to steep uphills. The descent from the mountain involves a great deal of walking and carrying your bike. This is not what most cyclists would call a fun downhill. Ranger Creek Trail descends a steep drainage with severe switchbacks, most of which are too tight to ride. Huge root obstacles are common. We counted over 30 unrideable sections of trail (not including countless dabs). Ranger Creek Trail spits you out onto White River Trail for 3 sweet miles of challenging single-track. The trip ends with 3.2 miles on the highway.

There are excellent views of the White River Valley, Crystal Mountain, and Mt. Rainier on this ride. Clear-cuts dominate the road miles, but the trails pass through lovely stands of old-growth timber. The stretch on White River Trail is a superior piece of technical single-track.

General location: This ride begins approximately 5 miles south of Greenwater, Washington.
Elevation change: The elevation at the trailhead is 2,160′. A high point of 5,500′ is attained on Dalles Ridge Trail. Undulations on the roads and trails add about 500′ of climbing to the loop. Total elevation gain: 3,840′.
Season: The roads and trails are usually free of snow from late June through September. Avoid the route when it is wet—trail damage and slick roots are concerns. The highway is busy with traffic on summer weekends.
Services: There is no water on the ride. Water can be obtained seasonally at the Dalles Campground. Food, lodging, limited groceries, and gas can be found in Greenwater.
Hazards: The ride is long and demanding. You will be fatigued by the time you reach the highway. Remain alert for traffic on the roads; be especially careful on WA 410. The single-tracks are treacherous and full of obstacles. Steep drop-offs are commonplace on Ranger Creek Trail.
Rescue index: Help is available in Enumclaw.
Land status: Mt. Baker–Snoqualmie National Forest.
Maps: The district map of the White River Ranger District is a good guide to this ride. USGS 7.5 minute quad: Sun Top.

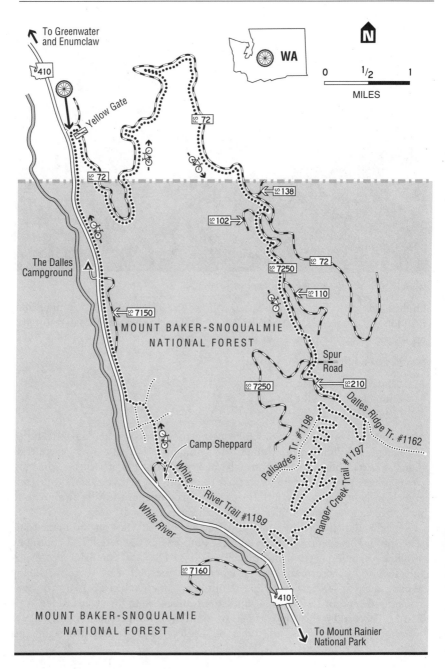

To Greenwater
and Enumclaw

410

Yellow Gate

FS 72

WA

N

0   1/2   1

MILES

FS 72

FS 138

FS 102

The Dalles
Campground

FS 7250

FS 72

FS 110

FS 7150

MOUNT BAKER-SNOQUALMIE
NATIONAL FOREST

Spur
Road

FS 7250

FS 210

Dalles Ridge Tr. #1162

Palisades Tr. #1198

Camp Sheppard

Ranger Creek Trail #1197

White River Trail #1199

White River

FS 7160

410

MOUNT BAKER-SNOQUALMIE
NATIONAL FOREST

To Mount Rainier
National Park

Cloud-cloaked view from Forest Service Road #72.

Finding the trail: From Greenwater, follow WA 410 south for 5.3 miles and turn left onto signed Forest Service Road 72. Go up the gravel road and park on the right (across from an unsigned spur road on the left).

Sources of additional information:

White River Ranger District
Enumclaw, WA 98022
(206) 825-6585

Notes on the trail: Carry your bike down the tight switchbacks on Ranger Creek Trail. Skidding around the turns is inappropriate; it causes severe trail damage. Attempting to roll through them does not cut it either—you may clean some of them, but you will miss frequently. When you miss, your foot comes down to catch your fall. Invariably, this damages the hillside above the trail and leads to slope failure (i.e., the trail gets trashed).

Pass through the yellow gate and ride up FS 72. Stay on the main road where spur roads branch off. Turn right onto FS 7250 where FS 72 continues straight (.4 miles beyond milepost 7). Follow FS 7250 for 2.1 miles to an intersection of three roads. An unsigned spur goes left, FS 210 goes straight ahead, and FS 7250 swings right. Continue straight onto FS 210. You will come to the end of FS 210 in .4 miles at a trailhead sign for Dalles Ridge Trail #1162. Proceed up this single-track for .6 miles to Ranger Creek Trail #1197, which cuts off just after the crest on Dalles Ridge Trail. Turn right and descend on Ranger Creek Trail for just over 1 mile to a hiker's shelter. Turn left, remaining on Ranger Creek Trail, where Palisades Trail #1198 goes straight. You will reach Little Ranger Creek Viewpoint in 2 miles. Visit the viewpoint, then continue with the descent. You will reach an intersection of trails in 2.5 miles; a sign on the left indicates that you have been following Ranger Creek Trail. Turn sharply to the right onto unsigned White River Trail. Soon you will find yourself paralleling the highway. Then you will arrive at a junction where a trail goes left and descends to the highway. Continue straight on White River Trail toward Camp Sheppard. In 1.1 miles you will reach an intersection where Buck Creek Trail goes left. Continue straight on White River Trail. You will come to another meeting of trails in .3 miles; continue straight on White River Trail and stay to the right at the next intersection, where a path branches left toward Camp Sheppard. Shortly you will pass through the back of the camp—stay on White River Trail. When you arrive at a grassy field, turn right onto a double-track. Immediately turn right into the woods to get back onto the unsigned single-track. (This turn is easy to miss— the double-track continues straight, following some telephone lines). Follow the signs at the next two intersections to remain on White River Trail. Turn right when you arrive at a clearing and power lines. Ride down to the highway. Turn right onto WA 410 and pedal 3.2 miles to FS 72. Turn right and ride to your vehicle.

RIDE 61 *HIGH ROCK LOOKOUT*

This is a 23-mile road loop. An 11-mile ascent takes you to Towhead Gap and High Rock Lookout Trail #266. The 1.6-mile hiking trail climbs 1,365 feet to the last manned lookout in the Packwood Ranger District. Views of Mt. Rainier, Mt. St. Helens, and Mt. Adams are outstanding. The ride ends with a long, fun descent.

The first nine miles are paved. The remainder of the loop is on gravel roads in mostly good condition. The trip starts with three miles of gently rolling terrain—a nice warm-up for the moderately difficult climb to Towhead Gap. The ascent contains some steep (but short) grades and many easy breath-catching stretches.

General location: This ride begins near Mt. Rainier National Park, approximately 14 miles east of Elbe, Washington.
Elevation change: The ride begins at 1,960′ and climbs to Towhead Gap, at 4,300′. Undulations on the route add an estimated 200′ of climbing to the loop. Total elevation gain: 2,540′ (hike not included).

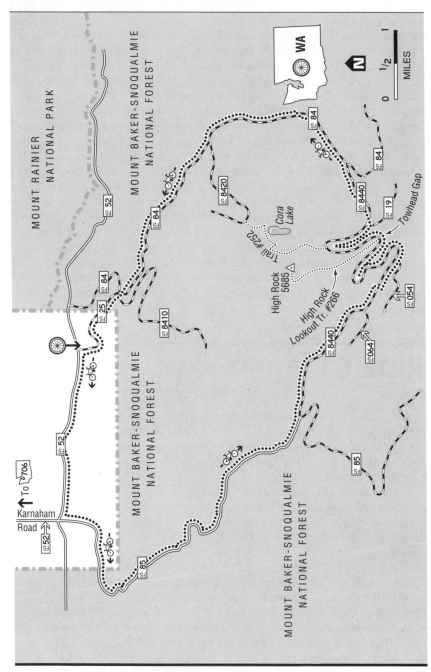

MOUNT RAINIER NATIONAL PARK

MOUNT BAKER-SNOQUALMIE NATIONAL FOREST

WA

N

MILES

0   1/2   1

FS 84

FS 84

FS 8420

Cora Lake

Trail #252

FS 8440

FS 19

Towhead Gap

FS 84

High Rock 5685

High Rock Lookout Tr. #266

FS 054

FS 52

FS 84

FS 25

FS 8410

FS 8440

FS 064

FS 52

MOUNT BAKER-SNOQUALMIE NATIONAL FOREST

To 706

Karnaham Road

FS 52

FS 85

FS 85

MOUNT BAKER-SNOQUALMIE NATIONAL FOREST

Towhead Gap.

Season: This ride is best on clear days from July through October.

Services: Limited groceries, gas, a pay phone, and espresso can be found in Ashford.

Hazards: The roads may be busy with logging and tourist traffic. Exercise caution when exploring on High Rock—the north face is a sheer 600′ cliff.

Rescue index: Help can be found in Ashford.

Land status: Mt. Baker–Snoqualmie National Forest lands, administered by the Gifford Pinchot National Forest.

Maps: The district map of the Packwood Ranger District of the Gifford Pinchot National Forest is a good guide to this route. USGS 7.5 minute quad: Sawtooth Ridge.

Finding the trail: From Elbe, follow WA 706 east to Ashford. Continue east from Ashford for about 2 miles to Karnaham Road/Forest Service Road 52 (on the right, just east of milepost 10). Turn right onto FS 52. Proceed on FS 52 for 4 miles to FS 25 (on the right, just east of milepost 4). Turn right onto FS 25 and park on the left.

Sources of additional information:

Packwood Ranger District
13068 Highway 12
Packwood, WA 98361
(206) 494-5515

Notes on the trail: Turn left out of the parking area onto FS 52. Continue on FS 52 to the intersection with FS 85 and turn left to follow the sign for High Rock Lookout. The pavement ends at a Y intersection 9 miles into the ride. Bear left onto FS 8440 toward the lookout. Keep left at the next two intersections, staying on FS 8440, until you reach Towhead Gap. Descend from the pass and stay on the main road when side roads branch off. You will pass Big Creek Trail #252, then FS 19 on the right. The next intersection signals the end of FS 8440. Continue straight onto FS 84, which is straight ahead and hard to the right. Stay on FS 84 for 5.3 miles to FS 25 (just beyond FS 8410 on the left). Turn left and follow FS 25 back to your vehicle.

Capitol State Forest

The 80,000-acre Capitol State Forest lies just south of Olympia, Washington, in an area known as the Black Hills. This forest is a favored destination for Puget Sound's more skilled and powerful mountain bikers. The northern half of the forest is an off-road-vehicle area, while the southern half is designated for hikers and equestrians (with some trails open to mountain bikes).

This recreation area contains miles and miles of demanding single-track. The woods are filled with unsigned and unmapped trails. Only seasoned locals really know their way around, but even the old hands spend part of their time getting un-lost.

Like many ORV areas, the trails take a beating, but they are well maintained. ORV permit fees and one percent of Washington gas tax revenues pay for off-road maintenance. A high clay content in the soils of Capitol State Forest makes for slippery conditions when the trails are wet. In places, cinder blocks have been set into the trail. Buried flush, the blocks provide excellent traction and help hold unstable ground in place.

RIDE 62 MT. MOLLY LOOP

The 8.3-mile Mt. Molly Loop is in the northern half of the Capitol State Forest. Locals consider this ride one of the area's easier outings, but in our opinion, it is difficult. The route follows single-track trails for over six miles and ends with paved and gravel roads.

Challenges and thrills are commonplace on this route. There is a lot of climbing, but most of it is moderately difficult to easy. The really steep stuff comes in short bursts, adding up to about one mile of strenuous climbing. There are some nice downhills, rolling terrain, and level stretches too. The circuit includes ditchlike conditions, deep ruts, mud holes, big rocks, roots, and howling motorcycles.

General location: Capitol State Forest is about 15 miles southwest of Olympia, Washington.
Elevation change: The ride starts at 180′ and tops out at 880′ near the halfway point of the loop. The trip is full of lesser undulations that add about 500′ of climbing to the ride. Total elevation gain: 1,200′.
Season: The early fall is a good time for a visit, especially on weekdays. The wettest seasons are typically the winter and spring. ORV use is heaviest on summer weekends.

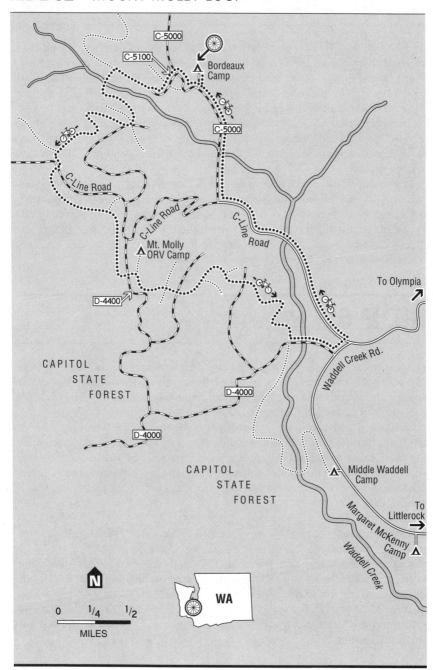

C-5000

C-5100

Bordeaux
Camp

C-5000

C-Line Road

C-Line Road

Mt. Molly
ORV Camp

C-Line Road

D-4400

To Olympia

Waddell Creek Rd.

CAPITOL
STATE
FOREST

D-4000

D-4000

CAPITOL
STATE
FOREST

Middle Waddell
Camp

Margaret McKenny
Camp

To
Littlerock

Waddell Creek

N

0   1/4   1/2

MILES

WA

Trail maintenance in Capitol State Forest.

Services: There is piped water at the trailhead in Bordeaux Camp. Gas and limited groceries are available in Littlerock. All services are available in Olympia.

Hazards: The trails are chock-full of obstacles and dangerous conditions (like deep ruts on severe descents). The tread is very slick when wet. Give motorized vehicles a wide berth. Be especially careful when crossing roads. The area is a maze of unmarked trails, and new trails are being blazed all the time. Getting lost is a real possibility. Travel with others and be prepared for emergencies.

Rescue index: Help is available in Olympia. The nearest pay phone is in Littlerock.

Land status: Lands administered by the Washington State Department of Natural Resources.

Maps: Check bike shops in Olympia for the latest editions of locally produced maps and directions. The Washington Department of Natural Resources no longer prints a map of Capitol Forest. USGS 7.5 minute quad: Littlerock.

Finding the trail: Follow Interstate 5 south from Olympia. Take Exit 95 and proceed west on WA 121 toward Littlerock. In Littlerock, go straight at the stop sign and keep going straight, following the sign for Capitol Forest. The road passes a gas station and a tavern, then crosses some railroad tracks. Drive .6 miles beyond the railroad tracks and bear right onto 128th Avenue

Miles of ORV trails run through Capitol State Forest.

at a Y intersection. You will immediately arrive at a stop sign; turn right onto unsigned Waddell Creek Road. Proceed for 4 miles to a T intersection at C-Line Road. Turn left and go another 1.3 miles to the end of the pavement at unsigned C-5000 Road. (The intersection is marked with an incomplete directional sign on the northwest corner and a "Dead End" sign on C-5000 Road.) Turn right onto C-5000 Road. Follow C-5000 Road for .8 miles; continue straight into Bordeaux Camp to park your vehicle.

Sources of additional information:

Department of Natural Resources
Central Region
1405 Rush Road S-3
Chehalis, WA 98532
(206) 748-2383

Notes on the trail: Ride out of Bordeaux Camp to C-5000 Road and turn right. Climb to C-5100 Road and turn left. Stay on the road as side trails branch off. Shortly, C-5100 Road enters the woods and becomes a wide single-track. Pedal into the woods for about .5 miles to an intersection of trails. Turn left and descend to a creek crossing. Cross the creek, then climb for .6 miles to an intersection where the trail meets a spur road. Several trails take off from here. Look to the right for a pile of roots blocking the road. Go around the roots on the right-hand side. This puts you on a switchbacking single-track that climbs away from the road. Ascend for .6 miles to a Y in the trail; bear left. When you arrive at a road, turn left then immediately bear right to get back onto the trail. (You will pass a rail fence soon after regaining the trail.) After a stretch of downhill riding and some easier climbing, you will reach another Y. Stay right and downhill—the trail skirts D-4400 Road and the Mt. Molly ORV Camp. Stay on the main trail as side trails branch off to access Mt. Molly Camp. Soon the trail crosses D-4400 Road. Cross the road and turn right at the T intersection of trails. Climb moderately, then drop a short way and continue straight across another trail to begin a more demanding and technical climb. The trail crosses a spur road, continues to climb, then arrives at a Y intersection of trails. Stay left and ascend steeply to the top of the climb. Crest and follow the trail downhill. (Some trails branch off, but they climb.) From the top, it is .25 miles to a Y intersection where both trails descend. Bear right, following the trail that is wider and less steep. Stay right at the next Y intersection, descend through a clear-cut, and cross a spur road. It is .4 miles from this spur road crossing to another road, unsigned D-4000 Road. Turn left onto D-4000 Road and ride out to paved Waddell Creek Road. Turn left onto unsigned Waddell Creek Road, then left again onto C-Line Road. Ride back to your vehicle at Bordeaux Camp (see "Finding the trail").

To expand your riding options in the Capitol State Forest, find single-tracks that take off from main roads. Use maps and a compass and allow plenty of time for route finding. A good way to quickly get to know some of the trails in the area is to tag along with local mountain bikers. Visit bike shops in Olympia; some of them conduct group rides in the forest.

Olympic Peninsula Area Rides

The 6,500-square-mile Olympic Peninsula is separated from the rest of Washington by salt water. The main access for the peninsula is US 101. The highway parallels the Pacific coastline on the west, the Strait of Juan de Fuca on the north, and the inland waters of Puget Sound on the east. You can also access the peninsula by ferry from Seattle or Victoria.

The area is unique and strikingly beautiful. It encompasses ocean beaches, windy ridges, precipitous mountains, snowfields, glaciers, deep gorges, and verdant forests.

Much of the peninsula lies within the Olympic National Forest. The forest contains a stunning variety of environments within short distances. In the 50 miles that stretch from the summit of Mt. Olympus to the Pacific, the vegetation changes from an arctic environment of lichen and rock to a temperate rainforest.

Precipitation on the Olympic coast averages over 12 feet a year! Rainfall amounts drop dramatically as you move east. Precipitation is heaviest in the winter, decreasing by spring. Summer is the driest time of the year.

While most of the riding on the Olympic Peninsula is on gravel forest roads, we direct your attention to three good trail rides. One trail that lies off the beaten path is the 11-mile long Wynoochee Lakeshore Trail, in the southern portion of the Olympic National Forest. The Spruce Railroad Trail, on the north end of the peninsula (and in Olympic National Park), is an easy outing beside beautiful Lake Crescent. Gold Creek Trail is a challenging and exciting path in the northeast corner of the peninsula.

RIDE 63   *WYNOOCHEE LAKESHORE TRAIL*

The single-track around Wynoochee Lake is 11 miles long and moderately difficult. There are some steep climbs, and pushing your bike will be necessary in several places. Some segments of the trail are technically demanding, while others are smooth and wide. The trail becomes exacting as it nears the north end of the reservoir. Obstacles like roots and rocks are more common, and the path switchbacks through some drainages. In places, the single-track narrows and drops off steeply to the side. The trail crosses the Wynoochee River at the

RIDE 63 *WYNOOCHEE LAKESHORE TRAIL*

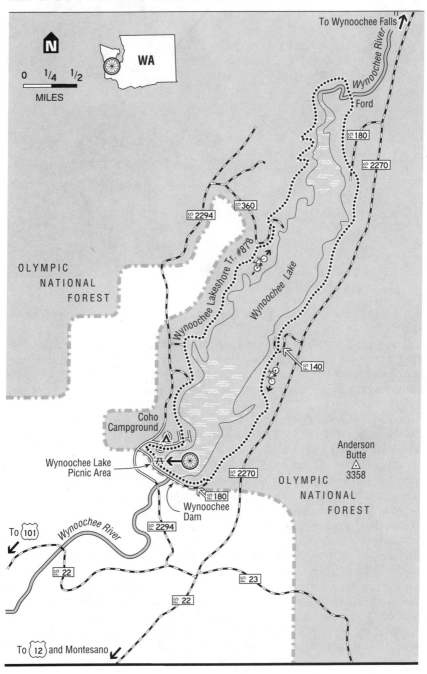

Wynoochee Lakeshore Trail.

north end of the reservoir. There is no bridge, so you must ford the river to continue the loop.

The scenery is lovely; the best views are at the south end of the lake. The trail offers glimpses of Anderson Ridge to the east and the Olympics to the north. Wynoochee Lakeshore Trail winds through a dense forest and past some magnificent old-growth specimens of Douglas fir and western hemlock.

General location: Wynoochee Lake is 37 miles north of Montesano, Washington, on the Olympic Peninsula.

Elevation change: The trailhead lies at 780′. The route climbs and drops over its entire length and reaches 900′ several times. The first half of the loop sees the most elevation gain—about 1,000′. The second half is easier and involves approximately 500′ of climbing. Total elevation gain: 1,500′.

Season: Trail conditions are normally best in the summer and fall. The trail is usually cleared of underbrush by midsummer. Prior to this maintenance, windfall can be a problem.

Services: Water is available seasonally at Coho Campground and year-round at the Visitor Center. There are no commercial services at Wynoochee Lake. Food, lodging, groceries, and gas can be obtained in Montesano.

Hazards: There are many small creek crossings. The larger creeks are spanned by simple bridges—one large log with a handrail. Carrying or pushing your bicycle over these bridges can be awkward. The trail takes a turn to the northeast near the north end of the lake and comes close to a high bank

North end of Wynoochee Lake.

of sand and gravel. Stay back from the edge of this unstable slope. The river level at the ford fluctuates; the river is generally too high to cross in the spring.
Rescue index: Help can be found in Montesano. There is a phone at the Wynoochee Dam Picnic Area that accepts collect or credit card calls. When using the phone, be patient; it may take 15 to 20 seconds for the operator to come on the line. The phone is located near the gate on Forest Service Road 180. You may be able to obtain assistance in the summer at the Wynoochee Dam Project Office or from the campground host at Coho Campground.
Land status: Olympic National Forest.
Maps: The district map of the Hood Canal Ranger District is a good guide to this ride. USGS 7.5 minute quad: Wynoochee Lake.
Finding the trail: From Montesano, drive west for 1 mile on US 12 and turn north on Wynoochee Valley Road/FS 22. Continue on FS 22 for approximately 35 miles to the major intersection with FS 2270. Turn left to stay on

FS 22. In .4 miles, turn right onto FS 2294. Follow FS 2294 for 1.2 miles and turn right onto FS 180 toward the Wynoochee Lake Picnic Area. Park in the day-use area.

Wynoochee Lake can also be accessed from US 101. The intersection of US 101 and FS 22 is approximately 30 miles north of Aberdeen and 20 miles south of Quinault Lake. Head east on FS 22, driving 21 miles to FS 2294 on the left. Turn left onto FS 2294 and go 1.2 miles to FS 180 on the right. Turn right onto FS 180 toward the Wynoochee Lake Picnic Area. Park in the day-use area.

Sources of additional information:

Hood Canal Ranger District
P.O. Box 68
Hoodsport, WA 98548
(206) 877-5254

Wynoochee Dam and Lake
City of Aberdeen
5120 Wynoochee Valley Road
Montesano, WA 98563
(206) 533-4100, ext. 361

Notes on the trail: Exit the day-use area and turn right onto FS 2294. Take the first right into the Coho Campground and follow the sign toward the boat launch. Just before you get to the lake, turn left onto the trail signed "Wynoochee Lakeshore Trail #878." After 2.7 miles, the single-track meets an abandoned road. There is a sign here that reads "Trail." Turn right onto this road and descend for .2 miles to an identical sign and the trail. Turn left onto the trail. You will come to the river crossing in about 2 miles. We were turned back by high water in May of 1993. We pedaled back to our vehicle, drove around to the other side of the ford, and continued with the trail. The path follows the lakefront for a couple of miles, then parallels FS 140. Soon the route crosses FS 140. The trail continues on the opposite side of the road. (It is hard to see; look for the sign.) The single-track ends at the south end of the lake, on the east side of the dam. Cross the dam to reach the day-use parking area.

RIDE 64 *SPRUCE RAILROAD TRAIL*

During World War I, the United States needed Sitka spruce for airplane production. The roadless forests of the western Olympic Peninsula held great

RIDE 64 *SPRUCE RAILROAD TRAIL*

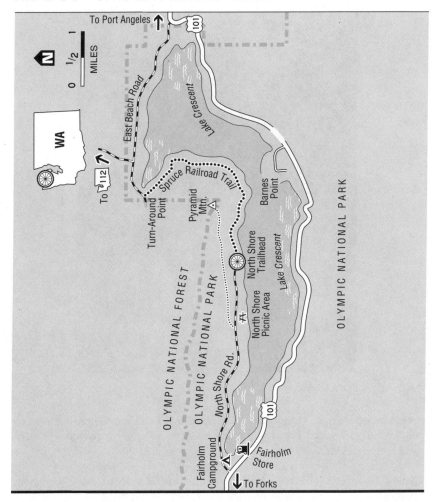

promise as a source of this valuable wood. A railway accessing the timber was built with dizzying speed but was completed 19 days after the war ended. A portion of this old railroad bed has been converted into the Spruce Railroad Trail.

This is an easy eight-mile out-and-back ride beside bucolic Lake Crescent. At one point the trail crosses an arched bridge over a lovely rock-walled inlet. Waterfowl may be observed along the shore of the lake, and deer are often seen in the woods. Views across the clear water are of forested hills backed by

Lake Crescent.

the majestic Olympic Mountains. Since the ride is in a national park, the scene contains no clear-cuts. The trip is spiced by a couple of short stretches of technical single-track.

General location: The trail begins on the north side of Lake Crescent, approximately 30 miles west of Port Angeles, Washington.
Elevation change: The trailhead lies at 800´. The route reaches a high point of 860´, and small hills add about 100´ of climbing to the ride. Total elevation gain: 160´.
Season: The low elevation of the ride makes it suitable for year-round use.
Services: There is no water on the trip. Water can be obtained at Fairholm Campground. Fairholm Store has limited groceries, gas, and a pay phone. All services are available in Port Angeles.
Hazards: Cougars have been encountered at close range in this area. Watch for poison oak growing beside the trail, and check your skin and clothing for

Lake Crescent local.

ticks. The trail surface does contain some obstacles like loose rocks, roots, and small creek crossings.

Rescue index: Help is available in Port Angeles. There are ranger stations (open during the summer only) at Fairholm Campground and Barnes Point.

Land status: Olympic National Park.

Maps: The Olympic National Forest and Olympic National Park map is an adequate guide. USGS 7.5 minute quad: Lake Crescent.

Finding the trail: From Port Angeles, follow US 101 west for about 25 miles to the west end of Lake Crescent. Pass the Fairholm Store (on your right) and take the next right onto North Shore Road. Follow the road to its terminus at the North Shore Trailhead of the Spruce Railroad Trail.

Sources of additional information:

Park Superintendent
Olympic National Park
600 East Park Avenue
Port Angeles, WA 98362
(206) 452-4501

Lake Crescent Ranger Station
HC 62, Box 10
Port Angeles, WA 98362
(206) 928-3380

Notes on the trail: The 8-mile round-trip starts at the North Shore Trailhead. Starting at the North Shore Picnic Area adds 3 miles to the tour. Beginning at Fairholm Campground makes for a 17-mile out-and-back excursion.

RIDE 65 *GOLD CREEK TRAIL*

Advanced cyclists will appreciate this demanding 18.3-mile loop. The trip begins with climbing on good gravel roads. Vistas into the snow-capped Buckhorn Wilderness get better as you gain altitude. Twelve miles of difficult climbing and screaming downhills bring you to Gold Creek Trail. The path begins in an area thick with rhododendrons. This single-track includes some short, strenuous climbs, but it is mostly downhill. The trail is exciting, with twists, whoop-dee-doos, major root drop-offs, and clifflike experiences.

General location: The ride begins near the first crossing of the Dungeness River on Forest Service Road 2860. This trailhead is approximately 15 miles south of Sequim, Washington, on the Olympic Peninsula.

Elevation change: The loop begins at 1,250′ and climbs 2,000′ in the first 4 miles. A series of descents nets a loss of 700′ in the next 4 miles and brings you to a bridge over the Dungeness River. The following 4 miles go up and down, adding up to 1,100′ of ascending and 400′ of descending. This puts you at the Gold Creek Trailhead at an elevation of 3,200′. Undulations in the trail contribute about 350′ of climbing to the trip. Total elevation gain: 3,450′.

Season: The Olympic Peninsula receives large amounts of precipitation, so predicting dry conditions is nearly impossible. The odds for fine weather improve in the late summer and early fall. The rhododendrons should be blooming in June.

Services: There is no water on the ride. Water can be obtained seasonally at nearby East Crossing Campground. Food, lodging, gas, and groceries are available in Sequim.

Hazards: The bridge over Silver Creek was under construction at the time of our research. Crossing the creek to continue on FS 2860 involved a 30′ carry over a big log high above the rushing water. This circuit is long and hard. You will be gassed by the time you reach the single-track. Gold Creek Trail presents obstacles like roots, rocks, extreme descents, and severe drop-offs. There are situations where a mistake could lead to serious injury. Anticipate others approaching from around the next bend—the trail is open to equestrians, hikers, and motorcyclists as well as mountain bikers. The lower end of the trail has some new switchbacks that are tight and steep. Walk your bike down

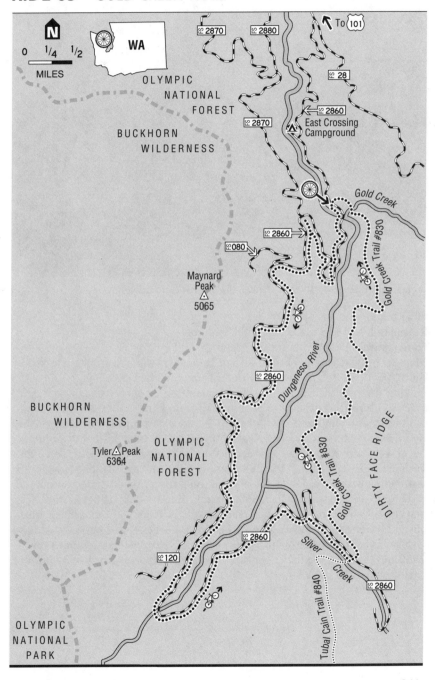

A view into Buckhorn Wilderness from Forest Service Road #2860.

these fragile sections of the trail.

Rescue index: Help can be found in Sequim.

Land status: Olympic National Forest.

Maps: The district map of the Quilcene Ranger District is a good guide to this route. USGS 7.5 minute quads: Mount Zion and Tyler Peak.

Finding the trail: From US 101, head inland on Louella Road, which is .2 miles south of the entrance to Sequim Bay State Park (about 5.5 miles south of the town of Sequim). Climb steeply for 1 mile and turn left onto Palo Alto Road at a T intersection. The road turns to gravel after 3.4 miles. Continue on gravel Palo Alto Road for 2 miles to a Y intersection. Bear left onto unsigned FS 28 where FS 2880 goes right toward Dungeness Forks Campground. Follow FS 28 for about a mile to another Y intersection and turn right onto unsigned FS 2860. At the time of our visit, FS 2860 was marked by an orange sign that read "Notice: Road 2860 closed 12 miles ahead for construction." Follow FS 2860 for 2 miles to the entrance of East Crossing Campground (on the right). Proceed past the campground on FS 2860 for 1 mile to the lower trailhead for the Gold Creek Trail #830 (on the left). Park on the right.

Sources of additional information:

Quilcene Ranger District
P.O. Box 280
Quilcene, WA 98376
(206) 765-3368

Notes on the trail: Gold Creek Trail has the potential to be greatly damaged by inappropriate use. Stay off the trail when it is wet, and tread lightly.

Ride uphill on FS 2860. Follow this road for 12 miles to the upper trailhead for Gold Creek Trail #830 on the left. Turn left onto the single-track. You will arrive at a Y intersection after 3.5 miles on the trail; stay left and downhill. The trail ends at your vehicle.

Northwest Washington Area Rides

The ambitiously named Mountain Loop Highway heads east out of Everett. This modest two-lane road takes travelers into the Darrington Ranger District of the Mt. Baker–Snoqualmie National Forest. Mountain bikers find the area laced with quiet gravel roads.

The paved portion of Mountain Loop Highway ends near Barlow Pass (one of several Barlow Passes in the Pacific Northwest). A double-track heads south from the highway and follows the Sauk River to the old mining town of Monte Cristo. The gravel road is quiet today except for the sounds of hikers and bikers. At the turn of the century, the towering granite peaks surrounding Monte Cristo were crawling with grizzled miners searching for gold. Today several footpaths lead from the town site into the Jackson Wilderness Area.

In close proximity to Monte Cristo is the Schweitzer Creek Loop. This ride takes in a mountain lake and passes over a short stretch of trail through old-growth cedar.

Swinging north, Mountain Loop Highway becomes a gravel road and heads toward Darrington. Most of the residents of this mill town hail from the hills and hollows of North Carolina. These fun-loving people have kept their rich southern Appalachian culture alive through quilting, bluegrass music, and gospel.

A good time can be had riding to the top of nearby North Mountain. A lookout tower on the summit gets you up over the treetops, revealing a countryside that is stunning in its beauty.

A similar ride is found north and west of Darrington at the foot of Josephine Mountain (east of Sedro Woolley). The pedal to the apex of Mt. Josephine is a demanding outing that features closeups of Twin Sisters, Mt. Baker, and Mt. Shuksan. Cinch down your helmet and hold on tight—the coast back to the trailhead is fast and furious.

Near the Canadian border are the city of Bellingham and an excellent bike path known as the Interurban Trail. This popular rail trail follows along the shoreline of island-studded Chuckanut Bay. It is a fun path for folks of all skill and fitness levels. At the south end of the trail, a closed gravel road heads steeply uphill to beautiful Fragrance Lake in Larrabee State Park.

Just south of Bellingham is Anacortes, the jumping-off point for the San Juan Islands. The islands are world renowned as a destination for outstanding bicycle touring. Strictly speaking, you won't find much mountain biking, but the road riding on the islands is great. If this prospect interests you, pick up a guidebook (there are several good ones on the market) and hop a ferry to some unforgettable back-road riding.

RIDE 66 *SCHWEITZER CREEK LOOP*

The majority of this l0.8-mile loop (which also includes an out-and-back leg) is on gravel roads in fair to good condition. There is no warming up on this ride; you begin with steep climbing. Steep grades quickly give way to moderate ones and then to easy uphill pedaling. The outing ends with fast, twisty downhills. There is some washboarding on the steep hills.

This loop is nice, though unremarkable. You climb past some pleasant, cascading creeks near the start of the ride. Logging operations have created some openings in the forest canopy; these gaps allow glimpses of snow-capped peaks in the Boulder River Wilderness. Rounding out the highlights are a stroll to a small lake and a short trail through a stand of old-growth cedar.

General location: The trip begins near Schweitzer Creek, approximately 33 miles east of Everett, Washington.
Elevation change: The circuit starts at 1,380' and climbs to a high point of 2,800'. Undulations on the route add an estimated 200' of climbing to the outing. Total elevation gain: 1,620'
Season: The early fall is a nice time for a visit to this portion of the forest. Forest Service Road 4020 is busy with vehicles traveling to hiking trailheads, especially in the summer.
Services: There is no water on the ride. Water is available at the Verlot Public Service Center and seasonally at Turlo Campground (across from the service center). Gas, food, lodging, and pay phones are available in Granite Falls.
Hazards: Traffic can be heavy. Stay alert and control your speed on the descent. The route contains some blind corners.
Rescue index: Help can be found at the Verlot Public Service Center during office hours and in Granite Falls. There is a pay phone at the service center.
Land status: Mt. Baker–Snoqualmie National Forest.
Maps: The district map of the Darrington Ranger District is a good guide to the forest roads followed on this ride. The ski trail connecting FS 4020 to FS 4021 is not shown. USGS 7.5 minute quad: Mallardy Ridge.
Finding the trail: From Everett and Interstate 5, take Exit 194 to US 2 east. Travel east on US 2 for about 4 miles to WA 9. Turn left (north) onto WA 9 and follow it for approximately 3.5 miles to WA 92. Turn right (east) onto WA 92 toward Granite Falls. Stay on WA 92 for about 8.5 miles to the inter-

RIDE 66 *SCHWEITZER CREEK LOOP*

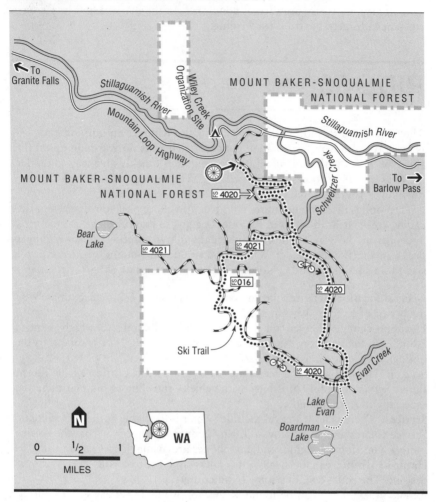

section of WA 92 and Mountain Loop Highway in Granite Falls. Turn left (north) onto Mountain Loop Highway. Drive approximately 11 miles on Mountain Loop Highway to the Verlot Public Service Center (on the left). Continue past the service center on Mountain Loop Highway for 4.7 miles and turn right on FS 4020. A sign here reads "Ashland Lakes Trails—5, Bear/Pinnacle Lakes Trails—6." Follow the dirt road uphill for .3 miles and park in the pullout on the right. There is a double-track jeep road to the left, opposite the pullout.

Checking the map at Lake Evan.

Sources of additional information:

> Darrington Ranger District
> 1405 Emmens Street
> Darrington, WA 98241
> (206) 436-1155 or (206) 259-7911

> Verlot Public Service Center
> Granite Falls, WA 98252
> (206) 691-7791

Notes on the trail: From the pullout, follow FS 4020 uphill. Continue on the main road past signed FS 4021 on the right. (You will be returning on this road.) The trailhead for Boardman Lake and Lake Evan is on the left, 4.7 miles into the ride. FS 4020 rolls up and down from this point. When the road swings north and descends, approximately 1.3 miles from the Lake Evan trailhead, look to the left for blue diamond-shaped symbols nailed on trees. These blue diamonds mark the start of a single-track ski trail. Turn left onto the trail and follow it into the woods. You will reach an abandoned road in about .3 miles. The road is built out of dark, crushed rock. Turn right onto the road and go over a two-plank bridge that spans the first of several ditches. After the ditches, you will reach a dirt road with a sign for Ashland Lakes Trailhead; turn left here. Shortly you will come to unsigned FS 4021. There is a sign here for Ashland Lakes Trail and Bear/Pinnacle Lakes. Turn right onto

FS 4021. At the intersection with FS 4020, turn left. Follow FS 4020 back down to your vehicle.

RIDE 67 *MONTE CRISTO*

Monte Cristo is an old mining town near the headwaters of the South Fork of the Sauk River. This easy out-and-back ride is nine miles long. It covers gentle terrain with a couple of short, moderately difficult hills. The trip follows a compacted dirt and gravel road in good condition. Repairs to flood-damaged sections of the road have been made with coarse rock; there are a few of these brief, extremely bumpy sections of road.

This area was the site of the Cascades' greatest gold rush. Millions of dollars worth of gold and silver ore were produced here in the late nineteenth and early twentieth centuries. A free map and walking tour brochure is available as you enter the town site. The pamphlet describes some of the town's history and provides insights into the lives of the miners. There are walking paths to old structures and relics of the "boom." The town sits below 7,000-foot peaks. Hiking trails lead into the surrounding Henry M. Jackson Wilderness.

General location: The trailhead is at Barlow Pass, about 50 miles east of Everett, Washington.

Elevation change: The ride starts at 2,360′ and reaches a low point of 2,300′ in the first mile. The road ascends to a high point of 2,760′ in Monte Cristo. Additional ups and downs over the course of the ride add approximately 50′ of climbing to the route. Total elevation gain: 570′.

Season: The road to Monte Cristo is generally free of snow from late May through October. The area sees its greatest influx of visitors in the summer.

Services: There is no water on this trip. Water is available at the Verlot Public Service Center and seasonally at Turlo Campground (across from the service center). Verlot is on Mountain Loop Highway on the way to the trailhead. Food, lodging, groceries, and gas are available in Granite Falls.

Hazards: Short, rocky sections of road can cause handling problems, particularly on the return descent. Use extra caution while riding over these rough areas or walk your bike through them. Extend courtesy to others on the road—this is a popular day hike. Although traffic is usually very light, you may encounter motorists traveling to homes in the area.

Rescue index: Help can be found at the Verlot Public Service Center during regular business hours. The nearest pay phone is at the service center.

Land status: Forest lands and private property within the boundaries of the Mt. Baker–Snoqualmie National Forest.

RIDE 67   *MONTE CRISTO*

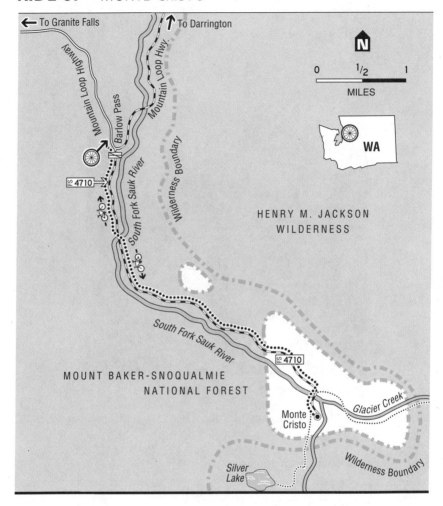

Maps: The district map of the Darrington Ranger District is a good guide to this ride. USGS 7.5 minute quads: Bedal and Monte Cristo.

Finding the trail: From Everett and Interstate 5, take Exit 194 to US 2 east. Travel east on US 2 for about 4 miles to WA 9. Turn left (north) onto WA 9 and follow it for approximately 3.5 miles to WA 92. Turn right (east) onto WA 92 toward Granite Falls. Stay on WA 92 for about 8.5 miles to the intersection of WA 92 and Mountain Loop Highway in Granite Falls. Turn left (north) onto Mountain Loop Highway. Drive approximately 31 miles on

Peaks in the Henry M. Jackson Wilderness.

Mountain Loop Highway to Barlow Pass. There are parking areas on both sides of the highway.

Sources of additional information:

Darrington Ranger District
1405 Emmens Street
Darrington, WA 98241
(206) 436-1155 or (206) 259-7911

Verlot Public Service Center
Granite Falls, WA 98252
(206) 691-7791

Monte Cristo Preservation Association
P.O. Box 471
Everett, WA 98206

Notes on the trail: Pedal east from the parking area toward the beginning of Forest Service Road 4710/Monte Cristo Road. Turn right onto FS 4710. Walk your bike around the gate and follow the road to Monte Cristo. Explore Monte Cristo on foot; no bikes on the trails, please. Return the way you came.

RIDE 68 NORTH MOUNTAIN

This out-and-back ride is 13.6 miles long. The ascent to the summit of North Mountain involves mostly easy pedaling. The climb is on a nicely graded gravel road in good condition. Near the top, the road gets steeper and a little rougher.

A lookout tower at the summit of North Mountain gives you one of the finest vantage points in the Pacific Northwest. Prominent features to the southwest are Whitehorse Ridge and Three Fingers. To the east lie the Sauk Prairie and the Sauk and Suiattle rivers. On a clear day you can see Mount Baker, the Olympics, and Puget Sound.

General location: This ride begins near Darrington, Washington. Darrington is 32 miles east of Interstate 5, approximately halfway between Seattle and Bellingham.

Elevation change: The ride starts at 1,960′ and reaches 3,824′ at the lookout. Total elevation gain: 1,864′.

Season: The road is usually clear of snow from May through October.

Services: There is no water available on the ride. Water, food, lodging, groceries, and gas can be obtained in Darrington.

Hazards: Expect some traffic on this trip, especially around sunset. Assume that sight-seeing motorists will be preoccupied. Control your speed on the descent, and watch for loose gravel.

Rescue index: Help can be found in Darrington.

Land status: Mt. Baker–Snoqualmie National Forest and state forest lands. There is also a stretch of public right-of-way through a small parcel of private property.

Maps: The district map of the Darrington Ranger District is a good guide to this ride. USGS 7.5 minute quads: Darrington and Fortson.

Finding the trail: From Bellingham, drive south on I-5 for about 45 miles to Exit 208. From Seattle, travel north on I-5 for approximately 45 miles to Exit 208. Follow WA 530 east for 32 miles to Darrington. Proceed east through Darrington to the intersection of WA 530 and Mountain Loop Highway. Turn left (north) to continue on WA 530. You will pass the Darrington Ranger Station on the left, then you will cross two sets of railroad tracks. FS 28 intersects with WA 530 immediately north of the second set of tracks (1.1 miles

RIDE 68 *NORTH MOUNTAIN*

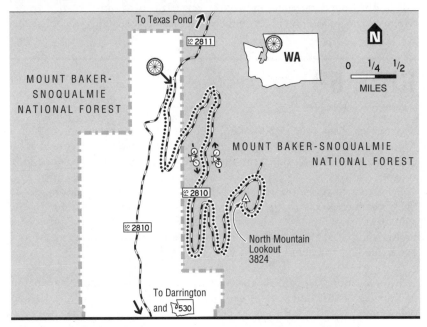

north of the intersection of WA 530 and Mountain Loop Highway). Turn left and follow FS 28 for 3 miles to FS 2810. Turn right onto FS 2810. You will arrive at FS 2811 (on the left, at a switchback in FS 2810) after 3.8 miles on FS 2810. Park your vehicle on FS 2810, on the outside of the switchback and just uphill from FS 2811.

Sources of additional information:

Darrington Ranger District
1405 Emmens Street
Darrington, WA 98241
(206) 436-1155 or (206) 259-7911

Notes on the trail: Ride uphill on FS 2810. Shortly you will pass milepost marker 4. Just beyond milepost marker 10, you will arrive at an intersection of roads. Stay to the right and continue to climb on the main road. (A rough spur road goes left and descends here.) Follow the main road to the lookout tower. Return the way you came.

View south from the lookout tower on North Mountain.

RIDE 69 *MT. JOSEPHINE*

This out-and-back ride is an 18-mile round-trip over gravel roads in fair to poor condition. The ascent is long and tiring, with a lot of moderate climbing and some short, steep pitches. The last couple of miles below the summit are the toughest. Rocky stretches of road make the return technical in places.

Although clear-cuts feature heavily in the picture, the panoramic view from the summit of Mt. Josephine is good. Twin Sisters, Mt. Baker, and Mt. Shuksan dominate the northern horizon. On a clear day you can spy Puget Sound and the Olympics to the west.

RIDE 69 *MOUNT JOSEPHINE*

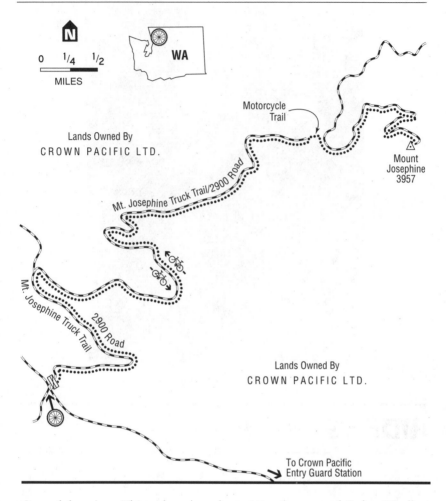

General location: This ride starts about 15 miles east of Sedro Woolley, Washington.

Elevation change: The ride begins at 570′ and tops out on Mt. Josephine at 3,957′. Total elevation gain: 3,387′.

Season: Snow may linger near the top of the mountain until the middle of the summer.

Services: There is no water available on the ride. Water, food, lodging, gas, and groceries can be obtained in Sedro Woolley.

Looking north to Twin Sister from Mt. Josephine.

Hazards: Watch your speed on the descent, and anticipate changing road conditions. The area is popular with ORV riders.

Rescue index: Access to the ride is gained through a controlled entry point at a guard station. Help can be summoned at the Crown Pacific guard station or in nearby Hamilton. To reach Hamilton, drive east on WA 20 from Cabin Creek Road and turn right after .6 miles.

Land status: Lands owned by Crown Pacific.

Maps: USGS 7.5 minute quads: Lyman and Hamilton.

Finding the trail: Take Interstate 5 to Exit 230 and follow WA 20 east through Burlington and Sedro Woolley. It is 17 miles from I-5 to Cabin Creek Road. (You have gone too far if you pass Crown Pacific's Hamilton office on your right.) Turn left (north) onto Cabin Creek Road and follow it for .2 miles to a stop sign. Turn right and proceed for .3 miles to an unsigned intersection. Turn left and travel .2 miles to a Crown Pacific entry guard station to obtain an entrance permit. Continue along the main road for another 2.5 miles to the gated Mt. Josephine Truck Trail on the right. An obscure wooden sign reads "Truck Trail/SW—HO—2900." Park on the side of the spur road that goes left here.

Sources of additional information:

Crown Pacific
P.O. Box 28
Hamilton, WA 98255
(206) 826-3951

Notes on the trail: Crown Pacific encourages recreational use of its forest lands in places where such use will not conflict with logging operations. Please obtain an access permit at the guard station or the company's Hamilton office.

Ride up the 2900 road. At intersections, follow the main road or signs that keep you on the 2900 road. Much of the cycling is through logged or burned areas that offer open views. The road enters shady woods after 5.5 miles and ends at a couple of streams in another 1.9 miles. Look to the right for a rough motorcycle trail. Take this path through the wet area and around a trench. This path will bring you to a gravel road; turn right. Stay left at the next three intersections. The road ends just below the summit. Turn right onto an old double-track trail that switchbacks up to the top. Return the way you came.

RIDE 70 *INTERURBAN TRAIL AND FRAGRANCE LAKE*

The Interurban was an electric railway that linked the communities of Bellingham and Mt. Vernon, Washington. It ran from 1912 to 1930. In 1987, the 5.8-mile Interurban Trail was opened to pedestrians, equestrians, and cyclists.

Linking up the Interurban Trail with Fragrance Lake Road creates a good out-and-back ride (16 miles round-trip). The pedaling on the compacted dirt and gravel trail is mostly easy. The path narrows and begins to zigzag as it drops into Arroyo Park. The climb out of the park is steep, short, and fun. There is one other short, steep hill before you arrive at the south end of the trail.

The gravel road to Fragrance Lake starts out as a gentle grade, but it soon becomes a very steep climb. Fragrance Lake Road is in good condition and is closed to public motor traffic. Your primary concern will be looking out for descending cyclists as you weave and waver your way to the top. After 2.3 miles you reach the end of the road and a trailhead. A short hiking trail leads

RIDE 70 INTERURBAN TRAIL AND FRAGRANCE LAKE

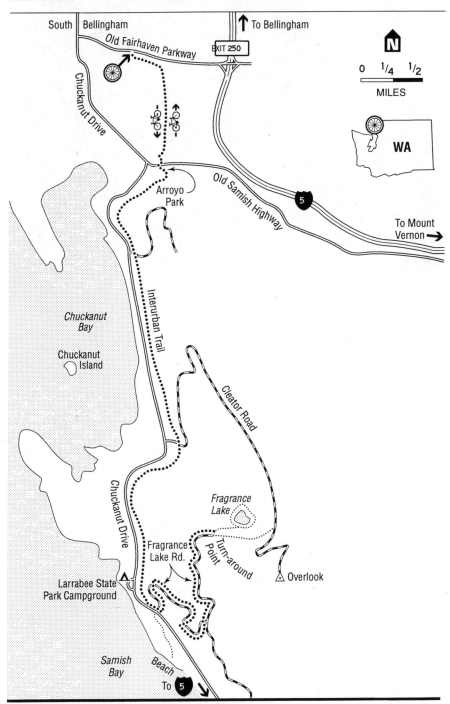

South Bellingham

Old Fairhaven Parkway

To Bellingham

EXIT 250

N

0   1/4   1/2
MILES

WA

Chuckanut Drive

Old Samish Highway

5

To Mount Vernon →

Arroyo Park

Chuckanut Bay

Chuckanut Island

Interurban Trail

Cleator Road

Fragrance Lake

Chuckanut Drive

Turn-around Point

Fragrance Lake Rd.

Overlook

Larrabee State Park Campground

Samish Bay

Beach

To 5 ↓

Sandy beach on Samish Bay.

to and around picturesque Fragrance Lake. The return road descent is exhilarating. Back at the Interurban Trail, you can lock your bike to a tree and walk down to a beach on Samish Bay. This hike is a one-mile round-trip.

General location: This ride starts from Old Fairhaven Parkway in South Bellingham, Washington.

Elevation change: The Interurban Trail begins at 100′ and climbs to 250′. Fragrance Lake lies at 1,170′. Ups and downs over the course of the trip add about 200′ of climbing to the ride. Total elevation gain: 1,270′.

Season: This ride can be enjoyed at any time of the year. July and August are nice—the route is well shaded, and ocean breezes help moderate the summer heat.

Services: There is no water on this ride. All services are available in Bellingham.

Hazards: Trail use is heaviest on summer holiday weekends. There are some blind corners in Arroyo Park—expect other trail users to be approaching. You may be sharing the trail with equestrians. Places where the trail crosses roads are poorly marked from both the cyclist's and the motorist's perspective. Be alert for intersections and approach them cautiously. Control your speed, and watch for loose gravel while descending from the lake. Although Fragrance Lake Road is closed to most traffic, you may encounter a Larrabee State Park

Fragrance Lake.

patrol or maintenance vehicle.

Rescue index: Help is available in Bellingham. In an emergency, assistance may be available at the campground in Larrabee State Park (off Chuckanut Drive). The campground has a pay phone and is staffed by a host.

Land status: State park lands and public right-of-way through private property.

Maps: A map by Rex N. Brainard called "Chuckanut Mountain Roads and Trails" is a good guide to this route and can be purchased at local bike shops and sporting goods stores. USGS 7.5 minute quad: Bellingham South.

Finding the trail: From Interstate 5 near Bellingham, take Exit 250 and follow the signs toward Chuckanut Drive and the Old Fairhaven Historic District. This will put you on Old Fairhaven Parkway, heading west. The trailhead for the Interurban Trail is on the left side of Old Fairhaven Parkway, .5

miles from I-5. Park on the side of Old Fairhaven Parkway.

Sources of additional information:

Whatcom County Parks and Recreation Department
3373 Mount Baker Highway
Bellingham, WA 98226
(206) 733-2900

Notes on the trail: Follow the trail to its southern terminus at Chuckanut Drive. Stay on the east side of Chuckanut Drive and walk your bike south—parallel the road, but stay off the pavement. In .1 miles, bear left into a large parking area. Go to the left of the white gate and turn onto Fragrance Lake Road. Ride to the end of the road, hike to the lake, and return the way you came.

Methow Valley Rides

The Methow Valley sits in the center of northern Washington, just east of North Cascades National Park. The valley has the "east of the Cascades" advantage: dry weather. In summer, temperatures in the daytime are moderate, while nights are cool. Sunny days are the standard fare.

The drive to the valley on the North Cascades Highway/WA 20 is great. The highway takes off from Interstate 5 near Burlington, south of Bellingham. As it proceeds east, the highway passes between the north and south sections of North Cascades National Park through some of the highest and wildest mountains in the state; it is incredibly picturesque. This stretch of highway is also a favorite with experienced touring bicyclists.

Dropping 3,600 feet from Washington Pass, the highway enters the open spaces of the Methow Valley. The valley is world-famous for its network of cross-country ski trails. It is becoming equally well known for its mountain biking. Surrounding the valley is the Okanogan National Forest, which contains hundreds of miles of outstanding single-tracks and scenic forest roads.

The valley has long been courted for its downhill ski resort potential. Developers fancy the area's plentiful snowpack, rolling hills, and high peaks. Valley residents have resisted this type of growth for over 25 years. Many would like to see the continued development of trail-based resorts. (One such resort is the elegant and already thriving Sun Mountain Lodge.) Some envision gondolas to a mountaintop for access not to alpine skiing but to a massive trail system.

This "trail-friendly" attitude gives the area a wonderful ambience. The Methow Valley Sport Trails Association has been a catalyst for community pride and trail development. The association was originally formed to maintain the area's cross-country ski trails. Now its members maintain many of the bike routes in the region as well. The association produces an excellent quarterly newsletter, "Trails," and brings the popular Methow Valley Mountain Bike Festival to the valley each October.

Winthrop is the center of tourism in the Methow Valley. The town operates on a western theme—with wooden sidewalks, storefronts, hitching posts, etc. It is quaint and quirky, with many fine accommodations, restaurants, and interesting shops.

Less than three miles out of Winthrop is Pearrygin Lake. Nestled in sagebrush hills, this state park provides visitors with camping and hot showers. Camping is also plentiful in the surrounding forests. Stop in at the national forest ranger stations in Twisp and Winthrop for information.

261

Twisp River Trail.

RIDE 71 *TWISP RIVER TRAIL*

The first half of this moderately difficult 13-mile loop is on a good single-track trail. The remainder is on well-maintained paved and gravel roads. Although the river is often audible from the trail, views of the water are rare. Clearings offer excellent vistas to Reynolds Peak in the Lake Chelan–Sawtooth Wilderness. Open, sunny areas are jammed with wildflowers in the spring and summer.

The Twisp River Trail #440 maintains a rather consistent elevation along its course. The pedaling is still demanding, however. The trail parallels the river on a forested hillside. There are no mountains to climb, but there are still plenty of ups and downs. Exposed roots, rocks, scree slopes, narrow sections,

Stiletto Peak and Twisp River Road.

steep drop-offs, and creek crossings are encountered along the way.

General location: The trailhead is 23 miles west of Twisp, Washington.
Elevation change: The trail starts at 3,400′ and quickly reaches a high point of 3,500′. Overall, the trail loses elevation as it heads east through many lesser hills and valleys. The road riding begins at 2,860′ and returns to 3,400′. Undulations add approximately 500′ of climbing to the ride. Total elevation gain: 1,140′.
Season: Wildflower displays in the spring and summer are often spectacular. Call ahead to check on the condition of the trail—specifically, whether or not it is dry.
Services: Water can be obtained seasonally at the Poplar Flat Campground. All services are available in Twisp.
Hazards: You will encounter obstacles and conditions typical of single-track

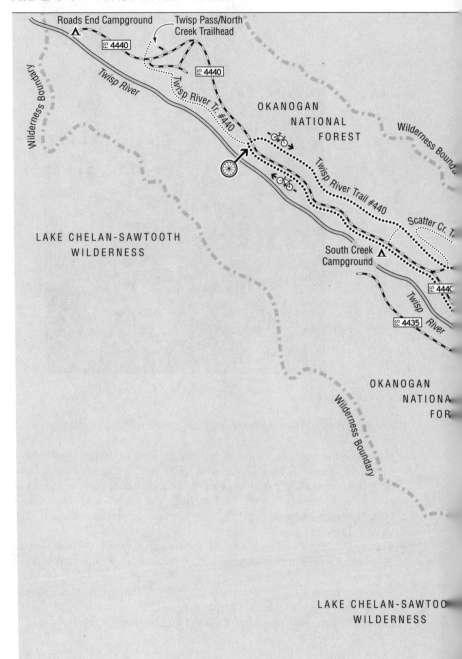

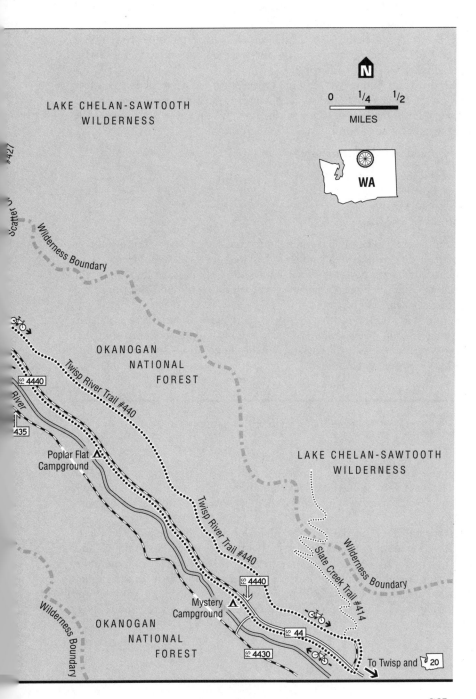

LAKE CHELAN-SAWTOOTH
WILDERNESS

N

0   1/4   1/2
MILES

WA

#427

Scatter Cr.

Wilderness Boundary

OKANOGAN
NATIONAL
FOREST

Twisp River Trail #440

FS 4440

River

435

Poplar Flat
Campground

Twisp River Trail #440

LAKE CHELAN-SAWTOOTH
WILDERNESS

Wilderness Boundary

Slate Creek Trail #414

FS 4440

Mystery
Campground

FS 44

Wilderness Boundary

OKANOGAN
NATIONAL
FOREST

FS 4430

To Twisp and 20

trails. Walk your bike across scree slopes.

Rescue index: The nearest help is in Twisp.

Land status: Okanogan National Forest.

Maps: The trail was built in 1991 and was not delineated on Forest Service maps or USGS quads at the time of our research. Check with the Twisp Ranger District for updated maps.

Finding the trail: From WA 20 in Twisp, turn west onto Twisp River Road/Forest Service Road 44. Stay on the north side of the river and drive 23 miles; park in the pullout on the left where the Twisp River Trail crosses the road, 1.4 miles west of South Creek Campground.

Sources of additional information:

Twisp Ranger District
P.O. Box 188
Twisp, WA 98856
(509) 997-2131

Notes on the trail: The official trailhead for the Twisp River Trail is another mile west of the parking area/trailhead that we have suggested. Heavy spring runoff had damaged portions of the trail and made passage difficult at the time of our visit. The Forest Service was in the process of building bridges and relocating segments of the trail.

The ride starts on the north side of the road, across from the recommended parking pullout. You should have little trouble finding your way along the Twisp River Trail—it is well marked. When you get to FS 44, turn right and pedal back to your vehicle.

RIDE 72 *LIGHTNING CREEK TRAIL*

Half of this 16-mile loop is a climb on gravel roads. The other half is a fun, fairly technical descent on single-track Lightning Creek Trail #425. The trip is short on views, but the cycling is pleasant as you pass through an open, sunny forest.

Overall, the climb on the forest roads is long and demanding. The ascent includes 4.5 miles of easy pedaling, 2.4 miles that are moderately difficult, and 1.3 miles that can be described as strenuous. There are also some short stretches of downhill and level riding. The road and trail surfaces are in good condition. Lightning Creek Trail passes through some rocky sections and some sandy areas. There are a couple of creek crossings where you are likely to get your feet wet.

RIDE 72 *LIGHTNING CREEK TRAIL*

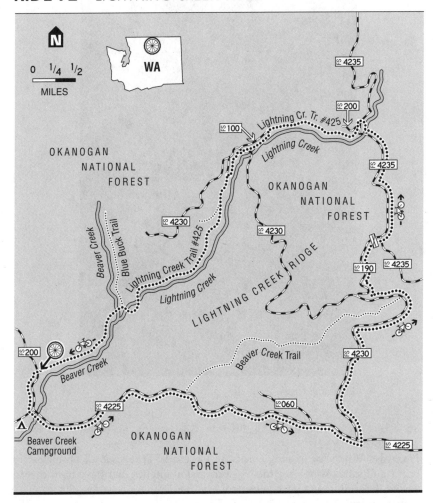

General location: The trailhead is 15 miles southeast of Winthrop, Washington, and 10 miles northeast of Twisp, Washington.

Elevation change: The ride starts at 2,800′ and reaches a high point of 5,200′ near the Lightning Creek Trailhead. Undulations add about 300′ of climbing to the loop. Total elevation gain: 2,700′.

Season: The trail is usually free of snow from mid-June through October. Avoid cycling here during hunting season.

Lightning Creek Trail.

Services: There is no water on this ride. All services can be found in Twisp and Winthrop.

Hazards: Watch for logging trucks on the roads. Primary trail obstacles are rocks and sand. Watch for the small diversion ditches that have been carved across the trail in an effort to control erosion.

Rescue index: The nearest help is in Twisp.

Land status: Okanogan National Forest.

Maps: The district map of the Twisp Ranger District is a good guide to this ride. USGS 7.5 minute quads: Blue Buck Mountain and Loup Loup Summit.

Finding the trail: From Winthrop, drive south through town on WA 20. Turn left onto Eastside Winthrop–Twisp Road where WA 20 swings right to cross a steel bridge over the Methow River. (Stay on the east side of the river and follow the signs for the airport.) Proceed on Eastside Winthrop–Twisp Road for 6.5 miles to Balky Hill Road on the left. Turn left onto Balky Hill Road and travel 4.5 miles to Upper Beaver Creek Road. Go left on Upper Beaver Creek Road and drive 3.4 miles to the intersection of Forest Service roads 4225 and 200. Bear left up FS 200 and drive .4 miles to a group of campsites on the right. Turn right and park.

From Twisp, drive east on WA 20. Turn left to stay on WA 20 where WA 153 goes right toward Wenatchee. In another 2.9 miles, turn left onto Beaver Creek Road (a sign points left toward Beaver Creek). Travel 5.9 miles to the intersection of FS 4225 and FS 200. Bear left up FS 200 and drive .4 miles to a group of campsites on the right. Turn right and park.

Sources of additional information:

Twisp Ranger District
P.O. Box 188
Twisp, WA 98856
(509) 997-2131

Notes on the trail: Coast down FS 200 and turn left onto FS 4225. Follow FS 4225 for 4 miles and turn left onto FS 4230. Pedal another 2.8 miles and make a right onto FS 190. After 1.2 miles on FS 190, you will pass through a gate and reach unsigned FS 4235. Turn left onto FS 4235, and stay on this road as spur roads branch off. FS 4235 crosses Lightning Creek after 1.4 miles, then intersects with FS 200 in another .2 miles. Go left onto FS 200 and immediately bear left to pick up the Lightning Creek Trail (do not follow FS 200). After 1.4 miles, the single-track trail enters a clear-cut and becomes more roadlike. (The trail follows closed FS 100 here.) Next, the trail crosses a couple of trenches and deposits you at unsigned FS 4230. Turn right on this main road and descend a short distance (.1 miles) to a spur road on the left (closed FS 125). Turn left onto the old road and pass through a couple more trenches. (You are now back on unsigned Lightning Creek Trail.) In another .8 miles you will arrive at a Y intersection. Stay to the left and follow the trail to your vehicle.

RIDE 73 METHOW TRAIL / SUN MOUNTAIN TRAILS

The 6.3-mile Methow Trail is a combination of single-tracks, double-tracks, gravel roads, and a touch of pavement. All of these parts form a link between the town of Winthrop and a concentrated network of loops known as the Sun Mountain Trails. The Sun Mountain Trails comprise 30 miles of single-tracks, double-tracks, and gravel roads used by equestrians, hikers, runners, cyclists,

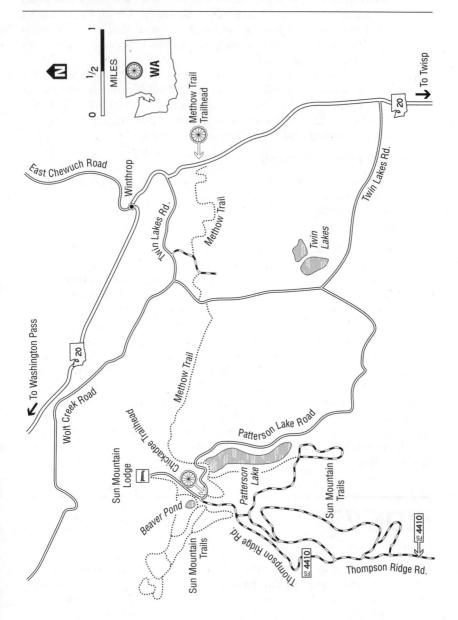

Little Wolf Trail on Sun Mountain.

and cross-country skiers. You would be hard-pressed to find an area with a greater variety of routes and settings.

From the valley floor, the Methow Trail climbs west toward Patterson Lake and into the mountains. The difficulty of the climb and the technical difficulty of the trail vary constantly. There are 2.7 miles of easy, 1.2 miles of moderate, and .3 miles of steep ascending. In addition, there are over two miles of level and downhill terrain. The hardest stretch of uphill comes after about three miles of pedaling, where a double-track stair-steps up a drainage. Most of the ride is on good surfaces, but there are many sections of loose and/or embedded rocks and a couple of short sandy stretches.

Sun Mountain Trails offer circuits suitable to all ability levels. The easiest loops are via Chickadee, Beaver Pond, and Little Wolf trails. Pathways that branch off from these easier routes offer cyclists some intermediate challenges.

Tougher routes include the Overland, Criss-Cross, Inside Passage, Meadow Lark, and Patterson Lake trails.

General location: The Methow Trail begins in Winthrop, Washington.
Elevation change: The trailhead for the Methow Trail lies at 1,760′. The Chickadee Parking Lot trailhead for the Sun Mountain Trails lies at 2,600′. Ups and downs along the way add about 200′ of climbing to the ride. Total elevation gain: 1,040′. Rides on the Sun Mountain Trails can involve negligible amounts of elevation gain (Beaver Pond Loop) or sizeable doses of climbing (Thompson Ridge Road tops out at about 3,640′).
Season: It is often dry enough to ride here in the late spring. Snow may begin falling in October.
Services: There is no water available on the ride. Water and all services can be found in Winthrop. The Sun Mountain Lodge offers dining and accommodations.
Hazards: Note the location of the barbed-wire gate you pass through while climbing on the Methow Trail—you will approach it from around a corner on the return. Watch for traffic on the roads. Yield to horses and pedestrians.
Rescue index: Help can be found in Winthrop.
Land status: The Methow Trail crosses private property on its way to public lands; the general public is encouraged to use the trail responsibly. The Sun Mountain Trails are in the Okanogan National Forest.
Maps: These trails are not delineated on National Forest maps or the USGS quads. We recommend the Methow Valley Sport Trails Association's "Sun Mountain Ski Trails" map and the "Summer Hiking and Mountain Biking Trail Map and Guide" produced by the Sun Mountain Lodge.
Finding the trail: The trailhead for the Methow Trail is next to WA 20 in Winthrop. To find it, drive south through town on WA 20. Follow the highway as it swings hard to the right, crossing a steel bridge over the Methow River. After you cross the bridge, bear left, staying on WA 20. From the bridge, it is about .5 miles to the trailhead (on the right side of the highway, across from the Marigot–Best Western Hotel). There is no room to park on the west side of the highway near the trailhead. Turn around and head north on the highway. Turn right and pull well off the highway to park near the "Rodeo" sign (just south of the Evergreen Grocery and Hardware).

To drive to the Chickadee trailhead and day-use parking for the Sun Mountain Trails, drive south through Winthrop on WA 20. After crossing the steel bridge over the river, bear right and follow the signs for Sun Mountain Lodge. The parking area is on the left about .5 miles beyond the Patterson Lake Cabins (about 9 miles from town).

Sources of additional information:

Twisp Ranger District
P.O. Box 188
Twisp, WA 98856
(509) 997-2131

Winthrop Ranger District
P.O. Box 579
Winthrop, WA 98862
(509) 996-2266

Methow Valley Sport Trails Association
P.O. Box 147
Winthrop, WA 98862
(509) 996-3287

Sun Mountain Lodge
P.O. Box 1000
Winthrop, WA 98862
(509) 996-2211

Notes on the trail: Some of the Sun Mountain Trails are closed to bikes. Kraule and Ridge are off-limits to cyclists at all times. Sunnyside and Beaver Pond are closed after 5 P.M.

At the time of our research, the Methow Trail was well marked and easy to follow. Although the Sun Mountain Trails were marked, a map and a compass were helpful directional aids.

RIDE 74 *BUCK LAKE LOOP*

This 13-mile loop is moderately difficult and involves about 4.5 miles of climbing. These uphills are evenly divided between easy and moderately difficult grades; one-quarter mile is strenuous. Nearly 70 percent of the ride follows level terrain or descends. About half of the route is paved; the other half is on compacted dirt roads and gravel roads in good condition. There is a short uphill stretch of degraded double-track where you must push your bike.

Buck Lake is a nice place to camp, fish, or enjoy a picnic lunch. Deer and other wildlife are often observed near the shore. The sun-drenched hillsides south of the lake are awash with wildflowers in the spring and summer. There are some nice views of the Cub Creek and Chewuch River drainages from Forest Service Road 140.

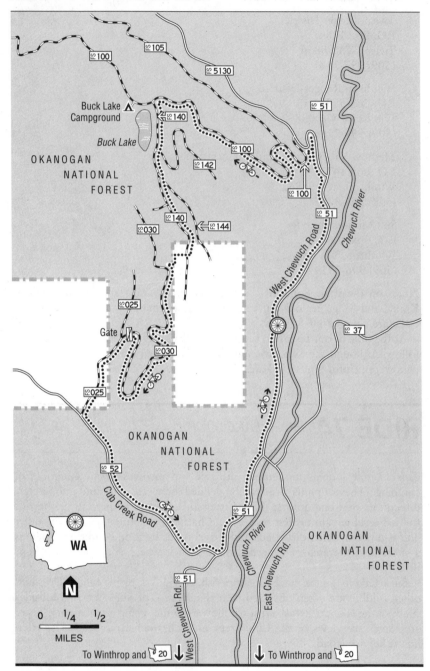

Buck Lake Loop.

General location: This ride starts approximately 8 miles north of Winthrop, Washington.

Elevation change: The ride begins at 2,080′ and climbs to a high point of 3,260′. Ups and downs encountered along the route add about 200′ of climbing to the ride. Total elevation gain: 1,380′.

Season: The roads around Buck Lake are usually free of snow by June. Locals enjoy mountain biking from the late spring through the fall. The Methow Valley is busy with tourists during the summer.

Services: There is no water on this ride. Water and all services are available in Winthrop.

Hazards: Be extra careful on the paved roads. They are quite narrow, and traffic moves along at a good clip. Wear shoes that provide good traction for the push up the double-track that connects FS 140 to FS 030; it is steep, rutted, and sandy. There are two cattle guards: one across FS 140 at Buck Lake, and one across FS 025 near its intersection with Cub Creek Road.

Rescue index: Help is available in Winthrop.

Land status: Okanogan National Forest lands and public right-of-way through private property.

Maps: The district map of the west half of the Winthrop Ranger District is a good guide to this ride. USGS 7.5 minute quad: Lewis Butte.

Finding the trail: In Winthrop, turn north onto West Chewuch Road/FS 51 (across from the Red Barn auditorium). Follow it for 7.8 miles to signed FS 015 (on the right, .9 miles north of the intersection of West Chewuch and East Chewuch roads). FS 015 leads downhill into the defunct Memorial Campground. Turn right onto FS 015 and park on the roadside.

Sources of additional information:

Winthrop Ranger District
P.O. Box 579
Winthrop, WA 98862
(509) 996-2266

Methow Valley Sport Trails Association
P.O. Box 147
Winthrop, WA 98862
(509) 996-3287

Notes on the trail: Follow West Chewuch Road north. Turn left onto paved FS 5130 (marked by a sign that points left toward Buck Lake), then turn left onto gravel FS l00. Climb to FS 140 and turn left to follow the sign for the boat ramp (right goes to the campground). Follow the road along the lakeshore. You will cross a cattle guard and then arrive at an unmarked intersection at the south end of the lake. Turn right. Soon the road starts to descend; follow the main road downhill. About 1 mile beyond the lake, the double-track emerges from the woods onto grassy hillsides. Ride through this more open environment for a short distance to an intersection in a group of pine trees. Look to the right for a large rock and a double-track that goes right and climbs very steeply up the hillside. Turn right and push your bike up this double-track. It tops out in .1 miles, swings to the left (south), and promptly comes to an intersection with another double-track that goes right (west). Continue straight and in a southerly direction; you are now on unsigned FS 030. From here, portions of the route are marked with bike route symbols. Descend on FS 030 to a locked gate. Pass around the side of the gate and immediately come to the unsigned intersection of FS 030 and FS 025. Stay left and downhill, on FS 025. You will cross a cattle guard before arriving at unsigned, paved Cub Creek Road. Turn left and follow Cub Creek Road down to West Chewuch Road. Turn left onto West Chewuch Road and pedal back to your vehicle.

RIDE 75 GOAT WALL LOOP

Goat Wall is a huge granite outcropping that looms high above the western end of the Methow Valley. The views from the top of this escarpment are outstanding. Below you are pasturelands and residences bordering the Methow River; above are the jagged peaks that surround Washington Pass. Fit cyclists with a taste for vistas will appreciate this demanding 28-mile road ride.

The first seven miles switchback up 2,560 feet. The ascent is evenly divided between easy and moderately difficult climbing, with about one-half mile of steep hills. This climb is followed by a 1.5-mile descent into Black Pine Basin. Then the road rolls up and down through the basin for close to three miles and climbs again for two miles. You descend from this point to meet Lost River Road. The last eight miles are an easy paved road ride back to your vehicle.

Most of the roads are gravel and in good condition. The four miles that descend from the mountain are on a weathered dirt road that drops off like a high dive.

General location: This ride begins approximately 11.5 miles northwest of Winthrop, Washington.

Elevation change: The ride begins at 2,240′ and climbs to 4,800′ atop Goat Wall. A high point of 5,000′ occurs after the climb out of Black Pine Basin. Undulations on the ride add an estimated 500′ of climbing to the trip. Total elevation gain: 3,260′.

Season: The ride is best from the late spring through the fall.

Services: There is no water on this ride. Water is available seasonally at the Early Winters Campground on WA 20. Phone, gas, limited groceries, and espresso are available at the Mazama Country Store. All services can be found in Winthrop.

Hazards: Stay in control while descending on Forest Service Road 100; it is a steep and degraded dirt road. Ride defensively and watch for traffic at all times.

Rescue index: Help can be found in Winthrop. You may also be able to obtain assistance in Mazama.

Land status: Okanogan National Forest.

Maps: The district map of the west half of the Winthrop Ranger District is a good guide to this route. USGS 7.5 minute quads: Rendezvous Mountain, Mazama, and McLeod Mountain.

Finding the trail: From locations to the west, drive east on WA 20 from Early

RIDE 75   GOAT WALL LOOP

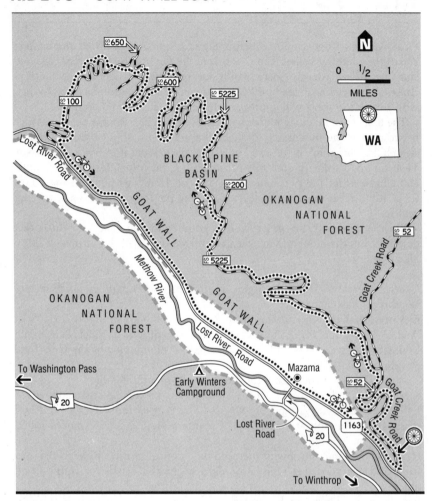

Winters Campground. In 1.9 miles, turn left onto Lost River Road toward Mazama. Cross the river and bear to the right onto County Road 1163 in Mazama. Turn left onto gravel Goat Creek Road/FS 52 in another 1.9 miles. From locations to the east, travel west from Winthrop on WA 20. After 7 miles on WA 20, turn right onto CR 1163 (just before the bridge over the Winthrop River), where a sign directs you toward Hart's Pass and Goat Creek Road. Drive 4.5 miles on CR 1163 and turn right onto Goat Creek Road/FS 52. Proceed down FS 52 for .3 miles and turn right onto a spur road. Park in the clearing.

The Methow Valley from Goat Wall.

Sources of additional information:

Winthrop Ranger District
P.O. Box 579
Winthrop, WA 98862
(509) 996-2266

Methow Valley Sport Trails Association
P.O. Box 147
Winthrop, WA 98862
(509) 996-3287

Notes on the trail: Continue on FS 52 for 2.3 miles to an intersection where FS 5225 breaks off hard left and FS 52 goes straight. Turn left onto FS 5225 toward Goat Peak Lookout. Stay on the main road as spur roads break off to the left and right. Notice the mileposts that mark this road—the Goat Wall viewpoint is .3 miles beyond milepost 4. After checking out the view, continue on FS 5225 for nearly 5 miles to a Y intersection at signed FS 600. Turn right onto FS 600 and climb to the high point of the ride, which occurs at a cattle guard and a green gate. FS 600 descends briskly from this spot. Slow down after FS 600 switchbacks hard to the right, 1 mile past the cattle guard. Descend for another .5 miles to unmarked FS 650, which is marked by an orange, diamond-shaped symbol on a tree; the road crosses a wet, open area. Turn right onto FS 650; bear left at a fire ring and left again where an overgrown road goes right at a T intersection. You are now on unsigned FS 100. Rag-doll down the hill for several miles; you will emerge into a meadow near two vault toilets. Continue straight, then turn left onto unsigned, paved Lost River Road. Follow the pavement back to FS 52 and your vehicle.

Colville National Forest

The relatively remote Colville National Forest is fast developing a reputation as a good destination for mountain biking. Tucked into the northeast corner of Washington, the forest shares borders with British Columbia to the north and Idaho to the east. Spokane lies to the south and supplies the forest with most of its visitors.

The old gold-mining town of Republic is the center of activity in the western part of the forest. South of town is the Lakes Area of the Republic Ranger District. Some of the roads and double-tracks in this part of the forest have been closed to motor traffic. These routes are slowly being absorbed back into the woods. Some are beginning to feel more like trails than roads.

The district hosts a fat-tire festival each year to promote all-terrain biking. Group rides of varying lengths and difficulties highlight the weekend. The event is held at Swan Lake Campground, an excellent base for exploring in the Lakes Area.

East of Republic on WA 20 is Sherman Pass. At 5,575 feet, it is the highest highway pass in Washington. Extending north and south from the gap is the 30-mile long Kettle Crest Trail. Many loops and shuttle rides can be created by combining Kettle Crest Trail with spur trails that drop off the ridge.

Continuing east on WA 20, you cross the Columbia River near Kettle Falls; pass through Colville, the region's largest community; and then enter the Little Pend Oreille Chain of Lakes Recreation Area. The region is packed with multi-use trails, good camping facilities, and resort services.

The extreme northeast corner of the forest is administered by the Sullivan Lake Ranger District. The riding on Hall Mountain above Sullivan Lake is an outstanding mix of gravel roads and single-tracks. Wildlife viewing is an added bonus in your travels through this part of the country.

Driving south from Sullivan Lake toward Spokane brings you past the Newport Ranger District. The rangers in this part of the forest are actively involved in promoting mountain biking. Cross-country ski trails and forest roads near Newport are seeing increased two-wheeled traffic from locals and visitors alike. There is an especially pleasant loop at Bead Lake; this outing features a single-track that drops out of the mountains to skirt the eastern shore of the lake.

RIDE 76 *SWAN LAKE TRAIL / LAKES AREA MOUNTAIN BIKE ROUTES*

The Lakes Area (south of Republic, Washington) offers many miles of pleasant cycling on gravel roads. Some of the roads are closed to motor vehicles, and several loops have been signed as mountain bike routes. Many of the outings are easy; others make good training rides. This chapter describes a relatively easy 7.6-mile loop. Beginners will find the circuit challenging. The route includes an excellent 1.6-mile single-track trip around Swan Lake.

The road conditions vary considerably. Much of the ride is on double-tracks that are slowly becoming trail-like. There is also riding on good gravel roads, rough spurs, and a short stretch of pavement. The trail around Swan Lake is in good shape. The single-track has some challenging sections, but pushing your bike through them is only moderately difficult.

General location: Swan Lake is approximately 15 miles southwest of Republic, Washington.

Elevation change: The ride begins at 3,700′ and descends to a low point of 3,320′ at Forest Service roads 350 and 100. From here, the route climbs to meet the Swan Lake Trail at 3,640′. Ups and downs on the roads add approximately 300′ of climbing to the trip. Swan Lake Trail adds about 200′. Total elevation gain: 880′.

Season: The period from spring through fall is the best time to ride in this area. Swan Lake is a popular destination on summer weekends. Avoid hunting season.

Services: There is no water on this ride. Water, food, lodging, groceries, and gas are available in Republic.

Hazards: Expect some traffic on the main forest roads. There are areas of sand and some large ruts on FS 640. You will encounter embedded rocks, roots, and log bridges on Swan Lake Trail.

Rescue index: Help can be found in Republic.

Land status: Colville National Forest.

Maps: A handout and map on the area's mountain bike opportunities can be obtained from the Republic Ranger District. USGS 7.5 minute quad: Swan Lake.

Finding the trail: From the intersection of WA 20 and WA 21 in Republic, follow WA 21 south. Turn right after 6.7 miles onto Scatter Creek Road/FS 53 toward Swan Lake. You will arrive at Swan Lake Campground in 7.3 miles. Continue straight on FS 53 for another .25 miles to a parking area on the left near a gate and the beginning of FS 075. Park on the left near the information board.

RIDE 76 *SWAN LAKE TRAIL /*
LAKES AREA MOUNTAIN BIKE ROUTES

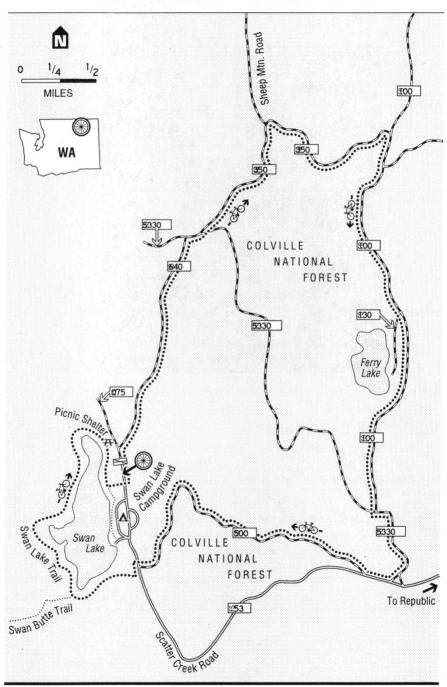

Swan Lake.

Sources of additional information:

Republic Ranger District
P.O. Box 468
Republic, WA 99166
(509) 775-3305

Notes on the trail: From the parking area, go through the open gate on FS 075, then immediately turn right onto unsigned FS 640. This old road is blocked by a couple of large rocks and is marked with a bike symbol (as is much of the route). You will reach unsigned FS 5330 after 1 mile of pedaling. Turn right, then immediately turn left onto FS 350 at a bike symbol. Stay on the main double-track for .8 miles to an intersection where Sheep Mountain Road goes left. Turn right to remain on FS 350. You will reach FS 100 at a T

Near the south end of Swan Lake.

intersection in another .5 miles. Turn right onto FS 100. Continue straight at the next juncture of roads, where FS 130 goes right toward Ferry Lake. Turn left onto FS 5330, toward Scatter Creek, at the next T intersection. After crossing a cattle guard, turn right at a Y intersection, then turn right again onto paved, unsigned FS 53/Scatter Creek Road. In .2 miles, turn right onto double-track FS 500, toward Swan Lake Road. Follow this road for 1.4 miles to paved FS 53/Scatter Creek Road. Turn left and immediately turn right onto Swan Lake Trail. Remain on Swan Lake Trail where Swan Butte Trail goes left, after .4 miles of single-track. Stay on the main trail to the picnic shelter at the north end of the lake. Continue past the shelter along the lakeshore. Just after passing the first beach, bear left onto a side trail, and stay to the left as you climb away from the water. Pass through a tent campsite; you will emerge onto FS 53 and your vehicle to the left.

RIDE 77 _KETTLE CREST / SHERMAN TRAIL_

This loop—a strenuous 17.2-mile ride—follows trails for 6.6 miles, gravel roads for 6.2 miles, and pavement for 4.6 miles. The most challenging part is the initial climb on Kettle Crest Trail. From Sherman Pass on WA 20, Kettle Crest Trail switchbacks up White Mountain for a mile; it is steep and hoof-worn in places. Short "breaks" between the most technical spots keep it rideable. This climb is followed by a gentle traverse around Columbia Mountain and some moderately difficult (but short) climbs near Jungle Hill. Much of the descent from Kettle Crest involves tight, rocky switchbacks. Sherman Trail ties into gravel roads that lead out to WA 20. The climb back up to the pass is on a two-lane highway—a grind only a touring cyclist could love. It is actually an easy grade, but you will be taxed after five miles of it.

The highlights of this ride are its challenging start and miles of pleasant single-track cruising. Climbing up the highway, you look out over 20,000 acres of wasteland—the result of the 1988 White Pine Mountain fire. On the highway there is an interpretive display about the fire. The display gives you a good excuse for taking a break from the climb, but it is hard to make devastation interesting.

General location: The trailhead is at Sherman Pass, approximately 17 miles east of Republic, Washington.

Elevation change: The ride begins at 5,600′ and tops out at 6,500′ on Kettle Crest Trail. The low point of the route is 4,260′. Ups and downs on the loop add approximately 300′ of climbing to the trip. Total elevation gain: 2,540′.

Season: The best riding here is in the summer, after the snow has melted and the trail has had a chance to dry.

Services: There is no water on this ride. Water, food, lodging, groceries, and gas are available in Republic.

Hazards: Obstacles on the trails include rocks, roots, and tight switchbacks. The gravel roads contain ruts and cattle guards. The riding on WA 20 is probably the most dangerous part of the trip. Traffic is usually light, but it moves along at a good clip.

Rescue index: Help can be found in Republic.

Land status: Colville National Forest.

Maps: The forest map for the Colville National Forest is a suitable guide to this route. The USGS topographic maps are more detailed and are a better source of information. USGS 7.5 minute quads: Sherman Peak, Edds Mountain, Copper Butte, and Cooke Mountain.

Finding the trail: From locations to the west, follow WA 20 east from Republic for 17 miles to Sherman Pass. From locations to the east, take WA

RIDE 77 *KETTLE CREST / SHERMAN TRAIL*

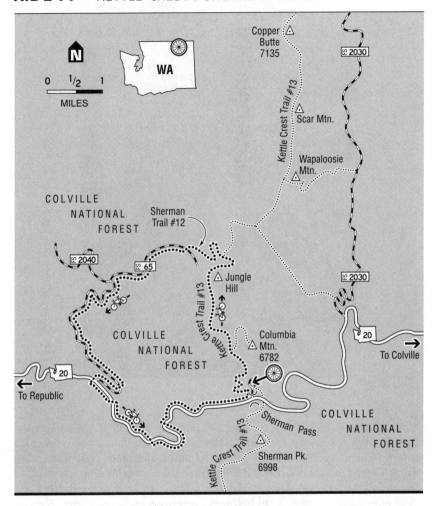

20 west from Colville for 36 miles to Sherman Pass. Turn onto FS 495 at the "Trailhead" sign. Follow FS 495 north to a cul-de-sac and park your vehicle.

Sources of additional information:

Republic Ranger District
P.O. Box 468
Republic, WA 99166
(509) 775-3305

Kettle Crest Trail.

Notes on the trail: From the parking area, ride back up FS 495 and turn right onto Kettle Crest Trail #13 North. After a little more than 2 miles, continue straight where Kettle Crest Trail meets Columbia Mountain Trail. Remain on Kettle Crest Trail for another 3.2 miles, through a switchbacking descent, to Sherman Trail #12. Continue straight onto Sherman Trail where Kettle Crest Trail goes right. Sherman Trail becomes overgrown and grassy after .6 miles. Continue straight; the trail soon switchbacks to the left and becomes obvious again. Turn right and descend when you reach FS 65. Both the descent and FS 65 end at unsigned FS 2040. Turn left onto FS 2040. Stay on the main road; you will reach WA 20 in 3.8 miles. Turn left onto the highway and climb back up to the pass.

RIDE 78 *FRATER LAKE*

Frater Lake is one of the eight glacial lakes that make up the Little Pend Oreille chain in northeastern Washington. Frater Lake Trail #150 is part of a 15-mile network of cross-country ski trails. This 4.3-mile loop serves as an introduction to the mountain bike opportunities in the area. The region is also home to the Little Pend Oreille Trails, a 75-mile system of multi-use trails designated for off-road motorcycling, hiking, horseback riding, and mountain biking.

About half of the route is on single-tracks in mostly good condition. The other half is on rough double-track roads. The loop has a fairly low elevation gain, but it does contain some steep ascents and rocky stretches. Overall, the terrain is rolling, with a significant number of ups and downs. The trail winds through dense forest and boggy areas and past rocky outcrops, meadows, and clear-cuts.

General location: Frater Lake is approximately 30 miles northeast of Colville, Washington.

Elevation change: The ride begins at 3,220′ and reaches a high point of 3,430′. Ups and downs add an estimated 200′ of climbing to the loop. Total elevation gain: 410′.

Season: The Little Pend Oreille Lakes region is known for its wild berries. Gorge yourself on huckleberries, gooseberries, and currants in July and August. The trails can be boggy in the spring and early summer. Avoid busy summer weekends.

Services: There is no water on the ride. Water, food, lodging, groceries, and gas can be obtained in Ione, approximately 10 miles northeast of the trailhead on WA 31.

Hazards: Portions of the trail are open to motorcycles; remain alert for approaching traffic. Ski trails are easier to follow in the winter; keep your eyes peeled for the blue diamond-shaped symbols affixed to the trees.

Rescue index: Help is available in Colville.

Land status: Colville National Forest.

Maps: The district map of the Colville Ranger District is a useful guide to this outing. USGS 7.5 minute quad: Ione.

Finding the trail: From Colville, at the intersection of US 395 and WA 20, follow WA 20 east toward Ione and Newport. Drive just over 29 miles to Frater Lake (on the left). You will pass a cross-country skier symbol just before the lake. Turn left off the highway to park in the pullout beside Frater Lake. From Ione, follow WA 31 south for 3.6 miles and turn right onto WA 20. Travel 6.3 miles to Frater Lake (on the right). A cross-country skier symbol is posted for

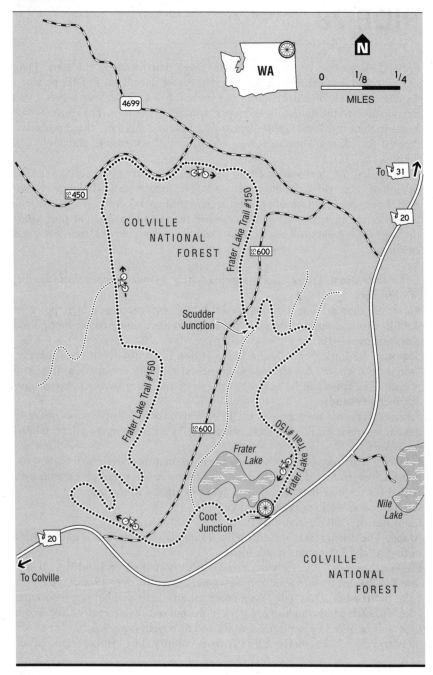

Frater Lake.

traffic approaching from this direction—you will pass it just before you reach the lake. Turn right to park in the pullout beside the lake.

Sources of additional information:

Colville Ranger District
755 S. Main
Colville, WA 99114
(509) 684-4557

Notes on the trail: From the parking area, pedal past the map and boat ramp, following a trail marked with blue diamond-shaped symbols. This trail will put you on a spur road that leads into a parking area. The trail continues at the end of the parking area—it is marked with blue diamonds. Turn left for Coyote Rock Loop when you reach Coot Junction. Cross a gravel road and continue the climb to Coyote Rock. Continue past the rock for .6 miles to a rutted multi-use trail on the left. Continue straight on the ski trail. The route gets boggy and then arrives at FS 450. Bear right and descend on the double-track for .3 miles to an indistinct trail on the right. (This trail is easy to miss. While descending on FS 450, look to the right for the faint trail marked by a blue diamond. You have overshot the trail by .1 miles if you arrive at a T intersection at a gravel road.) Follow the trail into the woods and chase the blue diamonds for .75 miles to Scudder Junction. Turn left for Tiger Loop. Shortly you will approach a fence bounding Teepee Seed Orchard. Do not pedal up the fence line; look farther to the right to find a blue diamond on a tree. Move toward it. The trail becomes more obvious and heads into the woods. Follow the blue diamonds. You will soon reach a Y intersection where both trails are signed with blue diamonds. Turn right. Choose the route marked with blue diamonds at the next two intersections. This will bring you to a barbed-wire gate. Pass through the gate and turn right onto a faint trail marked with a blue diamond (easy to miss). Parallel the highway back to your vehicle.

RIDE 79 *HALL MOUNTAIN LOOP*

Spectacular scenery and great single-track riding highlight this loop. You can see into Idaho and British Columbia from the top of Hall Mountain. There is also a good possibility of spotting Rocky Mountain bighorn sheep; a herd that ranges on the mountain is frequently seen from the trail. The ride is 24 miles long and suited to strong, experienced cyclists.

The first 8 miles follow pavement and hard-packed dirt roads—a nice warm-up for the 7.3-mile grind that follows. This long gravel road ascent is moderately difficult, with a few short, steep pitches. Dig deep at road's end for the 2.3-mile ascent on Hall Mountain Trail. It is moderately difficult, with some steep sections and some level riding. Descending on Hall Mountain Trail is fun, but dessert is served on Noisy Creek Trail. The first 1.5 miles feel like an E-Ticket ride at Disney World! Then, back to reality and two miles of creek crossings, rocky stretches, boggy areas, and technical climbs and descents. Noisy Creek Trail improves for a terrific 1.5-mile ending.

General location: The trailhead is located approximately 12 miles southeast of Metaline Falls, Washington.
Elevation change: The loop begins at 2,600' and reaches 2,880' at the intersection of Forest Service roads 22 and 500. It climbs steadily on FS 500 to Hall Mountain Trail at 5,280'. Hall Mountain Trail tops out at 6,323'. Ups and downs over the course of the ride add an estimated 300' of climbing to the ride. Total elevation gain: 4,023'.
Season: This ride is good from late June through September. Windfall may be a problem in the spring; find out if the trail has been cleared.
Services: Water is available seasonally at Noisy Creek Campground near the trailhead. There is a pay phone at the Sullivan Lake Ranger Station. Food, lodging, groceries, and gas can be obtained in Ione and Metaline Falls.
Hazards: Sullivan Lake Road is narrow and can get busy in the summer. In places Hall Mountain Trail narrows and drops off steeply to the side. Portions

RIDE 79 HALL MOUNTAIN LOOP

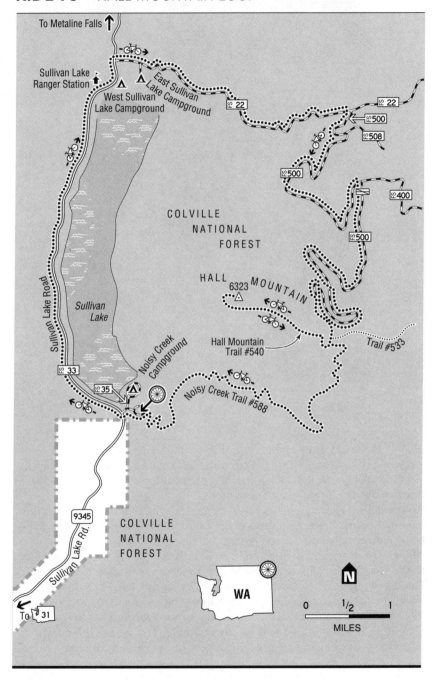

Hall Mountain Trail.

of Hall Mountain Trail contain logs that are hidden from view by tall grass. Sections of Noisy Creek Trail are narrow, scree-covered, steep, and extremely technical. Anticipate others approaching from around the next bend. Black bears and grizzly bears reside in the area.

Rescue index: Help can be found at the ranger station at Sullivan Lake during office hours. Emergency services are available in Ione and Metaline Falls.

Land status: Colville National Forest.

Maps: The district map of the Sullivan Lake Ranger District is a good guide to this ride. USGS 7.5 minute quads: Pass Creek and Metaline Falls.

Finding the trail: From the intersection of WA 20 and WA 31, follow WA 31 north. In 3.2 miles (.4 miles south of Ione), turn right onto County Road 9345/Sullivan Lake Road. This road is signed for Sullivan Lake and Sullivan Lake Ranger Station. Follow it for about 9 miles and turn right onto FS 35 into Noisy Creek Campground. Turn right in .1 miles onto a gravel road (marked by a hiker symbol). Follow this road past a vault toilet and park near the Noisy Creek Trailhead.

Sources of additional information:

Sullivan Lake Ranger District
12641 Sullivan Lake Road
Metaline Falls, WA 99153
(509) 446-2681

Notes on the trail: Ride back to Sullivan Lake Road and turn right. Follow the road around the lake. Pass West Sullivan Campground; in .3 miles, turn right onto FS 22. Stay on the main road for 3.3 miles and turn right onto FS 500. FS 500 ends at the trailhead for Hall Mountain Trail #540. Follow Hall Mountain Trail (an old double-track at first). Ride past Trail #533 (on the left); you will soon arrive at Noisy Creek Trail #588 (on the left). Continue straight toward Hall Mountain (you will follow Noisy Creek Trail later). The last .25 miles of the trail are unrideable. Park your bike and hike to the remains of the old lookout. Return down Hall Mountain Trail to the intersection with Noisy Creek Trail and turn right. Follow Noisy Creek Trail for 5 miles to your vehicle.

RIDE 80 BEAD LAKE LOOP

Bead Lake Loop is a scenic 17.7-mile ride recommended for intermediate and advanced cyclists. Gravel roads comprise 11.7 miles of the circuit; the first 2 miles are rough and steep. The rest of the climb up to Bead Lake Divide is easy to moderately difficult. The road surface improves too. Six-mile-long Bead Lake Trail varies in its condition. Most of it is a good, hard-packed dirt path. There are some precipitous scree slopes and five steep switchbacks on the descent to the lake. There is one monster climb in the last two miles of single-track.

The beginning of the ride features some nice vistas to the south of the Pend Oreille River and the Selkirks. Logging on Bead Divide has opened up some views. Below and to the west you can see Bead Lake. To the east are Idaho forests and mountains. Bead Lake Trail drops down to the water through a lush old forest. The route passes some huge white pines.

General location: The trail begins 10 miles northeast of Newport, Washington, which is 40 miles north of Spokane.
Elevation change: The ride starts at 2,865′ and reaches a high point of 4,400′. Ups and downs on the roads add approximately 300′ of climbing to the trip.

RIDE 80 *BEAD LAKE LOOP*

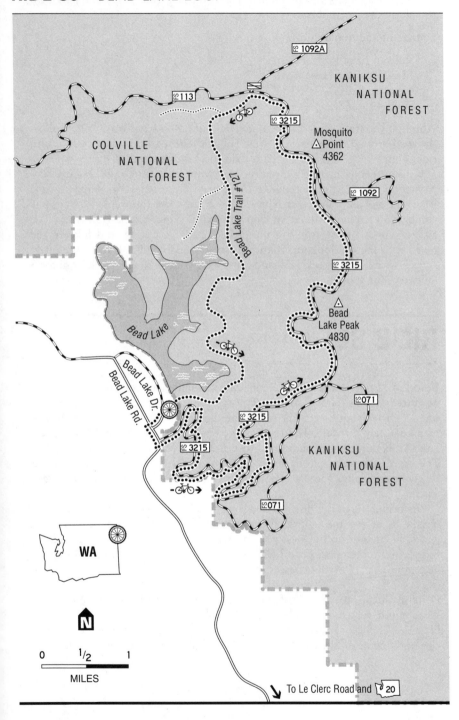

KANIKSU
NATIONAL
FOREST

COLVILLE
NATIONAL
FOREST

FS 1092A

FS 113

FS 3215

Mosquito
△ Point
4362

FS 1092

Bead Lake Trail #127

FS 3215

△
Bead
Lake Peak
4830

Bead Lake

FS 071

Bead Lake Dr.

Bead Lake Rd.

FS 3215

FS 3215

KANIKSU
NATIONAL
FOREST

FS 3215

FS 071

WA

N

0   ½   1

MILES

To Le Clerc Road and WA 20

Bead Lake Trail.

Undulations on the trail add about 500′. Total elevation gain: 2,335′.

Season: Portions of the trail become boggy during wet periods; plan on visiting in the summer or fall.

Services: There is no water on the ride. Water, food, lodging, groceries, and gas are available in Newport.

Hazards: The descent on Bead Lake Trail includes steep switchbacks and scree slopes. Some sections of the trail contain an abundance of forest litter. There is also some technical single-track along the lakeshore. Some segments of the path drop off steeply to the water, and some stretches are rocky. Stay alert for traffic on the forest roads. Black bears reside in the area.

Rescue index: Help can be found in Newport.

Land status: Colville National Forest.

Maps: The Colville National Forest map is a suitable guide to this route. USGS 7.5 minute quad: Bead Lake.

Finding the trail: From Newport, follow WA 2 east through Old Town, Idaho, and cross the Pend Oreille River. At the end of the bridge, turn left onto signed Le Clerc Road. Continue for 2.7 miles and turn right onto Bead Lake Road. Follow this road for 6 miles and turn right onto Bead Lake Drive. You will reach the trailhead on the right in .3 miles. There is room to park three or four cars. Do not block the gate.

Sources of additional information:

Newport Ranger District
P.O. Box 770
Newport, WA 99156
(509) 447-3129

Notes on the trail: Go back up the gravel road to the intersection with Bead Lake Road. Turn left and immediately turn left again onto Bead Lake Divide/Forest Service Road 3215. Continue on this main road for over 11 miles as spur roads go left and right. Just past the milepost 11 sign (on your right as you descend), at a clearing, look to the left for Bead Lake Trail #127. This is also the boundary between the Colville National Forest and the Kaniksu National Forest; here the road designation changes from FS 3215 to FS 113. Turn left onto the single-track. In .3 miles, turn left at a Y intersection where Divide Trail goes right. Continue straight at the next intersection (in 1.4 miles), where signed Bead Lake Spur Trail goes right. Stay on Bead Lake Trail to return to your vehicle.

Spokane Area Rides

Spokane, the largest city between Seattle and Minneapolis, is the commercial hub of a vast mining, lumbering, and agricultural region. Spokane is also emerging as one of the nation's fastest-growing bike-racing centers. City officials have been able to lure top-flight racing programs, like the 1984 and 1988 Olympic trials and the 1992 U.S. Nationals, to Spokane. Big-league mountain bike racing is scheduled to arrive here in 1994, in the shape of a Grundig World Cup event.

From its headwaters in northern Idaho, the Spokane River enters eastern Washington, then splits Spokane into two halves. Turning north, the river defines the western edge of the city. Here the riverside becomes a greenbelt of parks, arboretums, golf courses, and other open spaces for public enjoyment.

Riverside State Park is a wonderful recreation area on the Spokane River. Its 5,514 acres are tightly laced with single-tracks and closed roads. A foot-bridge near the park's campground crosses the turbulent river and offers access to the trails.

Another hotbed of mountain biking is found in Mt. Spokane State Park. Mt. Spokane sits in the middle of the park, and on summer weekends it crawls with mountain bikers plying their favorite trails.

RIDE 81 *RIVERSIDE STATE PARK*

Riverside State Park contains 8,000 acres of prime recreation land in the middle of Spokane. The area is crisscrossed with miles of trails, most of which are open to mountain bikes. The paths offer fun cycling to riders of all ability levels.

One of the most scenic trails follows the churning Spokane River past water-sculpted boulders and craggy cliffs. This 7.2-mile loop is moderately difficult. The route travels on 4.3 miles of single-track, 2.7 miles of dirt roads, and .2 miles of pavement. The trails and roads are in good condition, with some technical stretches of rock and sand.

General location: The park entrance is located approximately 6 miles northwest of downtown Spokane, Washington.
Elevation change: The ride begins at 1,580′ and follows the river downstream to 1,480′. You reach a high point of 1,640′ before dropping back to the trail-

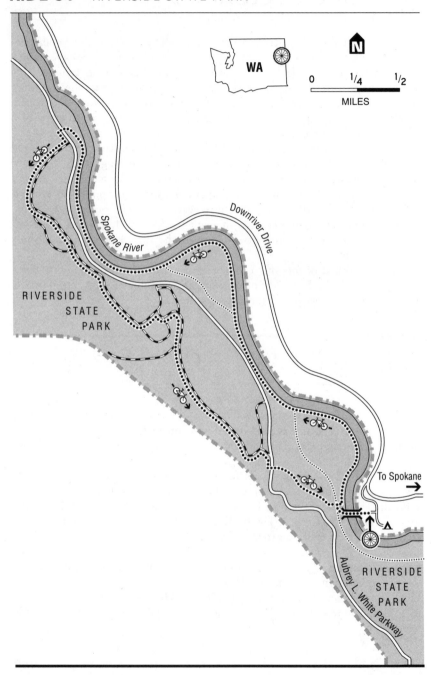

Jerry O'Neal, Ed Rockwell, and Kris Van Breda Kulff in
Riverside State Park.

head. Ups and downs add about 300′ of climbing to the loop. Total elevation
gain: 460′.

Season: The riding in the park is good from the spring through the fall.
Summer weekends can be very busy with fellow bikers, equestrians, runners,
and walkers. Anticipate other trail users at all times.

Services: Water, a pay phone, and toilets are located in the day-use area near
the beginning of the ride. All services are available in Spokane.

Hazards: Watch for rocks, soft surfaces, and other trail users. Control your
speed. The trails in the park are unsigned.

Rescue index: Help can be found at the park headquarters (near the campground). Emergency services are available in Spokane.

Land status: State park.

Maps: An excellent topo map of the park has been developed by the

Spokane River.

Washington State Orienteering Association. It can be purchased from the Recreational Equipment Inc. (REI) store in Spokane.

Finding the trail: From Interstate 90 in Spokane, take the Monroe Street exit. Drive north on Monroe Street for 1 mile to Boone Street (REI is located at this intersection). Turn left onto Boone and drive .4 miles, then turn right onto Maple Street. In three blocks, turn left onto Maxwell Street. Follow Maxwell Street as it swings right and becomes Downriver Drive. The road descends toward the Spokane River—stay to the left, traveling under the overpass at Meenach Drive. Continue along the east side of the river on Downriver Drive. Proceed past a municipal golf course (on the right) to the signed Riverside State Park entrance. Turn left to enter the park; follow the main road. Go past the first two day-use areas. Turn right at the third intersection—the road to the left goes to a pay phone, the campground, and park headquarters. Park in this day-use parking area.

Sources of additional information:

Riverside State Park
4427 Aubrey L. White Parkway
Spokane, WA 99205
(509) 456-3964

REI
North 1125 Monroe Street
Spokane, WA 99201
(509) 328-9900

Notes on the trail: You may wish to forgo these directions and simply rely on the recommended map and a compass. There are miles of trails and roads to explore.

From the day-use parking, find the paved path that leads toward the river; the path is across from the toilets. Ride down to the bridge and walk your bike across the bridge. Push your bike up the hill on the west side of the river. Stay to the right; you will pass a shelter. Bear to the right when you reach the top of the hill, and ride through the basalt outcrops. Shortly you will arrive at an intersection of paths at a wooden post in the trail. Turn right toward the river; soon the trail swings left, paralleling the water. As side trails branch off, choose the trail that keeps you beside the river. After about 3 miles of single-track, the trail climbs a hill and you can see some private residences on your right. Stay on the main trail as a faint trail goes right here. The trail climbs a little more, parallels a paved road, then turns left just beyond a white gate. You will find a trailhead sign on the right here. Turn left onto the pavement (Aubrey L. White Parkway) and ride .1 miles to the first gravel road on the right. Turn right onto this unsigned road. Stay on the main road (heading south) as side roads branch off. The gravel road comes close to the paved road near a gate. Stay on the main gravel road and reenter the woods. Pass a metal shed and turn left at the next intersection (the road becomes a double-track). Bear right at the next intersection and then left to stay on the main road. Begin a steep climb and stay to the right where a road comes in from the left. You will reach another intersection near the top of the hill—bear left. Descend sharply, following the main road. When you arrive at the paved road, cross it; you will regain the trail at three short, concrete posts. Stay on the trail as it hugs the hillside, climbs a little, and then descends the eroded hillside. Turn right when you come to the wooden post in the trail. Return the way you came.

RIDE 82 *MT. SPOKANE STATE PARK*

One of Mt. Spokane's chief attractions is winter recreation. Mountain biking and a spectacular summit view are the main draws for visitors during the summer months. The park's cross-country ski trails are popular with beginning mountain bikers, while miles of unmapped single-track trails delight more advanced riders.

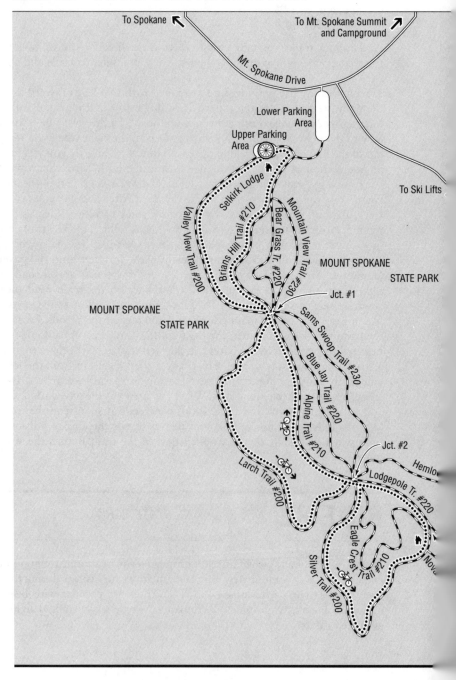

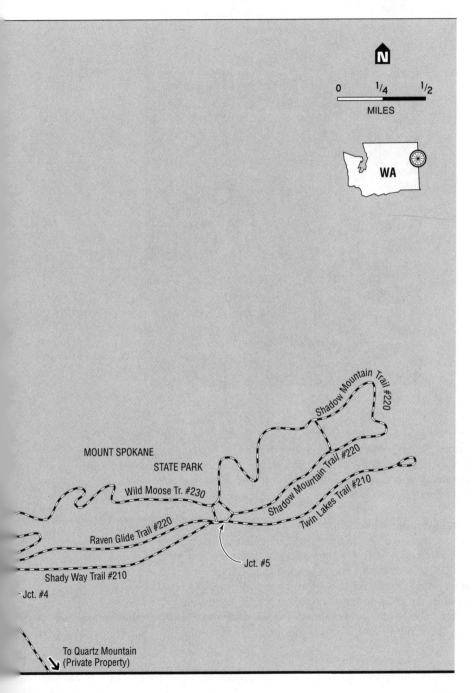

N

0   1/4   1/2

MILES

WA

Shadow Mountain Trail #220

MOUNT SPOKANE

STATE PARK

Wild Moose Tr. #230

Shadow Mountain Trail #220

Twin Lakes Trail #210

Raven Glide Trail #220

Jct. #5

Shady Way Trail #210

Jct. #4

To Quartz Mountain
(Private Property)

Mt. Spokane State Park.

This chapter is an introduction to the Nordic Ski Trail System on Mt. Spokane. Riders can create everything from easy outings to demanding circuits. We describe a moderately difficult 3.6-mile loop that follows double-tracks and gravel roads in good condition. Some intersections were unsigned at the time of our visit, but it looked like new signs were being installed.

General location: The trailhead for the Mt. Spokane Nordic Ski Trail System is approximately 25 miles northeast of Spokane, Washington.

Elevation change: The double-tracks take off from Selkirk Lodge at 4,500′. The high point of the trail network is about 4,800′.

Season: While some trails on the mountain may be crowded on summer weekends, the cross-country trails receive only light use.

Services: There is no water available on the ride. Water can be found seasonally at the campground. The campground consists of 12 sites that are available on a first-come, first-served basis. All services can be obtained in Spokane.

Hazards: Anticipate some rough stretches of road and some sandy conditions.

Rescue index: There is a pay phone at Selkirk Lodge. Budget cuts have reduced the park staff to a bare minimum—you may or may not be able to obtain help at the park office. The office is on your left, just past Kirk's Lodge, as you enter the park.

Land status: State park.

Maps: As this book went to press, a comprehensive map of bike trails on Mt. Spokane was unavailable. A map of the cross-country trails could be obtained, but it was inaccurate and hard to find. The folks in the bicycle department at the Recreational Equipment Inc. (REI) store in Spokane helped us track one down. The map in this book is a revised version of that cross-country trail map. USGS 7.5 minute quads: Mt. Spokane and Mt. Kit Carson.

Finding the trail: From Interstate 90 in Spokane, take Exit 281 and follow Division Street north through the city. After 6 miles, bear right onto US 2, following the signs for Mt. Spokane. In another 4.3 miles, turn right onto WA 206/Mt. Spokane Park Drive. You will pass Kirk's Lodge after about 15 miles on WA 206. Go 3.5 miles beyond Kirk's Lodge and turn right into a large gravel parking lot. Proceed uphill through the parking area for .3 miles, and turn right to enter the upper Sno-Park lot at Selkirk Lodge.

Sources of additional information:

Mt. Spokane State Park
North 26107 Mt. Spokane Park Drive
Mead, WA 99021
(509) 456-4169

Washington State Parks and Recreation Commission
7150 Cleanwater Lane, KY-11
Olympia, WA 98504-5711

Washington State Parks Information Line
(800) 562-0990 in Washington
(206) 753-2116 outside Washington
May 1–Labor Day: Monday–Friday, 8 A.M. to 5 P.M.

REI
North 1125 Monroe Street
Spokane, WA 99201
(509) 328-9900

Notes on the trail: The following description is one of many available routes in the Mt. Spokane Nordic Ski Trail System. Stay closer to the lodge for less demanding options.

Find Valley View Trail #200 in the southwest corner of the parking lot. Follow it to Junction 1. Stay to the right at Junction 1 and pick up Larch Trail #200. When you arrive at Junction 2, bear right to get on Silver Trail #200. After .8 miles on Silver Trail, you will come around the back side of Nova Hut and arrive at an intersection. Turn left and ride a short distance to Junction 3. Turn left and follow the main road back to the Sno-Park lot at Selkirk Lodge.

Turn right at Junction 3 for deeper explorations into the system of trails. We followed the main road to Junction 5 and went left to ride on Shadow Mountain Trail #220. We got lost several times on this trail—it is interlaced with ORV and snowmobile routes. There are some nice views to the south from this double-track.

Information about the single-track opportunities on Mt. Spokane is hard to find. The park staff is eager to promote the trail network but lacks funding for signage and maps. With the coming of a Grundig World Cup event, though, it shouldn't be long before someone produces a good guide to Mt. Spokane's trails.

Afterword

LAND-USE CONTROVERSY

A few years ago I wrote a long piece on this issue for *Sierra* magazine that entailed calling literally dozens of government land managers, game wardens, mountain bikers, and local officials to get a feeling for how riders were being welcomed on the trails. All that I've seen personally since, and heard from my authors, indicates there hasn't been much change. We're still considered the new kid on the block. We have less of a right to the trails than horses and hikers, and we're excluded from many areas, including:

a) wilderness areas

b) national parks (except on roads, and those paths specifically marked "bike path")

c) national monuments (except on roads open to the public)

d) most state parks and monuments (except on roads, and those paths specifically marked "bike path")

e) an increasing number of urban and county parks, especially in California (except on roads, and those paths specifically marked "bike path")

Frankly, I have little difficulty with these exclusions and would, in fact, restrict our presence from some trails I've ridden (one time) due to the environmental damage and chance of blind-siding the many walkers and hikers I met up with along the way. But these are my personal views. The author of this volume and mountain bikers as a group may hold different opinions.

You can do your part in keeping us from being excluded from even more trails by riding responsibly. Many local and national off-road bicycle organizations have been formed with exactly this in mind, and one of the largest—the National Off-Road Bicycle Association (NORBA)—offers the following code of behavior for mountain bikers:

1. I will yield the right of way to other non-motorized recreationists. I realize that people judge all cyclists by my actions.

2. I will slow down and use caution when approaching or overtaking another cyclist and will make my presence known well in advance.

3. I will maintain control of my speed at all times and will approach turns in anticipation of someone around the bend.

4. I will stay on designated trails to avoid trampling native vegetation and minimize potential erosion to trails by not using muddy trails or short-cutting switchbacks.

5. I will not disturb wildlife or livestock.

6. I will not litter. I will pack out what I pack in, and pack out more than my share whenever possible.

7. I will respect public and private property, including trail use signs and no trespassing signs, and I will leave gates as I have found them.

8. I will always be self-sufficient and my destination and travel speed will be determined by my ability, my equipment, the terrain, the present and potential weather conditions.

9. I will not travel solo when bikepacking in remote areas. I will leave word of my destination and when I plan to return.

10. I will observe the practice of minimum impact bicycling by "taking only pictures and memories and leaving only waffle prints."

11. I will always wear a helmet whenever I ride.

Now, I have a problem with some of these—number nine, for instance. The most enjoyable mountain biking I've ever done has been solo. And as for leaving word of destination and time of return, I've enjoyed living in such a way as to say, "I'm off to pedal Colorado. See you in the fall." Of course it's senseless to take needless risks, and I plan a ride and pack my gear with this in mind. But for me number nine smacks too much of the "never-out-of-touch" mentality. And getting away from civilization, deep into the wilds, is, for many people, what mountain biking's all about.

All in all, however, NORBA's is a good list, and surely we mountain bikers would be liked more, and excluded less, if we followed the suggestions. But let me offer a "code of ethics" I much prefer, one given to cyclists by Utah's Wasatch-Cache National Forest office.

Study a Forest Map Before You Ride
Currently, bicycles are permitted on roads and developed trails within the Wasatch-Cache National Forest except in designated Wilderness. If your route crosses private land, it is your responsibility to obtain right of way permission from the landowner.

Keep Groups Small
Riding in large groups degrades the outdoor experience for others, can disturb wildlife, and usually leads to greater resource damage.

Avoid Riding on Wet Trails
Bicycle tires leave ruts in wet trails. These ruts concentrate runoff and accelerate erosion. Postponing a ride when the trails are wet will reserve the trails for future use.

Stay on Roads and Trails
Riding cross-country destroys vegetation and damages the soil.

Always Yield to Others
Trails are shared by hikers, horses, and bicycles. Move off the trail to allow horses to pass and stop to allow hikers adequate room to share the trail. Simply yelling "Bicycle!" is not acceptable.

Control Your Speed
Excessive speed endangers yourself and other forest users.

Avoid Wheel Lock-up and Spin-out
Steep terrain is especially vulnerable to trail wear. Locking brakes on steep descents or when stopping needlessly damages trails. If a slope is steep enough to require locking wheels and skidding, dismount and walk your bicycle. Likewise, if an ascent is so steep your rear wheel slips and spins, dismount and walk your bicycle.

Protect Waterbars and Switchbacks
Waterbars, the rock and log drains built to direct water off trails, protect trails from erosion. When you encounter a waterbar, ride directly over the top or dismount and walk your bicycle. Riding around the ends of waterbars destroys them and speeds erosion. Skidding around switchback corners shortens trail life. Slow down for switchback corners and keep your wheels rolling.

If You Abuse It, You Lose It
Mountain bikers are relative newcomers to the forest and must prove themselves responsible trail users. By following the guidelines above, and by participating in trail maintenance service projects, bicyclists can help avoid closures which would prevent them from using trails.

I've never seen a better trail-etiquette list for mountain bikers. So have fun. Be careful. And don't screw things up for the next rider.

Dennis Coello
Series Editor

Glossary

This short list of terms does not contain all the words used by mountain bike enthusiasts when discussing their sport. But it should serve as an introduction to the lingo you'll hear on the trails.

ATB   all-terrain bike; this, like "fat-tire bike," is another name for a mountain bike

ATV   all-terrain vehicle; this usually refers to the loud, fume-spewing three- or four-wheeled motorized vehicles you will not enjoy meeting on the trail—except, of course, if you crash and have to hitch a ride out on one

bladed   refers to a dirt road that has been smoothed out by the use of a wide blade on earth-moving equipment; "blading" gets rid of the teeth-chattering, much-cursed washboards found on so many dirt roads after heavy vehicle use

blaze   a mark on a tree made by chipping away a piece of the bark, usually done to designate a trail; such trails are sometimes described as "blazed"

blind corner   a curve in a road or trail that conceals bikers, hikers, equestrians and other traffic

BLM   Bureau of Land Management, an agency of the federal government

buffed   used to describe a very smooth trail

catching air   taking a jump in such a way that both wheels of the bike are off the ground at the same time

clean   while this may describe what you and your bike won't be after following many trials, the term is most often used as a verb to denote the action of pedaling a tough section of trail successfully

combination   this type of route may combine two or more configurations. For example, a point-to-point route may integrate a scenic loop or out-and-back spur midway through the ride. Likewise, an out-and-back may have a loop at its farthest point. (This configuration looks like a cherry with stem attached; the stem is the out-and-back, the fruit is the terminus loop.) Or a loop route may have multiple

312

out-and-back spurs and/or loops to the side. Mileage for a combination route is for the total distance to complete the ride

dab   touching the ground with a foot or hand

deadfall   a tangled mass of fallen trees or branches

diversion ditch   a usually narrow, shallow ditch dug across or around a trail; funneling the water in this manner keeps it from destroying the trail

double-track   the dual tracks made by a jeep or other vehicle, with grass or weeds or rocks between; mountain bikers can ride in either of the tracks, but you will of course find that whichever one you choose, and no matter how many times you change back and forth, the other track will appear to offer smoother travel

dugway   a steep, unpaved, switchbacked descent

endo   flipping end over end

feathering   using a light touch on the brake lever, hitting it lightly many times rather than very hard or locking the brake

four-wheel-drive   this refers to any vehicle with drive-wheel capability on all four wheels (a jeep, for instance, has four-wheel drive as compared with a two-wheel-drive passenger car), or to a rough road or trail that requires four-wheel-drive capability (or a one-wheel-drive mountain bike!) to negotiate it

game trail   the usually narrow trail made by deer, elk, or other game

gated   everyone knows what a gate is, and how many variations exist upon this theme; well, if a trail is described as "gated" it simply has a gate across it; don't forget that the rule is if you find a gate closed, close it behind you; if you find one open, leave it that way

Giardia   shorthand for *Giardia lamblia*, and known as the "back-packer's bane" until we mountain bikers expropriated it; this is a waterborne parasite that begins its life cycle when swallowed, and one to four weeks later has its host (you) bloated, vomiting, shivering with chills and living in the bathroom; the disease can be avoided by "treating" (purifying) the water you acquire along the trail (see "Hitting the Trail" in the Introduction)

gnarly   a term thankfully used less and less these days, it refers to tough trails

hammer   to ride very hard

hardpack   a trail in which the dirt surface is packed down hard; such trails make for good and fast riding, and very painful landings; bikers most often use "hardpack" as both noun and adjective, and "hardpacked" as an adjective only (the grammar lesson will help you when diagramming sentences in camp)

hike-a-bike   what you do when the road or trail becomes too steep or rough to remain in the saddle

jeep road, jeep trail   a rough road or trail passable only with four-wheel-drive capability (or a horse or mountain bike)

kamikaze   while this once referred primarily to those Japanese fliers who quaffed a glass of saké, then flew off as human bombs in suicide missions against U.S. naval vessels, it has more recently been applied to the idiot mountain bikers who, far less honorably, scream down hiking trails, endangering the physical and mental safety of the walking, biking, and equestrian traffic they meet; deck guns were necessary to stop the Japanese kamikaze pilots, but a bike pump or walking staff in the spokes is sufficient for the current-day kamikazes who threaten to get us all kicked off the trails

loop   this route configuration is characterized by riding from the designated trailhead to a distant point, then returning to the trailhead via a different route (or simply continuing on the same in a circle route) without doubling back. You always move forward across new terrain, but return to the starting point when finished. Mileage is for the entire loop from the trailhead back to trailhead

multi-purpose   a BLM designation of land which is open to many uses; mountain biking is allowed

ORV   a motorized off-road vehicle

out-and-back   a ride where you will return on the same trail on which you pedaled out; while this might sound far more boring than a loop route, many trails look very different when pedaled in the opposite direction. Unless otherwise noted, mileage figures are the *total* distance out *and* back.

pack stock   horses, mules, llamas, et cetera, carrying provisions along the trails . . . and unfortunately leaving a trail of their own behind

point-to-point	a vehicle shuttle (or similar assistance) is required for this type of route, which is ridden from the designated trailhead to a distant location, or endpoint, where the route ends. Total mileage is for the one-way trip from trailhead to endpoint
portage	to carry your bike on your person
pummy	volcanic activity in the Pacific Northwest and elsewhere produces soil with a high content of pumice: trails through such soil often become thick with dust, but this is light in consistency and can usually be pedaled. Remember, however, to pedal carefully, for this dust obscures whatever might lurk below
quads	bikers use this term to refer both to the extensor muscle in the front of the thigh (which is separated into four parts) and to USGS maps; the expression "Nice quads!" refers always to the former, however, except in those instances when the speaker is an engineer
runoff	rainwater or snowmelt
scree	an accumulation of loose stones or rocky debris lying on a slope or at the base of a hill or cliff
signed	a "signed" trail has signs in place of blazes
single-track	a single, narrow path through grass or brush or over rocky terrain, often created by deer, elk, or backpackers; single-track riding is some of the best fun around
slickrock	the rock-hard, compacted sandstone that is *great* to ride and even prettier to look at; you'll appreciate it even more if you think of it as a petrified sand dune or seabed (which it is), and if the rider before you hasn't left tire marks (from unnecessary skidding) or granola bar wrappers behind
snowmelt	runoff produced by the melting of snow
snowpack	unmelted snow accumulated over weeks or months of winter—or over years in high-mountain terrain
spur	a road or trail that intersects the main trail you're following
squid	one who skids
switchback	a zigzagging road or trail designed to assist in traversing steep terrain: mountain bikers should *not* skid through switchbacks

talus	the rocky debris at the base of a cliff, or a slope formed by an accumulation of this rocky debris
technical	terrain that is difficult to ride due not to its grade (steepness) but to its obstacles—rocks, logs, ledges, loose soil . . .
topo	short for topographical map, the kind that shows both linear distance *and* elevation gain and loss; "topo" is pronounced with both vowels long
trashed	a trail that has been destroyed (same term used no matter what has destroyed it . . . cattle, horses, or even mountain bikers riding when the ground was too wet)
two-wheel-drive	this refers to any vehicle with drive-wheel capability on only two wheels (a passenger car, for instance, has two-wheel-drive); a two-wheel-drive road is a road or trail easily traveled by an ordinary car
water bar	an earth, rock, or wooden structure that funnels water off trails to reduce erosion
washboarded	a road that is surfaced with many ridges spaced closely together, like the ripples on a washboard; these make for very rough riding, and even worse driving in a car or jeep
whoop-de-doo	closely spaced dips or undulations in a trail; these are often encountered in areas traveled heavily by ORVs
wilderness area	land that is officially set aside by the federal government to remain *natural*—pure, pristine, and untrammeled by any vehicle, including mountain bikes; though mountain bikes had not been born in 1964 (when the United StatesCongress passed the Wilderness Act, establishing the National Wilderness Preservation system), they are considered a "form of mechanical transport" and are thereby excluded; in short, stay out
wind chill	a reference to the wind's cooling effect upon exposed flesh; for example, if the temperature is 10 degrees Fahrenheit and the wind is blowing at 20 miles per hour, the wind chill (that is, the actual temperature to which your skin reacts) is *minus* 32 degrees; if you are riding in wet conditions things are even worse, for the wind-chill would then be *minus 74 degrees!*
windfall	anything (trees, limbs, brush, or fellow bikers) blown down by the wind

LAURIE AND CHRIS LEMAN make their home in Ketchum, Idaho. Laurie was born in Vancouver, British Columbia and holds a degree from Simon Fraser University. She is employed as a waitress and freelance writer, and helps coach the Sun Valley Nordic Ski Team. Chris is from Detroit, graduated from Michigan State University, and earns a living as a carpenter. The two met while working as bicycle tour leaders in the Canadian Rockies.

DENNIS COELLO'S AMERICA BY MOUNTAIN BIKE SERIES

Happy Trails

Hop on your mountain bike and let our guidebooks take you on America's classic trails and rides. These "where-to" books are published jointly by Falcon Press and Menasha Ridge Press and written by local biking experts. Twenty regional books will blanket the country when the series is complete.

Choose from an assortment of rides—easy rambles to all-day treks. Guides contain helpful trail and route descriptions, mountain bike shop listings, and interesting facts on area history. Each trail is described in terms of difficulty, scenery, condition, length, and elevation change. The guides also explain trail hazards, nearby services and ranger stations, how much water to bring, and what kind of gear to pack.

So before you hit the trail, grab one of our guidebooks to help make your outdoor adventures safe and memorable.

Call or write
Falcon Press or Menasha Ridge Press
Falcon Press
P.O. Box 1718, Helena, MT 59624
1-800-582-2665
Menasha Ridge Press
3169 Cahaba Heights Road, Birmingham, AL 35243
1-800-247-9437

FALCON™

Menasha
Ridge Press